D0275580

Is the Planet Full?

Ian Goldin's Previous Books

The Butterfly Defect: How Globalization Creates Systemic Risks, and What to Do About It

Divided Nations: Why Global Governance is Failing, and What We Can Do About It

Globalization for Development: Meeting New Challenges

Exceptional People: How Migration Shaped our World and Will Define our Future

The Case For Aid

The Economics of Sustainable Development

Economic Reform, Trade, and Development

Modelling Economy-wide Reforms

Trade Liberalization: Global Economic Implications

Open Economies

The Future of Agriculture

Economic Crisis: Lessons from Brazil

Making Race

Is the Planet Full?

Edited by
Ian Goldin

OXFORD
UNIVERSITY PRESS

OXFORD
UNIVERSITY PRESS

Great Clarendon Street, Oxford, OX2 6DP,
United Kingdom

Oxford University Press is a department of the University of Oxford.
It furthers the University's objective of excellence in research, scholarship,
and education by publishing worldwide. Oxford is a registered trade mark of
Oxford University Press in the UK and in certain other countries

© Oxford University Press 2014

The moral rights of the authors have been asserted

First Edition published in 2014
Impression: 2

All rights reserved. No part of this publication may be reproduced, stored in
a retrieval system, or transmitted, in any form or by any means, without the
prior permission in writing of Oxford University Press, or as expressly permitted
by law, by licence, or under terms agreed with the appropriate reprographics
rights organization. Enquiries concerning reproduction outside the scope of the
above should be sent to the Rights Department, Oxford University Press, at the
address above

You must not circulate this work in any other form
and you must impose this same condition on any acquirer

Published in the United States of America by Oxford University Press
198 Madison Avenue, New York, NY 10016, United States of America

British Library Cataloguing in Publication Data
Data available

Library of Congress Control Number: 2013956090

ISBN 978–0–19–967777–1

As printed and bound by
CPI Group (UK) Ltd, Croydon, CR0 4YY

Links to third party websites are provided by Oxford in good faith and
for information only. Oxford disclaims any responsibility for the materials
contained in any third party website referenced in this work.

To the memory of
Dr James Martin
Visionary, Innovator, Entrepreneur, Philanthropist, Friend
Founder of the Oxford Martin School

Acknowledgements

Any edited volume is by nature a collective effort. I have been fortunate to be able to draw on the work of an immensely talented group of leading thinkers. I am most grateful to them for rising to the challenge and producing novel responses to the question as to whether our planet if full.

The volume arose out of a seminar series at the Oxford Martin School devoted to this topic. Many of the chapters found their initial expression in those seminars and were enriched by the contributions of panellists and participants from across the University of Oxford. The seminars were organized by Alison Stibbe and Clara Bowyer to whom I am most grateful. Alison took the lead in discussing the series with Oxford University Press. At the Press, Aimee Wright has proved highly effective in guiding this book from inception to the published volume. I am grateful too for Adam Swallow's continuing guidance and support. Brian Klaas and Chris Oates have provided excellent research assistance. Lindsay Walker has once again provided the necessary calm organization of my time to allow me to focus on this publication and ensure the timely delivery of the manuscript. My greatest debt is to David Clark who once again has demonstrated his extraordinary range of talents, from substantive questioning of the conceptual points being made to meticulous attention to detail in improving each chapter. This volume owes much to David's tremendous contribution to the editing.

This book is dedicated to the memory of James Martin who died during the preparation of the manuscript. The subject of the book is a question he posed repeatedly. Our interdisciplinary approach to the question is one he enthusiastically supported. This publication and the numerous other outcomes of research undertaken at the Oxford Martin School at the University of Oxford are proof of the extent to which Jim's legacy lives on. Jim Martin was a firm believer in the power of ideas and the need to provide fresh insights which can shape policy. My hope is that in addressing the question as to whether our planet is full this volume will arm readers with new insights that will allow them to shape their answer. As Jim Martin emphasized, humanity is at the crossroads, and it is up to us to choose which path we take.

Ian Goldin, Oxford, UK
October 2013

Contents

Contents

List of Figures

List of Tables

List of Abbreviations

2DS	2°C Scenario
AIDS	Acquired immunodeficiency syndrome
BRICS	Brazil, Russia, India, China, and South Africa
CCS	Carbon capture and storage
CERN	European Organization for Nuclear Research
CFCs	chlorinated fluorocarbons
CGIAR	Consultative Group for International Agricultural Research
CO_2	carbon dioxide
COURSE 50	Japan Iron and Steel Federation
DNA	deoxyribonucleic acid
EC	European Community (now the EU)
ERFs	Environmental Required Flows
EU	European Union
EU-ULCOS	Ultra-Low Carbon Dioxide Steelmaking (European Union Consortium)
FAO	Food and Agricultural Organization
FEMA	Federal Emergency Management Agency (United States)
g	gram
G8	Group of Eight
GDP	Gross Domestic Product
GM	Genetic Modification
GNI	Gross National Income
GNP	Gross National Product
GPP	Gross Primary Productivity
Gt	gigatonnes
HDI	Human Development Index
HIV	Human immunodeficiency virus
IEA	International Energy Association
IMF	International Monetary Fund

IPCC	Intergovernmental Panel on Climate Change
kJ	kilojoules
km^3	cubic kilometres
kW	kilowatts
m^3	cubic metres
MDGs	Millennium Development Goals
Mg	megagrams (tonnes)
Mt	million tonnes
MW	megawatts
NGO	non-governmental organisation
NHS	National Health Service (United Kingdom)
NPP	Net Primary Production
OECD	Organisation for Economic Cooperation and Development
R&D	research and development
REEs	rare earth elements
SARS	severe acute respiratory syndrome
SETAC	Society of Environmental Toxicology and Chemistry
SMART	Systematic Medical Appraisal, Referral, and Treatment
TB	tuberculosis
TFR	total fertility rate
TMR	total material required
TW	terawatt
UN	United Nations
UN-DESA	United Nations, Department of Economic and Social Affairs
UNDP	United Nations Development Programme
UNEP	United Nations Environment Programme
UN-HABITAT	United Nations Human Settlements Programme
UNHRC	United Nation Human Rights Council
US-AISI	American Iron and Steel Institute
US-DOE	(United States) Department of Energy
USGS	United States Geological Survey
W	watts
WCED	World Commission on Environment and Development
WHO	World Health Organization
WTO	World Trade Organization
YLDs	years lived with disability
YLLs	years of life lost

List of Contributors

Sir Anthony B. Atkinson, Professor of Economics and Fellow, Institute for New Economic Thinking, Oxford Martin School, University of Oxford.

Professor H. Charles J. Godfray, Hope Professor of Zoology, Director of the Oxford Martin Programme on the Future of Food, Oxford Martin School, University of Oxford.

Professor Ian Goldin, Professor of Globalization and Development and Director of the Oxford Martin School, University of Oxford.

Professor Sarah Harper, Professor of Gerontology and Director of the Oxford Institute of Population Ageing, Oxford Martin School, University of Oxford.

Anthony Hartwell, Director, NERC Mineral Resources Network, Department of Earth Sciences, University of Oxford.

Ian Johnson, Secretary General, The Club of Rome; formerly Vice President for Sustainable Development, World Bank.

Professor Yadvinder Malhi, Professor of Ecosystem Science, School of Geography and the Environment; and Director of the Oxford Centre for Tropical Forests, Oxford Martin School, University of Oxford.

Professor Mark New, Pro-Vice Chancellor and Director of the African Climate and Development Initiative, University of Cape Town, South Africa; Professor of Climate Science, School of Geography and Environment, University of Oxford.

Professor Robyn Norton, Co-Director, George Centre for Healthcare Innovation, Oxford Martin School, University of Oxford; and Professor of Public Health, Sydney Medical School, University of Sydney.

Dr Toby Ord, James Martin Fellow, Future of Humanity Institute, Oxford Martin School, University of Oxford.

1

Introduction

Ian Goldin

How Full?

Is the planet full? Over 7 billion people currently live on Earth. Sixty per cent live in Asia, 15 per cent in Africa, 11 per cent in Europe, 9 per cent in Latin America and the Caribbean, 5 per cent in North America, and less than 1 per cent in Oceania and elsewhere. In Singapore more than 7,000 people live per square kilometre, whereas in Australia three people on average inhabit the same area.[1]

The number of people and where they live is changing rapidly. The world's population has doubled over the past forty years, but the pace of growth is slowing, with the latest estimates suggesting that the population will increase by as many as 3 billion people to peak at between 9 and 10 billion people by 2050, before contracting after that (UN-DESA 2013a). In Europe, the population has already peaked,[2] and in many developed and developing countries (including China, South Korea, and Taiwan) fertility rates are well below replacement levels. Only sub-Saharan Africa and parts of India and South Asia are expected to see further rapid increases in population in the coming decades, with the growth elsewhere mainly due to rapid population ageing. As Sarah Harper explains in Chapter 4, this brings different challenges.

---

[1] Continental percentages are derived from UN-DESA (2013a), table I.4. The geographical groupings follow the 'Standard Country or Area Codes for International Use' adopted by the UN (ibid.: viii). The figure for Singapore is from SDS (2013). The population density for Australia has been calculated by dividing the population at the end of 2012 (ABS 2013) by the total area of Australia's states and territories (Geoscience Australia 2013).

[2] Following the United Nations, Europe is defined broadly to cover both Eastern European and Southern European countries including the Russian Federation. The latest statistics indicate that by 2005–10, almost all European countries (with the possible exception of Iceland and Ireland) had fertility rates well below replacement levels, confirming that population levels have indeed peaked (UN-DESA, 2013a: table A.22).

The impact of population growth will be felt acutely in the countries undergoing the most rapid transformation. The consequences are not, however, confined to any one group of countries. All our lives are increasingly intertwined across national borders. We share a global economy and a global commons. Both the opportunities and the risks associated with a fuller planet impact on all of us.

The distribution of effects is nevertheless uneven. At the same time that floods are destroying lives in some places, drought and water scarcity are laying waste to economies, withering crops, and sparking human tragedies elsewhere. This paradox is equally applicable to food: as the population grows, so does the average size of a person in the developed world. Obesity at one end of the spectrum is matched by starvation at the other.

Across the globe, the planet is full *and* empty. Resources are abundant *and* scarce. The problems of the planet reverberate everywhere in ways that are complex and often unpredictable.

In my book *The Butterfly Defect: How Globalization Creates Systemic Risks, and What to Do About It* I show that the number of people, together with the increasing density of our physical and virtual connections dramatically changes the propensity for systemic risks that we all face (Goldin and Mariathasan 2014). But equally, the opportunities are multiplied with increased physical and virtual connectivity. The extent to which the upside potential can mitigate the downside risks is a key determinant of judging whether the planet is full.

Rich and Poor

In considering whether the planet is full, the number of people on the planet is *not* the only or even most critical variable. It is *how* we live that matters. It is not a question of how many people there are but how our individual consumption and production impacts on the planet. The world could be 'overpopulated' with five billion people with unsustainably high consumption levels whereas over ten billion poor people with low consumption levels may not exhaust our planet's carrying capacity. This is not to say that poverty is good; quite the opposite is true and reducing poverty is the most important benchmark of global progress. Income growth and improvements in health, life expectancy, and other dimensions of human progress nevertheless have placed increasing pressure on the planet. The engine of economic progress over the past two hundred years has been fuelled by the burning of fossil fuels (Figure 1.1), but it is only in the last twenty years that scientists have unequivocally found that continuing on this trajectory will lead to disastrous climate change and that the atmosphere has exhausted its carrying capacity for carbon dioxide and other greenhouse gasses. The unsustainable use of other planetary resources—not least, the oceans, forests, and minerals—has

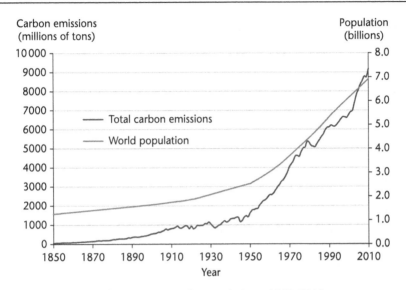

Figure 1.1. World population versus carbon emissions, 1850–2010
Sources: CDIAC (2013); UN-DESA (1999), table 1; UN-DESA (2013a), CD-Rom edition, file Pop/1-1.

given advanced economies a cheap ride to growth, unencumbered by the hidden costs of their growth patterns. While those in the more advanced economies must carry a significant part of the historic responsibility for exhausting the carrying capacity of the planet, the incremental pressure on planetary resources is increasingly coming from developing countries. It is in these countries that virtually all population growth and the lion's share of future income growth is anticipated.

The critical question we need to resolve is: how can we ensure that people born now and in the future are given the opportunity to live a high-quality life without wrecking the planet? Are current levels of consumption among the richer people sustainable and can we envisage an extension of such consumption patterns to all humanity without causing potentially catastrophic spillovers for everyone? If not, how can the imperatives of development be reconciled with the constraints of the planet? While the specific characteristics of questions and their answers vary from place to place, people and places are increasingly interconnected and the implications are global. Our focus is on the drivers of change that have a global or planetary impact.

Complex Lives, Complex Solutions

Our response to the question 'is the planet full?' draws on a variety of perspectives. By providing an interdisciplinary analysis of the question we aim to provide fresh insights. Real world challenges, and especially those as complex as our question, cannot be resolved through the narrow disciplinary lenses which too often bedevil scholarly approaches.[3] Complex challenges necessarily require insights from a wide variety of physical, life, and social science perspectives as well as from the humanities. Insights derived from philosophy, ethics, and history are just as valuable as those from hydrology or atmospheric physics. By bringing together these different disciplines, we offer fresh perspectives. In considering the prognosis for the future it is useful to be rooted in an understanding of history. The past is prologue—what happened before may give us clues to what will happen next. This is as true for individual lives as it is for society. One such extraordinary life is that of Fritz Haber.

In 1868, when Fritz Haber was born in Breslau, Germany, just over one billion people lived on Earth. Since then, population growth has soared dramatically, rising in the 20th century at a pace unparalleled in human history. Arguably, no individual contributed more to such rapid population growth than Haber, a German-born Jew who became a brilliant chemist.

From 1894 to 1911, Haber and his colleague, Carl Bosch, developed a process that created ammonia from hydrogen and atmospheric nitrogen when subjected to high pressure and high temperature. This breakthrough gave birth to large-scale industrial production of fertilizer, substantially increasing food production capacity and crop yields. It has since been argued that two billion people on Earth owe their continued survival to the Haber process (Charles 2005).

Less than five years after the discovery, Europe split apart in the 1914–18 World War. The Haber process—which gave life—also took it away. Just as it was used to make agricultural fertilizer, Haber discovered that he could develop lethal chlorine gas with the same method.

When the war ended, Haber was given the Nobel Prize. Then, as Germany began its devastating campaign against Jews, Haber was forced into exile. He died in 1934. A few years later, German scientists developed Zyklon B gas using the Haber process, and his breakthrough was used to exterminate millions in the Holocaust, including members of Haber's family.

Haber's process created 'bread from air', and sparked a population boom, through the development of fertilisers. It was also used to assist the largest genocide in history. This remarkable story illustrates the power of humanity, and at times, individuals, to affect population in dramatic ways. The lesson is important: innovation that may seem like progress can also have unexpected effects.

The story also reflects the scope, scale, and complexity of this volume, which asks: 'is the planet full?' Perhaps, without the Haber process and the

---

[3] The value added by interdisciplinary forms of research is discussed by Clark (2006), Harriss (2002), and Hulme and Toye (2006).

agricultural yields made possible by fertilizer, our answer would be a resounding 'yes!' but as the contributors make clear in this volume, answers are never quite so simple. Further technological developments to enhance agricultural yields or to create clean energy would make a dramatic difference to the answer. So too, as we show in the final chapter of this volume, would radical reforms in global governance.

Not a New Question

The question as to whether the planet is full is not new. Throughout history, intellectuals have sounded warnings of the imminent threat of overpopulation. 'What most frequently meets our view (and occasions complaint) is our teeming population. Our numbers are burdensome to the world, which can hardly support us...' Such a quote makes it sound like global collapse is imminent, yet the 'teeming population' referred to here was estimated to be around 190 million globally, and the alarmist thinker responsible is Tertullian, a resident of Carthage writing in the 2nd century AD (Osterfeld 1993).

For centuries the world population expanded slowly but steadily.[4] Thinkers such as Machiavelli and Otto Diederich Lutken echoed Tertullian's views and kept alive an ongoing debate. The issue was brought to the fore when Reverend Thomas Malthus published *An Essay on the Principle of Population* in 1798. Malthus (1798) warned that excessive population growth was slowing progress and derailing any chance of attaining a modern utopia. He argued that there were two forms of checks on population growth: positive checks (such as elevated death rates) and preventive checks (such as lowering the birth rate). These two checks, Malthus argued, were the key to avoiding poverty induced by overpopulation as well as natural corrections such as pestilence, war, and famine—phenomena that came to be known as Malthusian catastrophes (or checks). The impact of Malthus was widespread, infiltrating the intellectual context of nearly every field, from parliament passing new laws, to Darwin's writing on evolution, to literature, where Dickens' Scrooge insists: 'If they would rather die they had better do it, and decrease the surplus population' (Dickens 2009: 58).

Though Malthus wrote in England, scholars elsewhere issued similar warnings. For example, Hong Liangji, a Chinese philosopher, wrote about population pressures in his 1793 work, 'Zhi Ping Pian (治平篇, On Governance and Well-beings of the Empire)'.[5] Even though he wrote prior to Malthus's treatise, he reached similar conclusions: 'Small wonder that everywhere men die of

---

[4] For historical data spanning two millennia see UN-DESA (1999), table 1.
[5] See de Bary (2008: 88) and Dunstan (2006).

hunger and cold, in wind, storm and frost, and of the dew in the morning. Does Heaven know a remedy? Flood and drought, plague and pestilence are what nature offers us as remedies [to temper the population problem]...' (quoted in Silberman 1960: 262).

Malthus's writings influenced population debates long after his death. Their lasting legacy was challenged in the mid-1960s by Ester Boserup, a Danish economist. Boserup (1965) took aim at the core assumptions underlying Malthusian alarmism. Foremost, she inverted the Malthusian conclusion that food dictates population, suggesting that since 'necessity is the mother of invention,' population growth dictates food supply (p. 13). In other words, population growth should spur innovation. Humans, she argued, were innovative enough to figure out ways to feed an ever-growing population. Food supply is therefore not a fixed limit. For Boserup ostensible limits exist as catalysts to launch ingenuity; technological advancement out of necessity is a clear by-product of population growth. We can cope—even thrive—she argues, with our backs up against the proverbial global walls.

Not everyone shared Boserup's optimism. Earlier in the 1960s, a number of ecological works were published, including Rachel Carson's wake-up call, *Silent Spring* (1962). Paul Ehrlich's (1968) *The Population Bomb* challenged Boserup's rosy assumptions. Ehrlich adapted Malthus's work to the modern era (albeit with less moralizing) arguing that the pressures of population growth and elevated consumption would severely deplete resources and cause prices to soar. High food prices, he argued, would condemn millions, maybe billions, to famine.

Lester Brown was another prolific voice to enter the debate for the first time (but certainly not the last) in the mid-1960s. Brown, who has since written dozens of books warning of the environmental impacts of population expansion and unsustainable behaviour, published *Man, Land, and Food* in 1963. His analysis identified how food supply and demand trends would create a worldwide challenge of feeding an expanding population.

The rising concerns prompted the Club of Rome to commission the influential *The Limits to Growth* compiled by Meadows et al. (1972). For the first time, population ecology was put to the test of systematic and systemic computer modelling. As Ian Johnson, the current Secretary General of the Club of Rome, notes in Chapter 5 of this volume, these models offered a set of 'simulated scenarios, allowing the reader to gauge a series of potential outcomes on the basis of reasonable and plausible assumptions' about population growth, ecological impacts, consumption, and more. *The Limits to Growth* also introduced the concept of 'overshoot'; the notion that human population could exceed the environmental carrying capacity of the Earth. The report's impact was impressive; it sold millions of copies and was translated into thirty languages.

Policymakers also took note. Two years after *The Limits to Growth* was published, Henry Kissinger ordered the secret drafting of National Security Study Memorandum 200. The memo, later declassified, argued that population growth in the world's least developed countries posed a grave threat to American security interests. The logic, Malthusian at heart, suggested that swelling populations would spark conflict and destabilize regions, jeopardizing access to vital minerals and other resources for consumption in the United States (United States Department of State, 1974).

The debates concerning the merits of population growth and the future availability of resources continued to divide opinion well into the 1980s and beyond. Julian Simon (1981), for example, echoed Ester Boserup's earlier optimism by arguing that there is no resource crisis as technological breakthroughs and human adaptation—the 'ultimate resource'—can resolve the world's problems. At the heart of Simon's argument was the hypothesis that critical resources are becoming less scarce, as will be verified by lower prices. This controversial claim became the foundation of a famous ten-year wager between Simon and the author of *The Population Bomb*, Paul Ehrlich, in October 1980. Ehrlich formed a consortium with John Harte and John Holdren (energy and resource specialists at the University of California, Berkeley), and bet Simon $1,000 that the prices of five base metals—chrome, copper, nickel, tin, and tungsten—would rise over the next ten years. The debate continued to rage through the 1980s, but despite an increase in world population of 800 million, Ehrlich and associates eventually lost the bet (see Tierney 1990). The matter wasn't settled however, with Ehrlich pointing to the impact of the 1980s recession as an aggravating factor, and Simon refusing to accept the proposed terms of a second bet (see Ehrlich and Ehrlich 1996: 100–4).

Since the 1970s, debates on population limits and the implications of population growth have largely been launched within the borders of a single discipline. In philosophy, as Anthony Atkinson discusses in Chapter 2 and Toby Ord explores in Chapter 3, Derek Parfit's (1984) 'Repugnant Conclusion' renewed discussions of population ethics. In Economics, Elinor Ostrom's (1990) groundbreaking analysis of the commons established 'design principles' for effectively managing common pool resources.

Global actors began to devote attention to overpopulation in earnest in the late 1980s, marked in particular by the publication of the Brundtland Report (WCED 1987). The report coined the term 'sustainable development', which at its core was the imperative of meeting all current needs for the global population without damaging the ability of future generations to meet their own needs.

This contributed to the 1992 United Nations Conference on Environment and Development held in Rio de Janeiro, informally billed as the 'Earth Summit'. With representatives from 172 governments in attendance, the summit produced the 'Rio Declaration on Environment and Development', which enshrined 27 principles to guide global efforts for sustainable development. This conference marked an important change: global governance was beginning to come to terms with the strains of population growth on the environment and the prospects for future development efforts (UN 1992).

Twenty years after the original Rio summit, Rio + 20 (held in 2012) reaffirmed the principles of the original conference, adding an updated resolution called 'The Future We Want' to the already-agreed shared principles. The non-binding document encouraged member states to make sustainable development a priority, affirming that 'fundamental changes in the way societies consume and produce are indispensable for achieving global sustainable development' (UN 2012: 43, Article 224). The negotiations also highlighted the need to follow scientific advice when preparing policy related to population, growth, ecology, and environmental management.

Scientists were eager to give such advice. Rockström et al. (2009) provided a framework for the analysis of 'planetary boundaries'. Their analysis of the data suggests that we have already surpassed three of nine breaking points: climate change, rate of biodiversity loss, and interference with the phosphorous and nitrogen cycle (the last accelerated, no doubt, by heavy reliance on fertilizers made by the Haber process).

This 'on the brink' view is taken even further by *Ten Billion*, a recent work by Stephen Emmott. His outlook is the epitome of pessimism, perhaps best captured by his statement that: 'We urgently need to do—and I mean actually do—something radical to avert a global catastrophe. But I don't think we will' (Emmott 2013: 202). At the other extreme, Peter Diamandis and Steven Kotler (2012) echo Boserup's techno-optimism in their book *Abundance: The Future is Better than You Think*. They argue that leapfrogging technological breakthroughs mean that we will soon have the ability to meet and exceed the basic needs of everyone on the planet and that 'abundance for all is actually within our grasp' (ibid: 9). While Emmott sees the source of failure as self interest and failure to act, these issues are barely considered by Diamandis and Kotler.

Emmott is right that we need to change, but underestimates the extent to which radical change is already underway in key areas. Dorling (2013) suggests that population growth rates are falling more rapidly than the UN medium projections and that the world's population is likely to peak at around 9 billion by 2050 and then decline to below 7 billion by 2100.

A large part of the explanation is due to lower fertility rates. The trend has already begun; thirty years ago a sliver of the global population lived in countries below 'replacement' fertility rates (defined as 2.1 children per woman in populations with low mortality rates). Today, more than 60 per cent of the world population lives in countries with 'replacement' or below fertility rates, trends that hold true in China, and even areas of southern India (Winter and Teitelbaum 2013). As Sarah Harper explains in Chapter 4, there are three main reasons for this sustained drop. First, falling mortality rates (from better health care and less poverty) reduce the need to have a large number of children, as more will survive. Second, there is evidence that widespread access to contraception is reducing unplanned pregnancies and empowering women to have fewer children by choice. Third, there is significant evidence that urbanization, access to education, and entering the labour force are major drivers of lower fertility. This is a good thing. But declining fertility rates now will not have a major impact on global population trends for some time. Jeffrey Sachs (2006) nonetheless points out that promoting policies that accelerate the drop in fertility rates is also a wise investment in the short term, as 'High fertility represents a disaster for the children themselves, who suffer from profound under-investments in education, health and nutrition, and are thereby far more likely to grow up impoverished' (ibid: 42). Econometric studies, such as a recent publication by Ashraf, Weil, and Wilde (2011), concur, suggesting, for example, that a decrease in the fertility rate of one child per woman in Nigeria would boost per capita GDP by 13 per cent over the next 20 years, an illustration of the 'dependency effect'—having fewer children to look after, feed, clothe, educate, and care for, unleashes additional economic potential for the parents.

However, as the fertility rate drops, there is also evidence that it magnifies inequality. Education, urbanization, access to contraception, and entry into the labour force tend to be disproportionately the realm of the comparatively well off in any given developing society. So, even if the overall national fertility rate drops, the poor are more likely to continue being stuck in a fertility trap, while the middle and upper classes start having fewer children—exacerbating what are often already grotesque levels of inequality (Bloom et al. 2009).

This spillover effect is indicative of the complexity of population debates. Even though the falling fertility rate is positive, the complex challenges that lie ahead are daunting. Strategic and creative long-term thinking is required to address them.

Getting Out of the Silos

In recent decades, the debates on whether the planet is full have been echoing around disciplinary silos—economics, natural sciences, ethics, philosophy, politics, and even theology. In part, those debates revolved around forecasting and have been stuck in back-and-forth arguing over the merits of certain data. This is not necessarily bad; data are critical to discerning whether the planet is full. But it is a problem when the disciplinary silos and data obscure the larger picture.

This volume offers a remedy. By tackling the question, 'is the planet full?' from a range of disciplines, with attention paid to the interconnectedness and spillover effects of population changes, our ambition is to provide a multifaceted analysis of the problems facing humanity as we move forward from an Earth of just over 7 billion people to one that recent projections suggest will approach 10 billion people by 2050 (UN-DESA 2013a).[6]

Such projections paint a dramatic picture. While the developed world is likely to maintain a steady population, 'the 49 least developed countries are projected to double in size from around 900 million people in 2013 to 1.8 billion in 2050' (UN-DESA 2013b: 1). If current trends continue, India is poised to surpass China shortly as the world's most populous country. It is probable that there will be more Nigerians than Americans before 2050.

While there is inevitably great uncertainty about future outcomes, on the basis of the experience of the past sixty years we can be reasonably optimistic that average life expectancies will continue to increase by about two years per decade. As falling fertility takes time to be reflected in declining populations, this implies that at least for the coming forty years the global population will grow, with the global population currently rising by over 230,000 people per day, a total increase of 84 million every year (PRB 2012: 2). Virtually all this increase is in developing countries. Each additional person needs a place to live, food to eat, water to drink, air to breathe, health care to maintain them, and natural resources to support a modern lifestyle. Moreover, each additional person deserves the chance to live a decent life.

These considerations are central to how we answer the question: 'is the planet full?'. In a purely physical sense, the planet is not full; explore rural Montana, Australia, Mongolia, or Siberia and it would be hard to be overwhelmed by a sense of anything other than emptiness. The question is not, however, about physical space, nor is it about how many people occupy that space. Instead, it is about how many people there are and how those people live.

That most of the population growth is in countries where incomes are rising most rapidly is a source of tremendous optimism. More people have escaped poverty in our lifetimes than in any previous comparable period. Is this sustainable and what are the planetary implications? The Environmental Kuznets Curve depicts a stylized relationship between the growth in incomes and pollution. It shows that as development lifts more and more people out of

---

[6] These projections acknowledge uncertainty, with estimates ranging from low (8.3 billion) to high (10.8 billion) by 2050. The most likely outcome according to UN models, however, is that there will be roughly 9.6 billion people by that time. That number is cited most commonly.

poverty, they consume more resources and pollute more, extracting resources and damaging the environment (Grossman and Krueger 1995; Stern 2003). Pollution keeps increasing until societies reach middle-income levels. At these levels a 'tipping point' is identified; consumption of many (but not all) goods and services with high levels of negative spillovers begins to level off and as incomes rise the use of certain pollutants can even decrease. The archetypical example is economies transitioning from dirty, industrial production to services and investing in public transport and other pollution-reducing technologies. Underlying the analysis is an implicit view that poorer countries need to prioritize poverty reduction but as basic needs are satisfied societies have both the resources and the luxury of choice to consider the environment rather than simply survival.

As I show in *The Economics of Sustainable Development*, which I edited with Alan Winters, the Environmental Kuznets Curve and the notions underlying it have come in for fierce criticism as being overly simplistic (Goldin and Winters 1995). Not only is there a very wide range of pollutants, the production of which peak at different levels of income, but there is also a strong cultural and political foundation for decisions. Low-income countries have been shown to be capable of making decisions which are highly compatible with lower pollution, whereas many high-income countries have not. Nevertheless, underpinning the hypothesis of the curve are a number of robust observations regarding the increase in a range of externalities as incomes rise. With two-thirds of the world's population in countries which are making the critical transition to higher levels of income, where consumption of energy, food, water, and other planetary resources peaks, understanding the relationship between economic growth and environmental spillovers is vital. These relationships are not automatic and can be strongly affected by policy. However, they do imply in aggregate a sharply rising claim on our planet's resources by the rapidly growing world population.

As has been made abundantly clear by the lag associated with the burning of fossil fuel and our understanding of the consequences, and many other environmentally disastrous consequences of decisions that were taken in the past, we do not and cannot know the full consequences of our actions. The decisions taken today will be crucial in determining our future. Every time decisions are made regarding infrastructure or other major investments, the consequences are being locked in for years, if not decades, to come. Power plants built today typically are anticipated to have a thirty- to fifty-year life. If they are not green now, they never will be. Getting a better understanding of the potential outcomes and allowing prudence to become a part of our planning is urgently required. As with other explorations of risk and uncertainty, this calls for a multifaceted examination of the issues.

Innovative Thinking Required

In answering the question as to whether our planet is full this book draws on insights from economics, the physical and natural sciences, politics, philosophy, and other disciplines to find answers. For example, although questions of population size and sustainability are the realm of demographers and scientists, the subject is laced with normative and philosophical considerations. Would it be better to increase the aggregate amount of happiness on the planet by simply adding to the population, even if average individual happiness declines? Is it just and fair that the 19.5 million residents of New York State consume as much energy as the 800 million residents of sub-Saharan Africa? (IEA 2010: 10)[7]

Philosophical concerns bleed into economic ones; how does the quest for growth affect the sustainability of our consumption levels? Part of the explanation is to be found in a better understanding of the implications of technological change and the results of the latest findings of scientists. Ecology, biology, geology, and chemistry all make enormous contributions to our understanding of the implications of population growth. Without those contributions, we could never hope to forecast how resource depletion will affect biodiversity, or how deforestation will affect climate change, or how climate change will alter the global water supply. The insights that scientists provide to these questions feed back to the analysis provided by other disciplines, informing philosophical and ethical judgements and economic policymaking.

The judgements of ethics, principles of economics, and data from natural science are all of limited value without good governance. Problems cannot be solved without capable institutions. As I argue in my concluding chapter to this volume, knowing whether the planet is full or not is inconsequential unless something can be done.

Drawing on ethics, economics, natural science, and governance, the authors of the chapters of this book collectively answer the question: 'is the planet full?'. In addressing this question they respond to four underlying questions:

1) What are the ethical implications of population growth?
2) How will population growth affect incomes, inequality, and resource allocation?
3) What is the current physical state of the planet and the ecosystem, and how is this likely to change with population and income growth?
4) What can individuals, firms, and governments do to stop the negative effects of population growth and harness the positive effects?

---

[7] The figure for sub-Saharan Africa excludes South Africa.

This Book's Contribution

In answering these four questions, this volume breaks through the stale debates on overpopulation and contributes to the literature in three main ways.

First, it provides a long-overdue update to the debates on population growth. There has been remarkably little written, for example, on how *The Limits to Growth* fared as a predictive tool over the forty years since it was written.[8] This volume fills that gap, by not only providing up-to-date facts, figures, and forecasts across a wide array of subjects, but by going further to provide fresh perspectives. This is an essential contribution, particularly given the impact that technological advancement has had on key projections. After all, Malthus could never have predicted that pestilence could spread into a global pandemic in just 48 hours, as a result of global aviation networks, and *The Limits to Growth* could not have included the million-fold improvement in computing power over the past forty years in its modelling.[9]

A noteworthy forerunner to this book is Joel Cohen's (1995) *How Many People Can the Earth Support?* Cohen considers the history of population growth and asks what is known about the future of human population. At the time of his writing the global population stood at 5.6 billion and had expanded by at least 1.6 per cent per annum since 1950 (a rate that implies the population will double in size in less than 44 years) (Cohen 1995: 8, 13, 18). Over the last thirty years population growth has steadily slowed (averaging 1.4 per cent between 1980 and 2013) and even the United Nations' high estimate for 2013–50 (1.3 per cent per annum) is well below the post-1950 average reported by Cohen (UN-DESA 2013a: table I.3). Indeed, Cohen himself warns against the long-term accuracy of population projections. In short, the time is ripe for a reassessment.

Cohen also revisits a large number of historical and contemporary attempts to estimate the human carrying capacity of the Earth. In particular, he scrutinizes some of the 'unstated assumptions' behind these estimates, which vary widely. He argues that any estimate of the planet's carrying capacity can only be valid at a given point in time. This is because any estimate depends on the choices we make now and in the future, as well as environmental and resource constraints. He concludes

---

[8] A noteworthy exception is Turner (2008).
[9] The growth in the potential for infectious diseases to cross borders and the rapid expansion in computer processing power are both manifestations of globalization, and are discussed further by Goldin and Mariathasan (2014). The increasingly rapid spread of disease and computing power have both been identified as critical issues likely to shape the future of humanity and to pose potentially grave challenges by the Oxford Martin Commission for Future Generations (2013).

...that estimates of human carrying capacity may usefully serve as dynamic indicators of humans' ever-changing relations to the Earth. At any given time, a *current* but changing human carrying capacity is defined by the *current* states of technology; of the physical, chemical and biological environment; of social, political and economic institutions; of levels and the styles of living; and of values, preferences and moral judgements (Cohen 1995: 17, original emphasis).

Instead of taking a firm stand on the question of whether or not the planet is full (or is likely to reach maximum human-carrying capacity in the foreseeable future), Cohen attempts to provide a balanced assessment of available scientific knowledge and understanding from the perspective of a demographer. He tentatively suggests an 'infrastructure for problem solving' in place of concrete 'proposals for action' (p. 12) and reviews the suggestions of others for tempering population growth and easing resource constraints. In keeping with the present volume, Cohen's pragmatism and emphasis on the importance of critical choices underline the importance of good governance and sound management for expanding the carrying capacity of the planet. In contrast to Cohen, however, many of the chapters in this volume offer more decisive answers to the central question—is the planet full?—from a variety of disciplines and perspectives that transcend demography and engage with the factors identified by Cohen as 'defining' the planet's capacity to sustain a sizeable population.

Second, unlike most works that focus on one aspect of the planet's carrying capacity, from the outlook of a single discipline (such as Cohen's brand of non-technical demography), this volume is holistic, merging different perspectives to inform our answer. Derek Parfit may have pioneered modern population ethics, but his essays do not incorporate the lessons of population ecology or climate chemistry; Rockström et al. (2009) have provided new ways of understanding the planetary balances and highlighted the dire state of affairs in our physical environment, but their work gives little attention to how we can get ourselves out of our predicament. This is not a criticism; scientists are supposed to do scientific research, and philosophers are supposed to address moral questions. However, as global challenges are interconnected, full of feedback loops, and rife with spillover effects, interdisciplinary thinking is required.

Third, this book examines the externalities of population growth with reference to the most recent scientific evidence which, as it is evolving so rapidly, did not inform the debates of previous decades. Externalities refer to the spillover effects of population growth and resource consumption; a principle illustrated simply by the fact that upstream run-off from farming in Minnesota and other states along the Mississippi River is extinguishing life in an 8,000-square-mile dead zone in the Gulf of Mexico—thousands of miles away (Dell'Amore 2013). The fact that what happens in one place reverberates across the globe is not a new idea, but it has been conspicuous by its absence from the debate on overpopulation. Moreover, the understanding of climate change adds a critical new component that we bring to bear on the population debate. It affects everything—from our ethical obligations to future generations to current water supplies to economic distribution and global governance. Relying on Malthus, or even the forty-year-old *The Limits to Growth*, as our starting point is no longer appropriate, given that neither work paid enough attention to externalities and could not take into account our newfound appreciation of complex interdependencies.

Is the Planet Full? The Answer in Ten Chapters

Our answer to the question: 'is the planet full?' is broken down into ten chapters. The first chapters, 2 and 3, are devoted to debate on whether the planet is full, with a consideration of ethical, resource, and economic questions. Chapters 4 and 5 discuss the population issues. In Chapters 6, 7, and 8 the authors analyse resource availability before considering, in Chapters 9, 10, and 11 some of the broad challenges, political considerations, and possible solutions.

The book examines the question of whether our planet is full from a wide variety of disciplinary perspectives. Part of the originality of this volume is that we are able to bring together insights from leading scholars of economics, ethics, philosophy, physics, earth sciences, geography, biology, zoology, medicine, and demography, to provide a rounded response to our question. To this end, the book proceeds as follows.

In Chapter 2, the eminent economist Sir Anthony Atkinson brings the question 'is the planet full?' to the crossroads of economics and ethics. After establishing that the question is best grounded on an 'optimum-quantity-of-people' approach, he highlights the failings of classical utilitarian models and the 'Repugnant Conclusion' that they impel us to draw—that the pursuit of maximum utility warrants extreme population growth, even if individual lives are miserable. To cope with what he regards as this misguided way of thinking, Atkinson suggests that Amartya Sen's conception of poverty as the denial of capabilities is a useful compass to guide us as we grapple with the question of population growth. With Sen's approach other considerations become central, such as whether the allure of technological advancement and creative and economic dynamism justify higher population levels; in other words, 'In a larger population, one is more likely to find a new Shakespeare, . . . a new Mozart' or a new Bill Gates. Atkinson concludes by arguing that inequality—both between and within countries—is a crucial but often overlooked factor as we decide whether to answer 'yes', or 'no' as to whether the planet is full.

Following Atkinson's insights, philosopher Toby Ord in Chapter 3 argues that population ethics is too often focused solely on the costs of population growth while ignoring the instrumental and intrinsic benefits of having more people on Earth. He suggests that instrumental benefits—such as the added value brought by information goods (including things like intellectual property and medical breakthroughs)—must be considered alongside the intrinsic value of the joys and loves of human lives. As Ord contends, those benefits cannot be adequately weighed using the scales of the discredited 'total happiness view' or 'average happiness view', of population ethics. Instead, emerging theories must weigh the instrumental and intrinsic benefits of additional lives against the costs of capacity, which should be defined in terms of 'soft limits' and 'hard limits'. While the hard limits may be absolute, Ord suggests that technological advances can be coupled with social and behavioural changes to shift the soft limits of population capacity. Given this malleability of population constraints, Ord calls for a re-evaluation of population ethics, with more attention paid to the benefits of larger populations.

After exploring the prevailing ethical considerations, in Chapter 4, Sarah Harper provides perspectives on demographic transitions—particularly with regard to fertility rates, consumption, and environmental impact. She outlines how global demographics are changing and how the world population is becoming more urban, more mobile, and older. These changes are not uniform, though—fertility rates vary substantially, from 0.99 children per woman in Hong Kong to 7 children per woman in Niger. Harper explains that the outliers such as Niger are dotted across sub-Saharan Africa, where the 'demographic transition' toward replacement-level fertility rates has stalled. Harper highlights that the key to lower fertility rates is lower child mortality, access to family planning, and women's empowerment through education. Climate change, Harper concludes, accentuates the problems associated with high fertility and sees more rapid progress with the demographic transition as a key element in addressing the devastating impact of climate change, particularly in the lowest-income countries.

In Chapter 5, Ian Johnson surveys what has changed since *The Limits to Growth* first appeared in 1972. Johnson identifies how the concept of 'overshoot' advanced by Meadows et al. launched a new era of systemic thinking about human sustainability and highlighted the implications of 'business as usual'. In the subsequent years, free market ideologies have become more widespread, Johnson argues, at the expense of an understanding of the public costs of market behaviour. Johnson explores the consequences with reference to oil exploration and the pricing and distribution of water resources. The failures of modern consumption, Johnson contends, could be addressed by a return to a more systemic, holistic paradigm that departs from a too narrow concept of GDP growth and returns to the moral philosophy about human wealth advanced in early economic history.

Chapter 6 explores the issue at the centre of Boserup's critique of Malthus: global food. Charles Godfray explains how population growth will affect global food supply and distribution. We live in a paradox; the world is burdened with a pandemic of obesity in tandem with malnourishment and hunger. These pressures—on both ends of the scale—are likely to intensify. Similarly, citizens in developed countries spend less, proportionately, than ever on food, while higher food prices have, Godfray points out, 'triggered civil unrest in a number of low-income countries'. Volatility may rise in equal measure from the 'nutritional transition', as additional wealth (and urbanization) pushes the world's current poor into a more varied, richer, and more resource-intensive diet. Add the challenge of climate change, and Godfray outlines a recipe for a global calamity. Thankfully, he also provides insights on how this may be avoided: sustainable intensification of food production; altering global diets (particularly reduced avoidance on high-intensity meat production); reducing food waste and production inefficiency, and addressing global governance issues that warp world food markets. If we do not adopt these measures, Godfray warns, the planet may become full, but the stomachs of its people will not be.

Food is of little use without water. In Chapter 7, Mark New explores the implications of continued population growth for water availability, particularly under the new stresses of climate change. After differentiating between blue, green, and grey water, New explains that per capita water consumption mirrored population growth until 1945, but that subsequently per capita water usage has increased sharply due to increased irrigation, urbanization, and expanding middle classes across the developed world. New shows that since the 1980s total demand has soared while per capita usage has declined, as behavioural change and government regulation have mitigated water stress in developed economies. In developing countries, meanwhile, the challenge continues to become more intense as income and population growth place growing stress on global water supplies and ecological balance. Climate change is predicted to make water scarcity 'hotspots' more widespread and more acute. New concludes, however, that there is still hope: the virtual water trade, efficiency gains and water reuse, and a renewed drive for desalination powered by green energy could ensure that there is adequate global water supply for generations to come, even if the planet is home to many more people.

What determines how much food and water are needed to support us? In Chapter 8, Yadvinder Malhi provides a whole-system approach. He explains that the two vital resources for human survival—food and water—are also affected by the level of human activity and the resulting metabolic demands of our lifestyles. All biological organisms from bacteria upwards have a metabolism—the rate at which they process chemical energy to perform the processes that are required for survival and growth. Humanity is unusual in having an extended 'sociometabolism': we consume and process energy far beyond our direct biological requirements. This sociometabolism has grown through human history, with sharp transitions at the onset of agricultural and industrial activity. Globally, human sociometabolism is currently around 17 per cent of the metabolism of the land biosphere. This proportion is likely to double by 2050, and at some stage may exceed the natural metabolism of the land biosphere. Human sociometabolic history can be viewed as a constant struggle between metabolic limitation and innovation. The challenge of our time is to create the innovations in technology and governance that can sustain both humanity and planet at a time when the sociometabolism of a single species is approaching and surpassing the natural metabolic activity of the biosphere.

After exploring the direct physical constraints for supporting life (the equation of food, water, and metabolic rates), Robyn Norton turns to the escalating cost of health care in Chapter 9. The dangers posed by contagious diseases such as TB, malaria, and HIV/AIDS are well known (WHO 1996; Cockerham and Cocherham 2010; Gaimard 2013). These diseases are likely to remain 'global killers' and will inevitably contribute to the rising cost of health care. They may also become more of a challenge as population density, global connectivity, and climate change continue to accelerate; these phenomena typically spur the risk of pandemics, heighten concern about potential contamination of the food chain (with 'foreign' animal meats), or shift tropical disease boundaries further from the equator as cooler climates warm up. They also underline the need to tackle oligopolistic behaviour amongst drug companies and explore alternative models of high-return and low-cost health care models. Robyn Norton puts the very real dangers posed by contagious disease aside in order to focus on the burgeoning costs imposed by non-communicable diseases. She warns that the world will soon face a tsunami of rising costs of care in the developed world and increasing demands for cost-prohibitive models of health care in the developing world. Most people do not have access to safe, effective, and affordable care, and unless something drastic is done, life expectancy and quality of life could fall in the face of rising global population. Norton outlines current challenges: a surge of tobacco use, unhealthy eating, physical inactivity, and obesity in low-income countries. These concerns coincide with soaring costs of care, as health care technology advances begin to replace acute care and communicable disease deaths with expensive long-term chronic care. To avoid the impending crisis in health care, Norton shows that we need to make the transition to a model that revolves around task shifting from doctors to other health care professionals. Preventive care should be aggressively expanded and treatment in mobile settings and low-cost technologies should be deployed. In addition, afford-able medicines should be made available around the world. Norton believes it is feasible to ensure the provision of high-quality, low-cost care to the world's rapidly increasing population.

Beyond food, water, and basic health, we also need minerals. That is the focus of Chapter 10, as Anthony Hartwell delivers a mixed forecast for the impacts of population growth on mineral resources. Technological advance-ment has allowed humans to extract resources from places that previously were impossible to even explore. Deep-water resource mining has grown, and estimates of overall resource reserves are continually being adjusted upwards. So, if minerals are abundant, what's the problem? The answer, in its most singular form: climate change. Hartwell explains that mineral extraction is not only energy intensive itself, but that any vectors used to reduce climate change will require mineral resources to implement. Without major changes, a growing population will accelerate mineral demands, with cataclysmic con-sequences. Recycling offers an important opportunity; for some metals, such as aluminium, reuse requires only 5 per cent as much energy input as initial extraction. The planet may not be full, Hartwell concludes, but '[N]ew ways of designing, using, and re-manufacturing or reusing materials and products must be developed.'

Finally, I conclude the volume, arguing that governance is central to addressing every one of these challenges. We live in a 'global village', and we are at peril because we do not have village elders to guide us. The question 'is the planet full?' is not about numbers—how many babies are born or how many tonnes of emissions are produced—but about how those numbers are managed. Global governance substantially affects every major global chal-lenge. I draw on my book *Divided Nations: Why Global Governance is Failing and What We Can Do About It* (2013) to show that these challenges transcend national borders, yet supranational bodies and sovereign states have failed thus far to tackle them. The biggest challenge is the benign neglect of the planet. In a system punctuated with veto points, policy viscosity derails global solutions. I explore how this occurs with reference to climate change, food and water supply, and migration. These examples illustrate the extent to which national decisions alone cannot deal with the challenge and often may be counterproductive. Population growth and income growth are the result of globalization. The unprecedented benefits for humanity are, how-ever, matched by new systemic risks arising from the difficulties associated with managing an increasingly complex and interconnected world. These global risks invite global cooperation and provide ample opportunity for collective action. Whether the planet is full depends on our capacity to harvest the benefits of globalization to manage, mitigate, and adapt to the spiralling negative spillovers.

Our conclusion is neither alarmist nor complacent. The planet may not yet be full, but it is filling up. Our imperative is to understand the implications of our actions to ensure that the planet can continue to provide a home that can meet the aspirations of all the Earth's current and future citizens.

References

ABS (2013). '3101.0—Australian Demographic Statistics [December Key Figures]', Australian Bureau of Statistics. Last accessed 16 August 2013. <http://www.abs.gov.au/ausstats/abs@.nsf/mf/3101.0>.

Ashraf, Q., Weil, D. and Wilde, J. (2011). 'The Effect of Interventions to Reduce Fertility on Economic Growth', *NBER Working Paper No. 17377*. Cambridge, MA: National Bureau of Economic Research. Last accessed 13 August 2013. <http://www.nber.org/papers/w17377>.

Bloom, D., Canning, D., Fink, G. and Finlay, J. (2009). 'Fertility, Female Labor Force Participation, and the Demographic Dividend', *Journal of Economic Growth*, 14(2): 79–101.

Boserup, E. (1965). *The Conditions of Agricultural Growth: The Economics of Agrarian Change under Population Pressure*. London: Allen & Unwin.

Brown, L. (1963). *Man, Land, and Food*. New York: Arno Press.

Carson, R. (1962). *Silent Spring*. Boston: Houghton Mifflin.

CDIAC (2013). 'Global Fossil-Fuel CO_2 Emissions', Carbon Dioxide Information Analysis Centre, Oak Ridge National Libratory. Last accessed 16 August 2013. <http://cdiac.ornl.gov/trends/emis/tre_glob_2010.html>.

Charles, D. (2005). *Mastermind: The Rise and Fall of Fritz Haber*. New York: Harper Collins.

Clark, D. A. (2006). 'Development Studies in the Twenty First Century' in D. A. Clark (ed.), *The Elgar Companion to Development Studies*. Cheltenham: Edward Elgar, pp. xxvi–xli.

Cockerham, G. and Cockerham, W. (2010). *Health and Globalization*. Cambridge: Polity Press.

Cohen, J. (1995). *How Many People Can the Earth Support?* New York and London: W. W. Norton and Company.

de Bary, W. T. (2008). *Sources of East Asian Tradition: The Modern Period*. New York: Columbia University Press.

Dell'Amore, C. (2013). 'Biggest Dead Zone Ever Forecast in Gulf of Mexico', *National Geographic*, 24 June.

Diamandis, P. and Kotler, S. (2012). *Abundance: The Future is Better than You Think*. New York: Free Press.

Dickens, C. (2009). *A Christmas Carol*. New York: Bantam Classics.

Dorling, D. (2013). *Population 10 Billion: The Coming Demographic Crisis and How to Survive It*. London: Constable.

Dunstan, H. (2006). 'Official Thinking on Environmental Issues and the State's Environmental Roles in Eighteenth-Century China' in M. Elvin and T.-J. Liu (eds). *Sediments of Time*. New Haven: Yale University Press, pp. 585–616.

Ehrlich, P. (1968). *The Population Bomb*. New York: Ballantine.

Ehrlich, P. and Ehrlich, A. (1996). *Betrayal of Science and Reason*. New York: Island Press.

Emmott, S. (2013). *Ten Billion*. London: Penguin Books.

Gaimard, J. (2013). *Population and Health in Developing Countries* (2014 edition). London: Springer.

Geoscience Australia (2013). 'Area of Australia—States and Territories', Australian Government. Last accessed 16 August 2013. <http://www.ga.gov.au/education/geoscience-basics/dimensions/area-of-australia-states-and-territories.html>.

Goldin, I. (2013). *Divided Nations: Why Global Governance is Failing and What We Can Do About It*. Oxford: Oxford University Press.

Goldin, I. and Mariathasan, M. (2014). *The Butterfly Defect: How Globalization Creates Systemic Risks, and What to Do About It*. Princeton, NJ: Princeton University Press.

Goldin, I. and Winters, L. A. (eds) (1995). *The Economics of Sustainable Development*. Cambridge: Cambridge University Press.

Grossman, G. M. and Krueger, A. B. (1995). 'Economic Growth and the Environment', *The Quarterly Journal of Economics*, 110(2): 353–77.

Harriss, J. (2002). 'The Case for Cross-Disciplinary Approaches in International Development', *World Development*, 30(3): 487–96.

Hulme, D. and Toye, J. (2006). 'The Case for Cross-Disciplinary Social Science Research on Poverty, Inequality and Well-Being', *Journal of Development Studies*, 42(7): 1085–107.

IEA (2010). *Energy Poverty: How to Make Modern Energy Access Universal*. Paris: International Energy Association. Last accessed 17 August 2013. <http://www.unido.org/fileadmin/user_media/Services/Energy_and_Climate_Change/Renewable_Energy/Publications/weo2010_poverty.pdf>.

Malthus, T. R. (1778) [1993]. *An Essay on the Principles of Population* (Reprinted). Oxford: Oxford World Classics.

Meadows, D. H., Meadows, D. L., Randers, J., and Behrens, W. W. III (1972). *The Limits to Growth*. New York: Universe Books.

Osterfeld, D. (1993). 'Overpopulation: The Perennial Myth', *The Freeman*, September, 1993. Last accessed 13 August 2013. <http://www.fee.org/the_freeman/detail/overpopulation-the-perennial-myth>.

Ostrom, E. (1990). *Governing the Commons: The Evolution of Institutions for Collective Action*. Cambridge: Cambridge University Press.

Oxford Martin Commission for Future Generations (2013). *Now for the Long Term: The Report of the Oxford Martin Commission for Future Generations*. Oxford: Oxford Martin School. Last accessed 21 October 2013. <http://www.oxfordmartin.ox.ac.uk/commission>.

Parfit, D. (1984). *Reasons and Persons*. Oxford: Clarendon Press.

PRB 2012. '2012 World Population Data Sheet'. Washington, D.C.: Population Reference Bureau. Last accessed 13 August 2013. <http://www.prb.org/pdf12/2012-population-data-sheet_eng.pdf>.

Rockström, J., et al., (2009). 'A Safe Operating Space for Humanity', *Nature*, 461: 472–5.

Sachs, J. (2006). 'Lower Fertility: A Wise Investment', *Scientific American*, 295(3): 42 (21 August).

SDS (2013). 'Latest Data [Population & Land Area]', Singapore Department of Statistics. Last accessed 16 August 2013. <http://www.singstat.gov.sg/statistics/latest_data.html>.

Silberman, L. (1960). 'Hung Liang-Chi: A Chinese Malthus', *Population Studies*, 13(3): 257–65.

Simon, S. L. (1981). *The Ultimate Resource*. Princeton, NJ: Princeton University Press.

Stern, D. I. (2003). 'The Environmental Kuznets Curve', *Internet Encyclopaedia of Ecological Economics*. International Society for Ecological Economics. Last accessed 13 August 2013. <http://isecoeco.org/pdf/stern.pdf>.

Tierney, J. (1990). 'Betting on the Planet', *New York Times*, 2 December. Last accessed 19 August 2013. <http://www.nytimes.com/1990/12/02/magazine/120290-tierney-magazine.html?pagewanted=1>.

Turner, G. M. (2008). 'A Comparison of *The Limits to Growth* with 30 Years of Reality', *Global Environmental Change*, 18: 397–411.

UN (1992). *Agenda 21: Rio Declaration, Forest Principles*. New York: United Nations.

UN (2012). 'The Future We Want', *Resolution Adopted by the General Assembly 66/288*, 19 September. New York: United Nations. Last accessed 13 August 2013. <http://www.un.org/ga/search/view_doc.asp?symbol=A/RES/66/288&Lang=E>.

UN-DESA (1999). *The World at Six Billion*. New York: United Nations, Department of Economic and Social Affairs, Population Division. Last accessed 16 August 2013. <http://www.un.org/esa/population/publications/sixbillion/sixbillion.htm>.

UN-DESA (2013a). *World Population Prospects: The 2012 Revision, Volume 1 Comprehensive Tables*. New York: United Nations, Department of Economic and Social Affairs, Population Division. Last accessed 13 August 2013. <http://esa.un.org/unpd/wpp/Documentation/publications.htm>.

UN-DESA (2013b). 'World Population to Reach 9.6 billion by 2050 with Most Growth in Developing Regions, especially Africa', *World Population Prospects: The 2012 Revision, Press Release*, 13 June. New York: United Nations, Department of Economic and Social Affairs, Population Division. Last accessed 13 August 2013. <http://esa.un.org/unpd/wpp/Documentation/pdf/WPP2012_Press_Release.pdf>.

United States Department of State (1974). *National Security Study Memorandum 200: Implications of Worldwide Population Growth for US Security and Overseas Interests*, 10 December. Last accessed 13 August 2013. <http://pdf.usaid.gov/pdf_docs/PCAAB500.pdf>.

WCED (1987). *Our Common Future* (World Commission on Environment and Development). Oxford: Oxford University Press.

WHO (1996). *The World Health Report 1996: Fighting Disease, Fostering Development*. Geneva: World Health Organization.

Winter, J. and Teitelbaum, M. (2013). *The Global Spread of Fertility Decline*. New Haven: Yale University Press.

2

Optimum Population, Welfare Economics, and Inequality

Anthony B. Atkinson

The title of this volume asks a question: 'is the planet full?' When I was a student at Cambridge I was taught that the most important thing when taking an examination was not necessarily to answer a question but to *address* it: that is, consider how one *might* answer the question. As will become clear, I will not answer the question posed. What I shall try to do is to explain how economists have—over more than a century—sought to grapple with the issue of an 'optimum population'. I hope that my account, and critique, of how economists have approached the problem may help you think about what answer *you* would give.

The term 'optimum' population makes evident that a central ingredient is *welfare economics,* with which I begin. What is welfare economics? Welfare economics is concerned with the interplay between ethical values and economic analysis. Non-economists may be surprised to know that such interplay takes place—that economists have any interest in ethical issues. And it is true that the subject has been disgracefully neglected in recent years. When I was a student, welfare economics was a compulsory part of the curriculum, and leading economists were writing their doctoral theses on the subject. Today it is treated as an optional extra in most economics degrees.

But welfare economics is a central part of economics. John Broome recently wrote that

> Economics is a branch of ethics. At least much of it is. Part of economics is pure science . . . [but most economists] are interested in economic science because they are interested in finding better ways of running the economy, or of structuring the economic system, or of intervening or not intervening in the economy. All of that practical part of economics is a branch of ethics (Broome 2009: 7).

This may be too strong. I would rather say that welfare economics lies at the interface between economics and moral philosophy. But I fully agree with Broome that, for this reason, economists need to pay much more attention to the ethical basis of their analysis and to examine critically the values underlying their welfare analyses. As it was put by my teacher, Jan Graaff,

> welfare economics proceeds from a number of assumptions...which are seldom stated explicitly. If their nature were more widely appreciated by professional economists, it is improbable that the conventional conclusions of welfare theory would continue to be stated with as little caution as is at present the custom (Graaff 1957: 1).

This was written in 1957 but is even truer today. Hence the first section in my five-part chapter.

In the second section, I describe the classical utilitarian approach to the optimum population, showing how it may be taken as answering 'no' to the question posed, although it does not necessarily do so. However, there are many limitations to this analysis, which I discuss in the rest of the paper, beginning in the third section with the objections to utilitarianism. One of my criticisms of welfare economics is that it has remained rooted in utilitarianism and not taken account of alternative principles or evaluative bases. A second criticism is that important considerations are missing from the economic framework within which the question is posed. There is at present a tendency, encouraged by the practices of academic journals, to focus on one aspect of an economic problem, treating this aspect in depth but ignoring other, possibly more important, dimensions, as discussed in the fourth section. One of the most important missing elements is global inequality, which is the subject of the fifth section. Population growth is taking place in a world characterized by great inequality. Although economists like to assume in their models that everyone is identical—it makes life much simpler—this will not do when discussing the optimum population. The fact that new members of the population are entering a highly unequal world may change our answer to the question posed in this volume.

One final introductory remark concerns the global perspective of this book—which I very much welcome—and which is a distinctive feature of the Oxford Martin School as a whole. For much of the chapter, I adopt such a global approach to welfare and justice, asking whether there are too many people from the standpoint of the world as a whole. A global 'yes' is however quite consistent with the population being too *small* for individual countries, or whole continents, such as Europe. The organization Population Matters,[1] which believes that the world as a whole needs to contract its population, still

---

[1] Previously known as the Optimum Population Trust.

classifies some 46 countries as having the capacity to expand their population (Population Matters 2013).

The Welfare Economist's Approach

Why welfare economics? You may say that the question tackled in this book is a purely scientific one: is the current population of some 7 billion, or the 10 billion expected by 2100, the largest sustainable? Answering this question requires experts on water, food, natural resources, and health; topics covered by other chapters in this volume. I am not intending to trespass on their territory. But in asking 'is the planet full?' we are not simply asking whether the population is sustainable. A hundred years ago, the Swedish economist Knut Wicksell gave a lecture in The Hague, in which he argued that 'it is possible for a country to maintain for centuries a constant population and yet be terribly overpopulated' (1910: 208). As he recognized, any judgement about 'overpopulation' involves both technical issues and issues of value. It is rather like standing in Oxford's Banbury Road in the morning watching buses go by with 'Sorry, bus full' signs. We know that this does not mean that they could not take an extra passenger. Adding one more would not render the bus unable to move. Rather the bus driver is applying rules set by the bus company and by health and safety legislation. These rules reflect judgements about safety but also social norms about the acceptable degree to which passengers may be squashed together.

The question is not therefore only one of positive economics. We have to consider the underlying normative judgements. So, how do welfare economists think about this type of question? The first point I want to make is that judgements by economists take two different forms: the statements may be about

- Quantities: we have or do too much or too little;
- Distortions: people are not making their choices on the right basis.

Now it may seem to non-economists that the first is the key issue, and that the second is a distraction, or at best a sideshow. But for many issues the reverse is true. Indeed in many cases, the second statement seems the natural starting point. Suppose for example that I were to say 'there are too many books in the world'. This would probably be regarded as a strange statement. Why pick on books rather than some other consumer product? If one were to single out books, it could be because books are (in the United Kingdom) zero-rated for VAT, whereas other entertainment products such as CDs are taxed at 20 per cent. It could therefore be suggested that this differential tax treatment distorts people's choices. We should have a level playing field.

How is this relevant to population policy? Some years ago, I was a member of an EU High Level Group on the future of social policy in an enlarged EU, which came out arguing for a 'new demographic dynamism'. In this report we made the rather cavalier statement that

> history (the post-war period) and geography (the example of the United States compared with Japan) prove that demography is a key factor in the dynamism of a society: if we want to instil confidence and dynamism into our too-often gloomy societies, then we should:
>
> • develop more selective and better integrated immigration, and
> • allow young couples to have the number of children they desire.
>
> (European Commission 2004: 7).

This is an example of the second type of argument. We argued, citing evidence for a range of EU countries, that there was a significant shortfall of the number of children below the desired family size. Nor were we alone. In 2007, the OECD (2007: 36) reported that 'women generally have fewer children than they desire'.

Why we need to look at quantities

This is a 'levelling the playing field' argument. However, this approach now seems to me open to question. The first reason stems from the obvious point that decisions about fertility, unlike the choice between a book and a CD, are decisions that have significant consequences for others. The consequences may be negative, such as crowding, or positive, such as increased dynamism. There are potentially large differences between private and social costs (and benefits), referred to as 'externalities'.[2] Put in a stark form, if the EU High Level Group believed the dynamism argument then we should have made the case for encouraging population growth, and we should not have hidden behind the distortion argument. Or, the other way round, it may be that women in Europe may be choosing fewer children than they would like because they feel an obligation not to overcrowd the planet. They may have internalized the externalities.

The second reason for rejecting the distortion approach in the case of fertility is that the theory of the second best has long recognized that levelling one playing field is not enough, and may well be counter-productive, if other distortions exist. In the present case, this seems a serious risk. We know that the playing field is not level for women in the labour market. It could well be that the desired fertility is affected by the reduced opportunities that women

---

[2] See Birdsall (1988: 523–4) for a discussion of externalities in this context.

face in their professional lives. Removing obstacles to fertility, without removing unequal opportunities in the labour market, may not be a welfare improving reform. Indeed, the EU High Level Group's recommendation could be criticized on the grounds that it would reinforce gender stereotypes and make career advancement more difficult for women.

Third, in this field more than many others, preferences may be endogenous. Preferences cannot be taken as given. Preferences change as a result of education, of specific health and family planning advice, and of societal pressures. Since each of these may be influenced by public policy, we have to ask whether we wish to shift preferences in favour of reduced population size. We are back with an argument about quantities.

Finally, the argument of the High Level Group was made from the perspective of EU member states. But the consequences are global, and we need to allow for the difference between national objectives and a worldwide perspective. It may be, for example, that we need to shift the balance between the two elements, with EU countries seeking to maintain their dynamism by opening their doors more widely to immigration.

For all these reasons, I believe that the question is better posed in terms of quantities—is the planet too full?—rather than in terms of distortions of individual decisions.

The Classical Optimum Population Analysis

The quantity question has long preoccupied economists: '... the optimum concept ... was explicitly developed as an analytical tool by some of the path-breaking theorists who established the essential foundations of modern economics' (Gottlieb 1945: 291). One of those cited by Gottlieb was Wicksell, to whose lecture on 'optimum population' I referred to earlier. Another was Henry Sidgwick, who gave a very clear account of the classical utilitarian treatment, where the objective is to maximize the sum of utilities:

> For if we take Utilitarianism to prescribe, as the ultimate end of action, happiness on the whole ... it would follow that, if the additional population enjoy on the whole positive happiness, we ought to weigh the amount of happiness gained by the extra number against the amount lost by the remainder (Sidgwick 1874: 415).

Assuming for the moment that total consumption is fixed (an assumption relaxed below), the planet is too full if the average utility has fallen below the cost of an extra person.[3] The cost of an extra person is measured in terms of

---

[3] The following chapter by Toby Ord revisits Henry Sidgwick's work and provides a critical assessment of both the total and average views of utility from a philosophical perspective.

their consumption (assumed equal to the average—there is no inequality at this point) valued at the marginal utility of consumption. In symbols, if total resources are denoted by C, and the total population by N, giving consumption per head of C/N, then the planet is too full if

U(C/N) is less than U′(C/N) times C/N;

where U(C/N) is the average utility and U′(C/N) is the marginal utility. Alternatively, this can be expressed by saying that the average utility per unit of consumption per head is less than the marginal utility:

U(C/N) divided by C/N is less than U′(C/N).

The optimum population, given by maximizing N times U(C/N), is that where the average utility per unit of consumption per head is equal to the marginal utility.

Sidgwick's conclusion may be illustrated with a diagram—see Figure 2.1. Utility is derived from consumption per head, measured along the horizontal axis. With a fixed total consumption, the larger the population, the smaller is the consumption per head, so that as the population increases, one moves to the left in the diagram. The slope of the heavy curve at any point is the marginal utility from consumption, and the slope of the dashed line is the average utility per unit of consumption. At point A, these two are equal. At any point to the left of A, the average is less than the marginal, and the population is in excess of the utilitarian optimum. For this reason, I have shaded the area indicating the levels of population where the planet would be regarded as full. This is not, as noted earlier, the same as unsustainable, if we interpret the maximum sustainable population as that where utility falls to zero. A zero

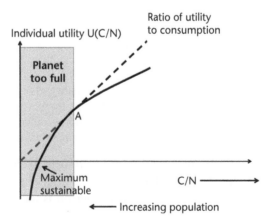

Figure 2.1. Optimum population to maximize the sum of utilities
Source: author.

level of utility is often taken to correspond to a 'neutral' life, defined to the borderline between 'a life worth living' and 'a life not worth living' (Blackorby, Bossert, and Donaldson 2005: 25). The optimum population is less than the maximum sustainable.

The discussion may seem far removed from reality, so let us put a little flesh on the bones, taking our cues from the global debate about poverty. First, let us follow the original Human Development Index (HDI) created by the United Nations Development Programme (UNDP 1990) and assume that well-being is governed by the (natural) logarithm of consumption per head. Secondly, let us suppose that the consumption per head is normalized by the level set in the Millennium Development Goals (MDG) target for extreme poverty. Since $\log_e 1$ is zero, this means that we are attributing the base of zero utility to a person living on $1.25 a day. I should point out that this choice differs from those made by others. For example, Broome (1996: 177) defines zero on the scale to be 'the well-being of a person who leads a life without any experience of any sort: a life lived in a coma throughout', and this might indeed be a better definition of neutrality.

Armed with this HDI/MDG specification, we can calculate that point A corresponds to a consumption level of $3.40 a day, some 2¾ times the MDG target (see Figure 2.2). (To maximize N times $\log_e(C/N)$, where N is total population and C is the (fixed) total of consumption, we have to set $\log_e(C/N) = 1$). This suggests that there remains considerable scope for expansion—that the planet is far from full, since today's world average consumption is more than seven times this amount. (This conclusion would be further reinforced if the neutral level of utility were to be set at a lower level of consumption.)

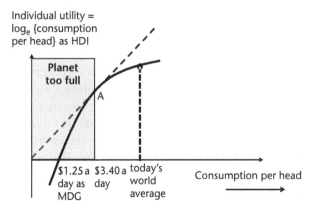

Figure 2.2. Utilitarian optimum population: an empirical application
Source: author.

Does utilitarianism favour large populations?

This calculation lends support to those who argue that the classical utilitarian analysis favours large populations. The problem is that 'it can recommend what could be regarded as overly large populations' (Dasgupta 2005: 424). This criticism underlies the 'Repugnant Conclusion' famously identified by Derek Parfit (1984) and much discussed in the philosophical literature.

> *The Repugnant Conclusion:* For any possible population of at least ten billion people, all with a very high quality of life, there must be some much larger imaginable population whose existence, if other things are equal, would be better, even though its members have lives that are barely worth living. (Parfit 1984: 388, original emphasis.)

As is often the case in economics, a lot turns on the phrase 'other things are equal'. The problem has to be fully specified in terms of what is being held constant. The formulation of the classical utilitarian problem above assumes that total consumption is fixed and that it is shared equally among everyone. An increase in the population reduces consumption per head, and hence utility, for everyone. In this context, it is evident that the recommended population depends on the form of the utility function. This is illustrated by Mulgan's demonstration of the Repugnant Conclusion:

> Begin with a world where ten billion people all have extremely good lives. Call it A. Imagine a second world, with twice as many people *each of whom is more than half as happy* as the people in A. Call this new world B. Total utility in B exceeds that in A. Now repeat this process until we reach a world where a vast population each have a life which is barely worth living. Call this world Z. As each step increases total utility, Z must be better than A.   (Mulgan 2004: 23, my emphasis.)

The key lies in the italicized assumption. It is easy to find utility functions for which this is true (for example, where U is the square root), but it is also easy to find cases where it does not hold. It fails for any utility function such that utility reaches zero at a strictly positive consumption, as shown in Figure 2.1. However, it remains the case that such functions can 'advocate very large populations' (Dasgupta 2005: 438), as he demonstrates for a plausible example where $U = B - (C/N)^{-\sigma}$, where B and σ are positive constants (this form is also used in Dasgupta 1969). But there is no necessity that this should follow. If we only require that the utility function be a non-decreasing, concave (not necessarily strictly concave) function, then we can find a utility function that generates any arbitrarily small population as the utilitarian optimum. This may be seen graphically in a diagram like Figure 2.1. Choose any point, with any arbitrarily small population, and draw the ray through the origin, which gives the ratio of utility to consumption per head. Concavity requires that a line joining any two points on the utility function lie everywhere below (or on) the utility function. This is satisfied by a function consisting of two straight line segments with a kink at the chosen point, such that the left-hand slope is greater than that of the ray and the right-hand slope is less than that of the ray. And with that utility function the chosen population is optimal.

There is therefore no presumption towards an answer 'yes' from classical utilitarians to the question posed in this book, even if it follows from the specific functional forms adopted in a number of studies. At the same time, the analysis is open to debate on several grounds. In investigating why it is controversial, and why the classical utilitarian argument may lead us astray, it is important to note that there are three key ingredients. The first are the social values that enter our judgement, or what I have referred to as the 'social welfare function'. The second is the economic model. The third is that we have not allowed for global inequality. I want to argue that these are all important, and different treatments may well change the way in which we answer the question.

Optimum Population and the Social Welfare Function

It may come as a surprise to non-economists to learn that much economic analysis today remains rooted in classical utilitarianism, but this is the case. Robert Lucas in his 2003 Presidential Address to the American Economic Association stated that

> To evaluate the effects of policy change on many different consumers, we can calculate welfare gains (perhaps losses, for some) for all of them, one at a time, and add the needed compensations to obtain the welfare gain for the group.
>
> (Lucas 2003: 1–2.)

Lucas appeared to regard this statement as self-evident: he described it as 'the general logic of quantitative welfare analysis' (Lucas 2003: 1). In this respect, he is followed by many economists. However, this statement disregards the many objections that have been raised to the utilitarian approach in the past century or more. It is as if a scientist were to analyse the economic consequences of climate change solely on the basis of reading Alfred Marshall's *Principles of Economics* (1890), approximately contemporary with Sidgwick's *The Methods of Ethics* (1874).

To begin with, we may not be content to add the welfare gains: the sum takes no account of how the utilities are distributed. In Amartya Sen's words (1973: 16), 'maximizing the sum of individual utilities is supremely unconcerned with the interpersonal distribution of that sum.' In order to allow for these distributional concerns, the sum can be replaced by a concave function of individual utilities, where the degree of concavity captures the extent to which we are concerned about the distribution. How would such a shift—from adding utilities à la Lucas to a concave function—change our views about population? It turns out, rather surprisingly, that it may lead us—in the present context with everyone identical (see below)—to favour a larger population, as has been shown by Dasgupta (2005). He comments that 'I have known this result for a long time, but still find it puzzling that the idea of *equality* should play such an influential role in normative population theory' (Dasgupta 2005: 438). Taking an iso-elastic function (with a strictly positive elasticity ϵ between zero and 1) of individual utilities (where positive), we find that the marginal utility is multiplied by ϵ, thus reducing the cost. Since the elasticity is less than unity, the optimum population is larger. Those concerned with equity, and not simply with summing utility, are less likely to say that the planet is full.

An alternative transformation of the utility function is that proposed by Blackorby and Donaldson (1984): 'critical-level utilitarianism is a one-parameter family of principles. The parameter is a *fixed* critical level of utility... and the criterion used to rank... is the sum of the differences between individual utilities and the critical level' (Blackorby, Bossert, and Donaldson 2009: 485, original emphasis). Rather than maximizing N times U(C/N), we maximize N times {U(C/N)-a}, where a is the critical level parameter. (They also propose critical-level generalized utilitarianism, which combines the introduction of the critical level with the concave transformation of utilities described in the previous paragraph.) As they note, a positive critical level is one route to avoid Parfit's Repugnant Conclusion. We can see too that the condition for the planet to be too full is that

U(C/N) is less than U'(C/N) times C/N + a.

The answer is more likely to be 'yes', the larger a is. With the HDI/MDG specification used earlier, the optimal consumption level becomes $(1+a)$ times \$3.40. With sufficiently large choice of a, the optimal population would be below the current level.

Capabilities

As Blackorby, Bossert, and Donaldson make clear in their discussion of the critical-level approach, they 'restrict attention to welfarist principles... defined on utility distributions' (2004: 47). More radical are proposals to shift the evaluative basis from utilities. A much-discussed example is provided by the capability approach, advanced by Amartya Sen, most recently in his book *The Idea of Justice* (2009). Broadly defined, capabilities refer to the freedom that people have to realize their potential: their opportunities rather than their outcomes. A shift to a capability approach can have major implications.

Here I simply refer to two of the important ways in which we may need to shift our perspective.

First, we have to link the mainly resource-based analysis of possibilities—as in the discussion of economic models to follow—to the impact on capabilities. As has been discussed in the literature on the definition of poverty, adoption of the capability approach means that an absolute concept of capabilities may translate into a set of resource requirements that depend on the society in question and may change over time.[4] Absolute capabilities may require relative resources. The resources required to be able to participate in society are no longer the linen shirt and leather shoes cited by Adam Smith in *The Wealth of Nations* (1776) but a mobile telephone. This in turn has implications for the specification of the consumption required to achieve a neutral life, and for the specification of the critical level just discussed. For the critical level, we may need to think not in terms of the absolute $1.25 a day of the MDGs, but of the higher level of resources required as a minimum to participate in a modern advanced society.

Second, in the capability approach there are many elements that determine the opportunities open to individuals. A number of these relate to personal resources, but they also depend on the provision of social goods and services. In their recent survey of 'functionings and capabilities', Kaushik Basu and Luis López-Calva say that

> in trying to empirically compare the quality of life achieved by different societies using the capabilities approach, we may need to focus on a few salient functionings...Do people in society x have the option of a long and healthy life? Are people able to live lives free of political oppression? Are people able to read and write?...Do people have enough to eat and drink?
>
> (Basu and López-Calva 2011: 155–6).

It is clear that in each of these a key role is played by public provision. In the case of the last, food is a personal good but access to food depends on public order and public infrastructure. Pressure on public infrastructure is indeed often invoked as a reason for resisting population growth. Put the other way round, those who are willing to invest more in public infrastructure are more likely to agree that the world population can be expanded. But this investment has a cost. In terms of the analysis here, we have to recognize that $1.25 a day refers to only one of the eight MDGs and that we have to add to this the cost of the required investments in education, health, and environmental sustainability to meet the other goals. The shaded rectangle in Figure 2.2 is expanded to the right, making it more likely we conclude that the planet is too full.

---

[4] See, for example, Sen (1983).

The adoption of the capability approach in place of classical utilitarianism may therefore render us more likely to respond 'yes' to the question whether the planet is full. However, the full implications of adopting the capability approach become clearer in conjunction with the two other extensions of the classic analysis. The relativity of the poverty line becomes important on account of the unequal world distribution (the subject of this chapter's penultimate section). The role of infrastructure becomes apparent when we consider how the world's resources are used. We cannot simply pose the problem in terms of dividing a cake of a given size. The ingredients have to be grown; the cake has to be baked; it has to be transported and distributed. The planet is affected by all of these activities, to which I now turn in the following section.

Optimum Population and Modelling the Economy

As Keynes famously said, 'economics is a science of thinking in terms of models joined to the art of choosing models which are relevant to the contemporary world' (Keynes 1973: 296). In modern economics, more attention seems to be paid to the first part of the sentence than to the second part. Much of modern economics treats some aspects of a problem in a highly advanced and specialized way, but in so doing often completely ignores other relevant dimensions of the problem. The subject has, in my view, become over-compartmentalized.

Among the key elements so far missing from the model are (a) the contribution of new people to production; (b) the necessary investment in private and public capital stock; (c) the using up of non-renewable resources and impact on climate change, and (d) the contribution of new people to advances in technology.

The first of these *has* been incorporated in the literature. James Meade, whose chapter on 'Optimum population and optimum saving' in *Trade and Welfare* (1955) is well worth reading today, took account of the contribution to production that new citizens would bring. This leads, in the framework employed here, to what Dasgupta (2005) calls the Sidgwick–Meade Rule. What this basically says is that the cost of an additional person is equal to what they consume minus what they produce. The planet is then too full if

$U(C/N)$ is less than $U'(C/N) \times \{C/N - \text{marginal contribution to production}\}$

Taking account of the contribution to production shifts the balance to the left in Figure 2.1. (In the case where the utility function is $\log_e(C/N)$, and where workers are paid their marginal product, we have to set $\log_e(C/N) = 1$ minus the proportionate share of wages.) The ratio of utility to consumption can now be less than the marginal utility. How much less depends on what one expects to be the contribution of new workers. James Martin (2011: 30), in his article in *Oxford Today* referred to a future time 'when conventional work is done by machines'. In that case, the optimal population will be smaller. In the other direction, robots may render humans more productive. Armed with new technologies, we may be able to make better use of the planet's resources.

But the contribution of new people to work is only part of the story. It is for this reason that it seems important to go beyond the Meade framework. The other considerations may operate in the opposite direction. We have already seen this to be the case with the requirement for additional costly infrastructural investments. Similarly, to the extent that an extra person reduces resources, or damages the environment, this imposes a cost. This cost term raises the right-hand side of the equation, and makes it more likely that an increase in population is undesirable. It is important here to stress that the relevant variable is the impact of an *additional person* on resources and the environment and on technological change. Of course, we are all today using up the resource base and damaging the environment, but we are asking whether policy should be directed to preventing new members joining the planet. At the same time, the impact of an additional person depends on the actions that we take and the policies pursued. In the case of resource use/ climate change, investment today in measures to limit use of nonrenewable energy per person will reduce the carbon footprint of the 9-billionth inhabitant. So a person who is willing to invest more in averting climate change (financed by reducing current consumption) is more likely to be relaxed about population growth than someone who does not believe that such investment should be made.

Technological advance

The impact on resources and the environment is the subject of other chapters in this book. Here I focus on the final element (d): technological advance. Historically, it is the case that consumption per head has grown as the world's population has increased. The idea that the growth rate of the economy depends positively on the growth of the population is in fact widely held. When the EU High Level Group, to which I referred earlier, argued that demographic factors made the economy more 'dynamic', it was this mechanism that they had in mind. Lack of population growth did not make a country poorer, but made it less likely to grow—hence the reference to Japan. Many years ago, the United States sociologist, Seabury C. Gilfillan argued that

> Increasing population and/or industry stimulate invention, because they increase the absolute need for a device, and the number of potential finders, while the cost of finding it remains the same. . . . More population does not help with more

portrait photographs, because more labor must go to make them...But as to invention, increasing population...entails that each inventor's work is more widely useful than before, at the same time that there are more inventors to work (1935: 58–9, quoted in Young, 1998).

At least over some range, growth may increase with population size. In their essay on 'Optimum human population size', Gretchen Daily, and Anne and Paul Ehrlich have argued that

> An optimum population would be sufficiently large to provide a 'critical mass' in each of a variety of densely populated areas where intellectual, artistic and techno-logical creativity would be stimulated. While creativity can also be sparked in sparsely populated areas, many cultural endeavours require a level of specialisa-tion, communication, and financial support that is facilitated by the social infra-structure characteristic of cities (1994: 471–2).

The insight that creativity may be positively related to population density has been embodied in a number of versions of endogenous growth theory, where there is a scale effect in the determination of the growth rate. The rate of technical progress is an increasing function of the size of the economy. This prediction of the theory has been criticized, but is a natural conse-quence if one treats invention and innovation as the outcome of an extreme value process. In other words, the productivity of an economy is determined by the 'best' idea to be identified. If the probabilities of making a discovery are independent, then the maximum achieved value is a non-decreasing function of the number of draws. In a larger population, one is more likely to find a new Shakespeare or a new Mozart. Or, more prosaically, the more people working in creative activities and innovation, the faster should be the growth rate.

The problems with this—seductive—argument are twofold. First, in theor-etical terms, the events are not independent. People interact, and people build on the work of others. This may mean that a larger country has a break-through, but is led in a direction where productivity gains are rapidly exhausted. They may be led into a cul-de-sac: for example, getting ever better at taking fingerprints, rather than supporting research in the totally different field of molecular biology that led to DNA as a source of identification. In any case, while the growth rate may increase with population size, it is not clear by how much. Is the effect proportionate, or less than proportionate, for example increasing with the square root of population size?

The second difficulty is that it is hard to find empirical evidence. Some empirical studies of growth simply assume away the possibility that growth increases with population size. As Robert Solow has remarked, such studies overlook the possibility of a scale effect on growth:

Usually, when we compare the R&D intensity of different economies, like Japan, the United States, and the EC, we look at R&D spending per unit of GDP. This has always seemed foolish to me.... If the United States has the same R&D–GNP ratio as Japan, it should produce more innovations than Japan, because it is larger (Solow 2000: 177).

In contrast, other empirical studies simply assume that technical advance is proportionate to population. When seeking to explain differences across countries in patent activity, it is common to examine patents per million of the population 'scaled to adjust for the size of the economy' (Falk 2004: 6), but not to include population as an explanatory variable. Variables such as R&D intensity, education, GDP per capita, and patent protection are included, but population is not. Scale effects are simply assumed to be proportionate: 10 billion people will generate twice as many patents as 5 billion. In fact, after reviewing the limited evidence, Young (1998: 43) concluded that 'the evidence of scale effects might best be described as inconsistent'.

My treatment of this subject is unduly cursory, and my main aim is to flag up the need to include this as part of the equation and to seek firmer evidence. The relation between population size and technological advance is a subject that needs further investigation.

Optimum Population and Inequality

Up to this point I have taken no account of inequality. Yet inequality can be an important factor influencing how we answer the question as to whether the planet is too full. Inequality has featured in the philosophical literature. Parfit (1986), for example, begins with societies A and B where everyone enjoys the same quality of life, but later introduces A+ where there are two unequal groups. Today's world is more like A+. It is made up of countries with very different per capita incomes, and within those countries incomes are unequally distributed. There is both between-country and within-country inequality.

In this section, I argue that (a) the *existence* of world inequality affects the conclusions drawn with regard to the optimum population; (b) population growth is projected to take place in countries that are poorer and more unequal, and (c) the answer to the question 'is the planet full?' depends on how far we are willing to increase world redistribution.

These are three separate arguments. To underline this, I begin by considering the case where population growth is spread evenly (each person is simply cloned) and where population growth leads to no further redistribution between rich and poor. People differ in the amount of resources received by them and people like them, denoted by c, where there is a distribution of c across the world population. The scale of the world population is denoted by N, so that each person belonging to the group with resources c is able to consume c/N. The condition for social welfare to be reduced if there is an increase in N is given by condition A: that the following expression, integrated (summed) over the distribution of c, be negative: $U(c/N) - U'(c/N).c/N$.

Suppose, for example, that we start from a situation of equality where everyone consumes c*/N and that the expression in condition A is zero for this value of consumption per head. In other words, we are at the optimum population. Let us also suppose that U takes the logarithmic form, as assumed in the earlier example, which means that the second term in condition A is equal to 1. In this special case, the impact of inequality operates through the impact on the level of utility. Let us introduce inequality by taking x from half the people and giving it to the other half, so that they consume $(c* - x)/N$ and $(c* + x)/N$, respectively. Total utility is the sum of ½ times $\log_e\{(c* - x)/N\}$ $+ ½\log_e\{(c* + x)/N\}$, which is equal to $\log_e\{c*/N\}$ and $½\log_e\{1 - (x/c*)^2\}$. The last term is negative where x is positive, which means that the level of utility is reduced, relative to the level with equality. This means that the expression in condition A becomes negative, so that the existence of inequality causes us to conclude that the population is too large. The impact on the optimum population in this case is illustrated in Figure 2.3, where the intersection of the dotted line (unity) with the average of rich and poor (on the dashed line) is to the right of the previous choice of A, indicating that the optimum population is smaller.

The effect of inequality does not, however, necessarily operate in this direction, as may be seen by replacing the choice of utility function by a quadratic. The expression in condition A then becomes proportional to

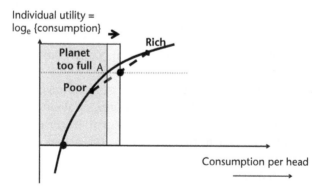

Figure 2.3. Classical utilitarian optimum population in the presence of inequality: special case of logarithmic utility function
Source: author.

$(c/N)^2$ minus a constant, the sum of which *increases* with the extent of inequality. More generally, we can appeal to the result of Rothschild and Stiglitz (1971: 67), which shows that the condition for a mean preserving spread of the distribution to reduce the expression in condition A is that the expression be a concave function of c/N. This property is not satisfied by the quadratic, but is shared by many social welfare functions used in the literature: for example, the form used by Dasgupta (1969, eq. 1.2) in much of his analysis. (A mean preserving spread is what the name suggests: taking consumption away from a poorer person and giving it someone better off. The example with x in the previous paragraph is a special case of such a spread.)

Insofar as the concavity property applies to the utility-specific functions employed in the literature, the introduction of inequality into the model is therefore one response to the concern that the classical optimum population analysis is biased in favour of large populations. What is more, it casts a different light on the implications of abandoning a simple summation of utilities. If the social welfare function becomes a concave function of individual utilities, then this concavity may reinforce the concavity of the expression in condition A, moving the optimum towards a smaller population. (For example, this happens with a transformation g() of the logarithmic utility function, where the first and third derivatives of g() are positive and the second negative.)

Where will population grow?

So far, I have assumed that world inequality remains the same as the population size varies. The above analysis posited a fixed degree of inequality and asked how this affected the welfare implications of a growing population. But inequality may rise as a result of population growth. The projected population growth is not spread uniformly. Taking the UN projections from 2011 to 2050 (the medium variant from the UN, 2011), we can see that there will be little or negative population growth in Europe. Growth in the United States is predicted as 110 million. This is part of the overall projected increase, from 7.1 billion to 9.7 billion, but only a modest part. The projected increase is much larger in India (plus 486 million) and in Nigeria (plus 230 million). These two countries account for over a quarter of the world's projected population growth. The increase in these countries is so large that I have left them out of Figure 2.4. This shows the 28 other countries where population is projected to increase by 20 million or more from 2011 to 2050 and their 2011 levels of Gross National Income per capita adjusted for differences in purchasing power (data from the World Bank 2013). Together these 30 countries (including India and Nigeria) account for over three-quarters of the 2.6 billion increase in population expected between now and 2050. As

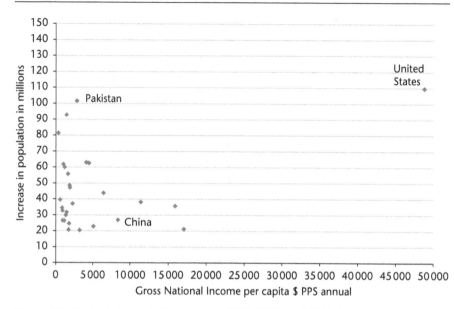

Figure 2.4. Projected population increase 2011–2050 and 2011 GNI per capita $PPP
Source: UN (2011) and World Bank (2013).

may be seen from Figure 2.4, the population growth is concentrated in low-income countries. Only 4 of the 30 countries had a per capita income above that of China in 2011.

The countries where population is projected to grow are also in many cases more unequal. That is, we have to bring in the second element that leads to global inequality: the differences within countries. The world is unequal both because Zambia is poorer than Britain but also because within Zambia there is high inequality. In Figure 2.5, inequality is measured by the Gini coefficient (or half the relative mean difference). Suppose that a new person in Zambia could have the income of anyone chosen at random from the Zambian population. What is the expected difference in their income from yours, where you are a randomly chosen citizen of Zambia? The expected difference, expressed as a percentage of mean income and divided by 2 gives the Gini coefficient. For Zambia, it is close to 50 per cent, according to World Bank data. On average the difference between the incomes of any two Zambians chosen at random is equal to twice 50 (= 100) per cent of the mean. Fifty per cent is quite high by international standards, as may be seen from Figure 2.5, which shows the distribution among all countries. What about the 30 countries where population is projected to grow by 20 million or more? Although there are a number of the 30 countries with values below 35 per cent, the median is above 40, and there are seven countries with values in excess of 45.

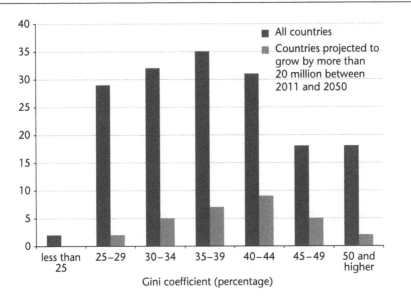

Figure 2.5. Gini coefficients in different countries, 2006

Source: Data supplied by François J. Bourguignon. See also Bourguignon (2011).

What does this mean?

Does this mean that only countries with above-average incomes or low inequality should be allowed to expand their populations? As Parfit (1986: 145) asked rhetorically, would it 'be best if in future only the best-off nation—such as the Norwegians—have children?' No, since there is a further element. The extent of global inequality is not immutable. The calculations above assume that the cost is borne by the country in question: the birth of an additional Zambian reduces the average consumption of Zambians but no one else. But if the cost is shared throughout the world, then the calculation may look rather different. An expansion of the world population may raise social welfare if it is accompanied by increased redistribution between countries. To revert to my transport metaphor, but switching from buses to the railways, it may be that a train cannot squeeze in any more passengers in standard class but that there are empty first-class seats. This may not be a problem if those in first class are willing to move their briefcases off the empty seats next to them and make room for some standard-class passengers.

The classical utilitarian analysis may have biased the conclusion in favour of overly large populations in part because it assumed that taxes and transfers would equalize incomes (see, for example, Meade 1955: 90). So far in this section I have gone to the opposite extreme and assumed that the existence of inequality has to be taken as given. This second-best view may be realistic, as was argued by Daily, Ehrlich, and Ehrlich:

we are sceptical that the incentives driving social and economic inequalities can ever be fully overcome. We therefore think that a global optimum should be determined with humanity's characteristic selfishness and myopia in mind (Daily, Ehrlich, and Ehrlich 1994: 471).

The train seat metaphor may give a misleading impression of the ease of making such transfers. There may be those who would be willing to reduce their own consumption but doubt whether the resources can be effectively transferred. For them, the deep-seated nature of global inequality may be a barrier to accepting population growth.

But this may be too pessimistic. The very fact that many of the increased world population will be found in countries that are both poor and highly unequal may lead to greater efforts to combat world poverty and inequality. People may therefore differ in their judgements about whether or not the planet is full according to their willingness to accompany an increase population with further redistributive transfers.

Conclusions: Is the Planet Full?

In this chapter I have argued that it is right to pose the question in terms of the number of people, not as a matter of levelling the field of individual choice. The central issue concerns the size of the world population, not untrammelled parental choice. The way in which economists have thought about the optimum population over more than a century has considerable value, but the standard classical utilitarian analysis has been criticized as biased in favour of large populations, as saying too readily 'no' to the question 'Is the planet full?'. I have argued, however, that such a response is not necessarily implied, and that the conclusion follows more from the specific assumptions than from the underlying framework.

At the same time, there remain serious shortcomings to the classical utilitarian analysis and I have examined three ways in which it needs to be developed: we need to take account of alternative social objectives, to enrich the economic framework within which the question is posed, and to consider the implications of inequality between and within countries. Each of these developments may incline us more towards saying 'yes'. With the critical-level utilitarian approach, we are in effect raising the bar, and making a 'yes' more likely. With a capability approach, absolute requirements in capability space may translate into a set of requirements for resources that are increasingly demanding, again shifting the baseline. The capability approach highlights the extra cost in terms of the need for social infrastructure. The impact of additional people on resources and climate adds to the cost side of the equation (although operating in the opposite direction may be a positive impact on technological creativity). The existence of inequality in the distribution of resources may well (although does not necessarily) give us pause about the desirability of expanding the world population. The pattern of population growth will tend, other things equal, to increase global inequality and poverty. Whether or not we welcome this population increase depends on whether we are willing to take steps to ensure that 'other things are not equal' by expanding global redistribution.

I said at the outset that I would not answer the question. I have, however, tried to identify some of the factors that are likely to lead to different conclusions: the answer depends on the following.

- The social welfare function: the classical utilitarian specification used by economists has tended to point towards saying 'no', but alternative approaches to evaluation may point towards 'yes';
- How important we expect labour to be as a productive factor in the future: people who believe that robots will largely replace humans are more likely to say 'yes';
- How far we believe that a large population leads to greater technological creativity: optimists are more likely to say 'no';
- How far we are concerned with global inequality: those with greater concern are more likely to say 'yes';
- How much global redistribution we are willing to undertake, or believe to be effective: those who believe in the desirability and effectiveness of more redistribution are more likely to say 'no'.

Acknowledgement

This chapter is based on the revised text of a paper presented at an Oxford Martin School seminar in November 2011. I am grateful to François Bourguignon for allowing the use of his data on the world distribution of income, to Adrian Wood for very constructive comments, and to Margaret Meyer for a most helpful discussion. None of them are to be held responsible for the views expressed.

References

Basu, K. and López-Calva, L. F. (2011). 'Functionings and Capabilities', in K. J. Arrow, A. K. Sen, and K. Suzumura (eds), *Handbook of Social Choice and Welfare* (vol. 2). Amsterdam: Elsevier, pp. 153–87.

Birdsall, N. (1988). 'Economic Approaches to Population Growth', in H. Chenery and T. N. Srinivasan (eds), *Handbook of Development Economics* (vol 1). Amsterdam: Elsevier, pp. 477–542.

Blackorby, C. and Donaldson, D. (1984). 'Social Criteria for Evaluating Population Change', *Journal of Public Economics*, 25: 13–33.

Blackorby, C., Bossert, W., and Donaldson, D. (2004). 'Critical-Level Population Principles and the Repugnant Conclusion' in J. Ryberg and T. Tännsjö (eds), *The Repugnant Conclusion: Essays on Population Ethics*. Dordrecht: Kluwer Academic Publishers, pp. 45–59.

Blackorby, C., Bossert, W., and Donaldson, D. (2005). *Population Issues in Social Choice Theory, Welfare Economics, and Ethics*. Cambridge: Cambridge University Press.

Blackorby, C., Bossert, W., and Donaldson, D. (2009). 'Population Ethics' in P. Anand, P. K. Pattanaik, and C. Puppe (eds), *Handbook of Rational and Social Choice*. Oxford: Oxford University Press, pp. 483–500.

Bourguignon, F. (2011). 'A Turning Point in Global Inequality...and Beyond' in W. Krull (ed.) *Research on Responsibility: Reflections on Our Common Future*. Leipzig: CEP Europäische Verlagsanstalt.

Broome, J. (1996). 'The Welfare Economics of Population', *Oxford Economic Papers*, 48: 177–93.

Broome, J. (2009). 'Why Economics Need Ethical Theory' in K. Basu and R. Kanbur (eds), *Arguments for a Better World: Essays in Honor of Amartya Sen* (vol. 1). Oxford: Oxford University Press, pp. 7–14.

Daily, G. C., Ehrlich, A. H., and Ehrlich, P. R. (1994). 'Optimum Human Population Size', *Population and Environment*, 15: 469–75.

Dasgupta, P. (1969). 'On the Concept of Optimum Population', *Review of Economic Studies*, 36: 295–318.

Dasgupta, P. (2005). 'Regarding Optimum Population', *Journal of Political Philosophy*, 13(4): 414–42.

European Commission (2004). *Report of the High Level Group on the Future of Social Policy in an Enlarged European Union*. Luxembourg: European Commission. Last accessed 8 August 2013. <http://www.pedz.uni-mannheim.de/daten/edz-fd/gds/hlg_social_elarg_en.pdf>.

Falk, M. (2004). 'What Determines Patents Per Capita in OECD Countries?' *WIFO Working Paper 242*. Vienna: Austrian Institute of Economic Research (WIFO). Last accessed 16 April 2013. <http://www.wifo.ac.at/jart/prj3/wifo/resources/person_dokument/person_dokument.jart?publikationsid=25390&mime_type=application/pdf>.

Gilfillan, S. C. (1935). *The Sociology of Invention*. Chicago: Follett.

Gottlieb, M. (1945). 'The Theory of Optimum Population for a Closed Economy', *Journal of Political Economy*, 53: 289–317.

Graaff, J. de V. (1957). *Theoretical Welfare Economics*. Cambridge: Cambridge University Press.

Keynes, J. M. (1973). 'The General Theory and After: Part II' in D. Moggridge (ed.), *The Collected Writings of John Maynard Keynes* (vol. 14). London: Macmillan.

Lucas, R. (2003). 'Macroeconomic Priorities', *American Economic Review*, 93: 1–14.

Marshall, A. (1890). *Principles of Economics*. London: Macmillan.

Martin, J. (2011). 'Turbulence Ahead', *Oxford Today*, 23(3): 26–30.

Meade, J. E. (1955). *Trade and Welfare*, Oxford: Oxford University Press.

Mulgan, T. (2004). 'Two Parfit Puzzles' in J. Ryberg and T. Tännsjö (eds), *The Repugnant Conclusion: Essays on Population Ethics*. Dordrecht: Kluwer Academic Publishers, pp. 23–44.

OECD (2007). *Babies and Bosses*. Paris: Organisation for Economic Cooperation and Development.

Parfit, D. (1984). *Reasons and Persons*. Oxford: Clarendon Press.

Parfit, D. (1986). 'Overpopulation and the Quality of Life' in P. Singer (ed.), *Applied Ethics*. Oxford: Oxford University Press, pp. 145–64.

Population Matters (2013). 'Overshoot Index 2011'. Last accessed 8 August 2013. <http://populationmatters.org/documents/overshoot_index_2011.pdf>.

Rothschild, M. and Stiglitz, J. E. (1971). 'Increasing Risk II: Its Economic Consequences', *Journal of Economic Theory*, 3: 66–84.

Sen, A. K. (1973). *On Economic Inequality*. Oxford: Oxford University Press.

Sen, A. K. (1983). 'Poor, Relatively Speaking', *Oxford Economics Papers*, 35: 153–69.

Sen, A. K. (2009). *The Idea of Justice*. London: Allen Lane.

Sidgwick, H. (1874) [1907]. *The Methods of Ethics*. London: Macmillan.

Smith, A. (1776) [1976]. *An Inquiry into the Nature and the Causes of the Wealth of Nations*. Chicago: Chicago University Press.

Solow, R. M. (2000). *Growth Theory: An Exposition* (2nd edn). Oxford: Oxford University Press.

UN (2011). *World Population Prospects: The 2010 Revision*, (online edition, file 1b), United Nations, Department for Economic and Social Affairs. <http://esa.un.org/unpd/wpp/index.htm>.

UNDP (1990). *Human Development Report 1990*. New York: Oxford University Press.

Wicksell, K. (1910). 'The Optimum Population', English translation by J. Overbeek. (1973). 'Wicksell on Population', *Economic Development and Cultural Change*, 21(2): 205–11.

World Bank (2013). 'GNI per capita, PPP (current international $)', World Development Indicators (online), <http://data.worldbank.org/indicator/NY.GNP.PCAP.PP.CD>.

Young, A. (1998). 'Growth Without Scale Effects', *Journal of Political Economy*, 106: 41–63.

3

Overpopulation or Underpopulation?

Toby Ord

Overpopulation has been one of the major global concerns of the last fifty years. The rapid rise of the world's population means many more mouths to feed, raising the possibility of mass famines, and making overpopulation a major humanitarian concern. The increased labour supply to non-Western nations and the projected increases in immigration have made it a major geopolitical concern. The projected increase in resource usage and associated pollution has made it a major environmental concern.

These are the main lenses through which rising population has been viewed. But they have missed a major part of the story.[1] In addition to its well known costs, increased population brings many *benefits*. It means more scientists to discover how our world works, more inventors and thinkers to help solve the world's problems, and more workers to put these ideas into practice. It means more great writers, musicians, and artists to explore the human condition, and to share their masterpieces. It means more people, more sons, daughters, fathers, and mothers, who get a chance to experience the world in all its richness—more beneficiaries for all the creations and improvements we hope to bring about.

It is impossible to have a nuanced and mature approach to population without considering these benefits alongside the costs. Do the costs strongly outweigh the benefits? If so, overpopulation is a big problem and we will need to work out how to prevent or manage it. Are the costs and benefits roughly balanced? If so, we should put less attention and effort into reducing population growth, for these resources could be better spent on other pressing issues. Or do the benefits outweigh the costs? If so, we may be

---

[1] Of course there are some well-known exceptions including Ester Boserup's (1965) historical analysis of the links between population density and technological change, and Julian Simon's (1981) argument about wealth creation countering dwindling resources.

facing *underpopulation*—having too few people—and strange as it may sound, we might face a duty to increase our population.

In this chapter, I aim to explore the question of the ideal number of people for the earth to bear. As the benefit of a larger population is a neglected area, it is there that I spend most of my time. I focus on the benefits of increased population for the creation of information goods, and on the intrinsic value of the new people themselves. I then consider several important questions about the various environmental limits, and on the distribution of the population increases. Finally, I consider how things might change in the future—how we might be able to relax some of the limits or increase some of the benefits.

No one person has the expertise to arrive at a final answer to the question of whether the benefits outweigh the costs, and I do not attempt to do so. My aim is instead to try to frame population policy in a way that takes account of benefits as well as costs, and in doing so, to help us confront the right questions.

Instrumental Benefits

The benefits of increased population can be split into two categories. The first is the instrumental benefits brought about by the presence of additional people. For example, if additional people produce new inventions which improve the lives of everyone, then this is a clear benefit of a larger population and must be weighed against any drawbacks. The second category is the intrinsic value of the lives of the additional people. It considers that it is good for those people to exist and to experience the joys, loves, and excellences that life can offer. It is much less clear how to assess this category. It involves many philosophical questions and there is some debate about whether bringing new people into the world can have intrinsic value at all. Let us therefore begin with the more concrete case of instrumental benefits and confront the philosophically charged intrinsic benefits later.

There are many ways in which creating additional lives can create instrumental benefits. Imagine a childless couple who, after some thought, decide to have a child. This child will make its parents lives better in various ways, chief among them is probably the special relationships they will form which the couple wouldn't have otherwise been able to experience. The child will of course have a financial cost to them, and will take up time that would have been spent on various leisure activities, but presumably the joy and satisfaction for the parents are often enough to outweigh the costs.

The child will also affect many other people in positive and negative ways through its personal relationships, its work, its purchasing decisions, its charitable contributions, and its environmental impact. I don't know how to determine whether these benefits outweigh the costs, but it would be irresponsible to deny that there are benefits being produced which need to be weighed against costs, and to not seek out the advice of specialists who could try to determine this.

One type of instrumental benefit deserves some special attention. *Information goods* may be the most important type of instrumental benefit. These include physical items like books, CDs, and DVDs where the value lies in the information encoded in the item. They also include downloadable software or music, where the pattern of information is once again key and where no underlying physical medium is actually traded. I shall also take the term to include other forms of valuable information, such as scientific discoveries, technological inventions, and novel systems for government or policy.

We can contrast information goods with *material goods*, such as hammers, cars, oil, or food. Consider the differences between hammers and (recorded) songs. Hammers are made of matter, while songs are fundamentally patterns which could be encoded in many different substrates. Each hammer must be laboriously made, perhaps in a smithy, or in a factory. In contrast, a lot of work goes into writing and recording a song, but once recorded, it can be very cheaply copied. Each hammer benefits a single user, so its value is roughly independent of the world's population. In contrast, each song can benefit everyone who desires it—potentially millions or billions of people. Thus unlike a hammer, a song becomes much more valuable the larger the population.

This is the key feature of information goods. Their value increases with the size of the population which both has access to them and could derive some benefit from them. In many cases there is a global appetite for the information and global distribution, so the value of an information good often increases with the size of the global population.

Over the centuries, we have shifted an increasing part of our economy to the production of information goods. They are now ubiquitous. They can be artistic, such as novels, poems, songs, films, or recipes. They can be technical, such as inventions, designs, and new techniques. They can be political, such as new political systems, ideology, or policy approaches. They include all the software that we use on more than a billion personal computers. They include all scientific discoveries, and more than that, they include all academic research in all disciplines.

Adding more people to the world will increase the number of people working to create information goods. This will increase the number of such goods, the variety, and also the peak of quality in many different areas. Additional medical researchers will develop cures for additional diseases; additional programmers will write new and better software; additional activists will develop new and better reforms to the political process. Additional artists will create new pop hits, and new masterpieces, launching new genres and styles. Of course they will also produce much more dross, but we are entitled to focus on the peaks instead of the troughs because we can by and large choose our preferred package of aesthetic information goods. With more people there will even be radio stations and critical reviews in more niches, increasing the quality and relevance of the music, novels, and films that reach you.

Of course it is not clear that twice as many people would produce twice as much value from information goods. Some of these goods will have only local reach or relevance, and many will have diminishing marginal value. We tend to pick the low hanging fruit of science and invention first, snapping up the easy-to-acquire improvements and leaving the more challenging or less beneficial ones for later.

Our cultural improvement will have diminishing marginal returns due to the crowding of our schedules. There are only so many plays or films we can watch, songs we can listen to, or books we can read. Better ones will crowd out worse ones, but if there are limits to the upper end of how much you can like a piece of art, then we will have diminishing returns as we move towards a situation in which you only watch, listen to, and read works that you consider masterpieces. However, we are still a long way from that point, and it sounds like a valuable point to reach!

If the diminishing returns are a major concern, one could also reap the benefits of information goods in another way. If we doubled the population, then instead of doubling the output of information goods, we could halve the input of labour to reach our current output. We could have information workers work 20 hours a week instead of 40, and still have access to the same rate of scientific, technological, and cultural output that we have today. This wouldn't change the proportion of people working to produce information goods, so it wouldn't lower the productivity of the material goods economy; it would simply allow us to have a lot more leisure time to spend as we wish.

A final way in which additional people could provide large benefits through information goods is that in addition to being information producers, they would be information consumers. This means that the markets for information goods would expand, making it more profitable for anyone to begin producing information goods. This would allow for more lavish budgets on mainstream films and albums, but perhaps more interestingly, it would mean more people in each niche of aesthetic taste. This would mean that some niches which are currently too small to have many works of art produced for them would have enough market power to entice artists and production companies to deliver more works. The same is true of non-aesthetic niches: there will be more good non-fiction works on currently obscure areas.

Intrinsic Benefits

Our lives contain significant value. While all our lives are marked in some way by hardship, grief, and pain, they are also filled with hope, joy, love, excitement, and contentment. In almost all cases, we judge that the good aspects outweigh the bad, and find intrinsic value in our lives.[2] The total value of someone's life consists of its instrumental value (the aggregation of all the intrinsic value they add to other people's lives) and its intrinsic value (the value of the life for the person himself or herself). We have discussed the first part, but we would be neglecting a major part of the question if we didn't consider the second.

It is common to hear overpopulation campaigners speak of the need to lower the population by a billion or more. I am yet to hear any discussion in the mainstream media of the lost intrinsic value in not having these people on this Earth. What is the intrinsic value of a billion people? Consider, if you will, the population of the islands that make up the United Kingdom and the Republic of Ireland. Think of the currently existing people who live there, in the small villages, the bustling towns and the thriving cities. Now add all the people who ever lived there before them, through the many centuries, with their different ways of life, all the way back in time until humans first arrived there. There have been a great many inhabitants—hundreds of millions—but the total is less than a billion.

Now consider whether there would have been something of value lost if they had never existed—if the islands had remained uninhabited and the rest of the world had gone on as usual. Of course there were various instrumental benefits for the rest of the world caused by these people (and harms too), but to my mind at least, there is also a great internal value: the intrinsic value of all of those hopes and joys and passions. Even if these people had been completely isolationist and had added nothing of instrumental value to the world, it would have been a great loss had they never existed.

This is the scale of the loss of intrinsic value there would be if we were to reduce the population by a billion. It is thus quite astonishing to see how casually reductions such as these are invoked in debates on population.

Consider your own life, and whether there is some value in it. Setting aside the effects you have on others, wouldn't the world be poorer without you— without your dreams and passions and experiences? If we had decided to radically slow population growth in the past, you might not be here. If you think your life is good, then something would have been lost.

---

[2] Many philosophers now use the technical terms 'final value' or 'noninstrumental value' where I use the less precise but more readily understood 'intrinsic value'.

I think that considerations like those above are often forgotten when talking abstractly about population. You are population too. As are your mother, father, brothers, sisters, friends, and lover. However, the term 'population' can be dehumanizing. It makes us forget that we are talking about you and me: about individuals with their own richly textured lives. It makes us forget about the intrinsic value in us all, and just focus on the aggregate costs such as pollution or crowding.

These questions about the intrinsic value of additional lives have recently received much attention within moral philosophy.[3] It first achieved prominence in the late 19th century in Henry Sidgwick's (1907) writings on utilitarianism. He pointed out that there is an important distinction between trying to increase the total happiness and trying to increase the average happiness (Sidgwick 1907: 415). If we are considering an ethical question where the population is fixed, then there is no significant difference between the total and the average: any action that increases one raises the other in the same proportion. However, if the population can vary, then the two come apart.

To use a heavily simplified example, suppose we could bring about one of two different outcomes:

(A) 5 billion people living very happy lives, or
(B) 10 billion people living lives that are almost as happy as those in (A).

The average happiness is greater in (A), while the total happiness is greater in (B). Over the last century, this distinction has risen to increasing prominence. Philosophers have come to several conclusions. First, this distinction is not just of interest for utilitarian theories of ethics. Whether or not one accepts utilitarianism, one should care about whether it is better if outcome (A) occurs or if outcome (B) occurs. However, in this general case, we shouldn't just think of the happiness in someone's life, but rather some measure of all the value in their life, which may include more than just happiness. Second, there are potentially far more than just two theories for the value of different populations (Parfit 1984; Arrhenius 2000b; Blackorby, Bossert, and Donaldson 2005; Arrhenius forthcoming). The study of these many different theories has come to be known as *population ethics*.

For now though, let us focus on these original two theories, that have come to be known as the *Total View*, and the *Average View*. These views give different recommendations in terms of the intrinsic value of people. According to the Total View, the value of a group of people is the value of each person put together. If we add a new valuable life to a population without changing anything else, it makes the population more valuable. Of course there will

---

[3] There has also been discussion of this question from a related angle in the economics literature, as explained by Tony Atkinson in Chapter 2 of this volume.

eventually come a point where adding a new person will have more costs for the others than it has benefits, making the other lives worse overall. This is a bad effect, but according to the Total View, the intrinsic value of this life may be enough to make up for the costs of overcrowding for others. The Total View recommends adding new lives until the point at which this would no longer increase the total value (because the combined instrumental and intrinsic values of the life turn out to be net negative).

In contrast, the Average View will typically recommend a smaller population size. It says that we should stop at the point where this would no longer increase the average value of a life. This could be because the intrinsic value of the new life would be below the average value (and wouldn't make up for this through instrumental benefits to others), or because the new life would impose enough costs on others to lower the average, or some combination.

It should be stressed that it is very unclear whether we have yet passed either notion of an optimal population. These ethical views explain what the intrinsic value of a population is, and thus what it would mean to have too many people. Much more empirical evidence on quality of life and environmental and economic issues would be needed to actually make use of either standard.

While these are the most well-known views on population ethics, they have both come under considerable attack. In 1984 Derek Parfit published a book called *Reasons and Persons*, which launched population ethics as a major strand in moral philosophy. In it he forcefully showed that the Total View leads to 'The Repugnant Conclusion' described in the previous chapter: the supposition that any expansion of a 'sizeable' and 'happy' population will be beneficial, even if the value of many lives in utility terms end up approaching zero and become 'barely worth living' (Parfit 1984: 388). For example, if the larger population had a thousand times as many people, and their lives were a hundredth as good, then it would contain more overall value according to the total view, though many of us would judge it as inferior. It is worth noting that the example populations we are considering here are not realistic options for our world. Restricting ourselves to realistic options would not allow us to create a choice as stark as this one, and it is through simple, clear thought experiments that philosophers try to judge whether there are problems for an ethical view.

Many philosophers believe that the Repugnant Conclusion makes the Total View implausible as a theory of population ethics. However, others argue that this is premature (Tännsjö 2002; Huemer 2008). For example, the Repugnant Conclusion asks us to imagine a world with a trillion or more people and our intuitions about such large numbers are notoriously shaky. When we try to imagine a trillion people, our mental image might not look very different from our image of a billion people, or even just a million people, whereas we find it easy to imagine people with much less value in their lives. This predictable failure of imagination could lead us to undervalue that outcome.

In contrast, the arguments against the Average View are so strong that to my knowledge there are no remaining philosophers at all who advocate it. The first challenge for the Average View is that it implies that the world would be improved by killing people whose lives are worse than average (at least insofar as this doesn't reduce the quality of life for the others). This is widely considered to be an absurd conclusion. However, this would only follow from an *instantaneous* version of the Average View, in which we look at the average quality of life at an instant. The Average View can also be interpreted in a *timeless* manner (Parfit 1984: 420; Broome 1992: 117). In this case, we consider all the lives that were ever lived and will ever be lived and try to increase the average of this vast 'timeless' population. Once someone is born, they are irrevocably part of this timeless population, so the average will not be improved by their death (unless their life is so bad for them that it has negative value, in which case it is much less clear that their death would be a bad thing).

However, there are numerous other problems for the Average View that the move to a timeless population does not solve. One of these is that it makes the ethics of our decisions more interconnected than seems plausible. For example, the question of whether a couple on an isolated island should have children now depends upon the world average, even if no one on that island ever effects the rest of the world, or vice versa. The move to the timeless population actually makes this worse, as we need to consider the timeless population average, which includes people in the distant past and in the distant future. We would need to study how many people have lived in the past and how good their lives were to make a decision, as well as predicting population size and quality in the future. Perhaps we would be compelled to produce more people now to increase the historical average quality.

The strongest argument against the Average View is probably the following hypothetical situation that Parfit presented in *Reasons and Persons* (Parfit 1984: 422):

Hell Three
Most of us have lives that are much worse than nothing. The exceptions are the sadistic tyrants who make us suffer. The rest of us would kill ourselves if we could; but this is made impossible. The tyrants claim truly that, if we have children, they will make these children suffer slightly less.

In this situation, the Average View says that it would be better to produce another hellish generation since this would slightly increase the average quality of life. However, since this would involve creating many new lives of negative value and has no compensating benefits, it seems very counterintuitive that this would be an improvement at all, and that the best thing people could do would instead be to have no more generations.

Examples like this have caused the Average View to lose all support among moral philosophers.[4] Since we also have reason to doubt the Total View, this has led to a wide proliferation of alternative views on how to value populations. While a full discussion of such views would take us well beyond the scope of this chapter, I shall briefly describe two of the most promising approaches.

Critical level theories are based around the idea that although lives which have negative value for that person are always bad to add to a population, lives with positive value for that person might not always be good to add (Blackorby, Bossert, and Donaldson 1997; Broome 2004). They could be neutral to add, or even bad to add if their value is sufficiently close to zero. This family of theories is similar in some respects to the Total View, but doesn't suffer from the Repugnant Conclusion as lives barely worth living will either have no value or negative value. However, there are other important problems for such theories, not least of which is that they can say that it is better to add lives that are not worth living than to add some larger number of lives which are worth living (Arrhenius 2000a).

Perhaps the most popular in recent years are the various *person-affecting* views. These are theories which are based around the intuition that a state of affairs can't be better (or worse) than another unless there is at least one person for whom it is better (or worse) (Narveson 1967; Glover 1977: 66).[5] These views say that certain kinds of merely potential people shouldn't enter into our assessment when comparing two outcomes. They differ in exactly how they spell this out, with some theories saying only presently existing people count, or that only the people who will actually end up existing count, or only the people who would exist in all alternatives count. While tempting, these theories have been shown to be open to a very similar set of devastating objections (Arrhenius 2009; Arrhenius forthcoming: 151–207).

In summary, there is no consensus on exactly how one should measure the intrinsic value of increases in population. The Average View is widely rejected, but there are reasons to be cautious about using the Total View. Other views are still very much under development, but those that have been proposed in the literature appear to have their own grave flaws. Indeed, there are even

---

[4] Curiously, it still seems to be used within economics. I suspect this is because the practioners are not familiar with the critical literature.

[5] In cases where there are the exact same people in both states of affairs this is akin to the economists' concept of a Pareto improvement. However, if the number or identity of the people can be different in the two cases it is far more controversial. For example, if we were to add people with hellish lives to a population, we intuitively think that this makes it worse even though there is no one for whom it is worse.

several compelling arguments that any approach to valuing a population will have to have at least one of a short list of undesirable properties (Arrhenius 2000a).

This does not mean that we can simply ignore the intrinsic value of additional people. As the initial intuitive arguments of this section show, we do have the intuition that subsections of our population can have considerable intrinsic value and failing to count them in an analysis of overpopulation would be morally reckless. For now though, there is no consensus on exactly how this is to be done.

Costs

I have spent considerable time discussing the instrumental and intrinsic benefits of higher populations as these topics are often neglected in discussions of overpopulation. Costs are much more commonly discussed—especially in the form of limits, such as the number of people that could be supported by the world's fresh water, by our food production, or by our mineral and fossil fuel resources. Chapters 6, 7, and 10 in this volume discuss such limits in detail.

Limits like these are really a form of cost. They are not typically binding constraints, but rather points at which we would have to change from business as usual. We might have to develop new forms of food production, or even just eat less meat, both of which would involve costs. Even without changing our food production, we could probably exceed a calculated limit, but only for a finite amount of time, before we paid a cost in terms of deaths due to starvation. There are also costs as we approach a limit. For example, if we were to get close to using all natural fresh water for drinking, we would need to exploit more and more of the wilderness surrounding sources of water, eventually including some of the most beautiful places which we would much rather preserve.

There is an important source of confusion here that can derail many conversations about the ideal population size. Consider the question of whether we are currently near the limit on food production. In one sense we are, for we are already using most of the world's arable land, and produce only slightly more food than is needed to feed all of the world's people. However, as Charles Godfray points out in Chapter 6 of this volume, meat production uses these natural resources very inefficiently. If we really wanted to feed as many people as possible, we could reduce meat production, or even abandon it completely.

So in one sense we are near the limit, while in another we are far from it. This can cause considerable confusion if a person using one sense engages in debate with someone using the other. The best way to see this is that the lower limit is a 'soft limit', where we can no longer pursue a business-as-usual approach without disaster ensuing, while somewhere above that is a 'hard limit' where—even when abandoning business as usual and using all techno-logical and policy measures available—we still can't exceed that population without disaster.[6]

As we exceed a soft limit and head towards a hard limit, there are two types of cost that we might encounter. One is that departing from business as usual will impose costs (such as those of researching and introducing a new tech-nology, or those of forgoing meat consumption). The other is potentially much worse. It is that even though we could safely exceed the soft limit were we to adjust our activities, we may well not have the will or the coord-ination to do so. For example, people in rich countries may refuse to abandon meat, and instead just pay the increasing costs of meat in a period of food scarcity, pricing those in poorer countries out of sufficient food to survive (Sen 1981).

These limits of political or social feasibility are harder to calculate than technical soft or hard limits, but they are no less important. If it really is socially impossible for rich countries to become vegetarian in order to let people in poorer countries survive, then we certainly want to find out and to factor this into our thinking on the ideal population. However, we should be careful in how we describe the problem. In that case, the situation could either be described as overpopulation, or as shocking selfishness of the world's rich. After all, even a population of just two people could count as overpopulated on that definition if the more powerful of the two demanded all the resources for his or her personal use. This issue frequently arises when people claim that with Western resource consumption the world can only sustainably support a fraction of the current population. This may be true, but it could just as well be interpreted as overconsumption instead of overpopulation.

We should also remember that not all limits take the form of global limits. For example, we might be able to support additional people in some regions or countries but not in others, or the costs of having additional people might be lower in some places than in others. Along these lines, people in poorer countries typically consume much less in the way of resources than those in richer countries, so the earth may be able to support more population growth in poor countries than in rich ones. Similarly, the benefits created by add-itional people in some places might be greater than those by additional people in other places. This means that even if we knew all the answers to the many complex empirical questions concerning overpopulation, the answer is

---

[6] While I describe this as a 'hard limit' in the sense of being unavoidable, it will be a vague rather than sharp boundary.

unlikely to be a simple 'yes'/'no', but more a complex set of policy prescriptions that could involve using different approaches in different places.

It is important to note that the costs and benefits of having a larger population are not static, but change greatly over time. For example, Paul Ehrlich (1968: xi) got it wrong when he opened his treatise on overpopulation by saying:

> The battle to feed all of humanity is over. In the 1970s and 1980s hundreds of millions of people will starve to death in spite of any crash programs embarked upon now. At this late date nothing can prevent a substantial increase in the world death rate...

Such a disaster may have ensued based on the business-as-usual limits of food production, but that period saw an extremely rapid rise in food production due to the so-called 'green revolution'. The use of irrigation, fertilizers, and pesticides, alongside the introduction of new high-yield cereals saw wheat yields per hectare dramatically increase (Evenson and Gollin 2003; Goldin and Reinert, 2012, table 5.5). These developments expanded the technical limits on how much food could be produced with the available arable land, and so changed the global picture regarding overpopulation.

It is in the nature of science and technology that it is difficult to predict whether and by how much we could raise other limits, but we should certainly bear this possibility in mind. For example, genetic engineering of crops or expansion of new farming methods such as aquaculture could again expand the available food supply, while any source of clean, cheap energy would relax a number of limits simultaneously. Consideration of technological improvements is important for planning and prediction purposes, and because we can direct funding towards finding ways to relax these limits. Indeed this might be one of the best policy levers for dealing with potential overpopulation. Expanding limits allows us to get the benefits of additional population without some of the costs, and may also be easier to achieve than preventing people from being born in the first place.

Technology is not the only way in which limits could be relaxed. As mentioned earlier, many of the soft limits we face are due to social limitations. We are near the soft limit on food production because we eat so much meat. We are exceeding our limits of CO_2 production because we aren't prepared to pay more to use the clean technologies that have already been invented. If we could make social progress on convincing people to change their behaviours to be more altruistic on these fronts, we could have as much impact as a technological breakthrough. Even if people were just altruistic enough to allow their governments to pass the appropriate legislation to disincentivize these activities, this could make a dramatic difference. Social change on this scale is not easy, but nor is it impossible, as examination of the rise of vegetarianism, civil rights, or the environmentalist movement shows.

Improvements in science, technology, and social change can also tip the balance in favour of larger populations by increasing the benefits of population as well as decreasing the costs. For example, the computer and the digitization of music and film have greatly reduced the costs for reproducing these information goods and have thus increased the benefits of large populations. Social reforms in intellectual property law might further increase the benefits by allowing more people to benefit from each new invention or artistic work.

Finally, it is possible that in the future the global population will trend downwards on its own. This was previously thought likely by the UN (2004: 13), though their updated report now suggests that this is less probable (UN 2011). The further the world's population were to fall, the more likely it would be that it would be underpopulated—that it would be better to have more people. If it fell sufficiently far, say to less than a billion people, then there would be widespread agreement that the world was underpopulated. However, the arguments that I have given as to the possibility of the world being underpopulated do not rely on a falling population. They show that population policy is best thought of not as maintaining the status quo, but as reaching an ideal level. Thus the world might be underpopulated even if the population is increasing.

Conclusions

As I have shown, a mature population policy cannot be constructed only from considerations of resource limits or the costs of additional people. We must consider the instrumental benefits that additional people will bring for the people who would have existed otherwise—especially from the creation of sharable information goods such as art, invention, and science. We must also consider the value of the additional people in and of themselves: their intrinsic value. There is active philosophical debate about exactly how we should take account of the intrinsic value of new people, but this does not mean that we can simply ignore this component of value. Instead, it means that there is considerable uncertainty in how we should assess the intrinsic value of differently sized future populations, and thus in how much we should add to their instrumental value in order to determine their overall value. However, even just properly accounting for their instrumental value alone may be enough to suggest that the planet might be underpopulated.

We have seen that the various limits on population due to resource constraints come in both soft and hard forms, and can be translated into the language of costs, to be weighed against benefits. We should also be aware that even the hard limits can potentially be raised with technological or social changes and we should consider attempting to raise limits as a very important policy option. We must also be aware that it can matter where the additional people are located: it is possible for some areas to have too many people while others have too few.

Most importantly though, we should stop looking at increasing population as just a problem to be managed, any more than our own lives are just problems to be managed. Like us, new people are the springs of great joy, novelty, and prosperity. The resources they consume may outweigh this, or they may not, but we certainly don't know the answer to this yet and would need to investigate much more fully. We should see increasing population as an opportunity as well as a challenge.

References

Arrhenius, G. (forthcoming). *Population Ethics*. Oxford: Oxford University Press. (Page numbers refer to unpublished manuscript).

Arrhenius, G. (2009). 'Can the Person Affecting Restriction Solve the Problems in Population Ethics?' in M. Roberts and D. Wasserman (eds), *Harming Future Persons: Ethics, Genetics and the Nonidentity Problem*, London and New York: Springer, pp. 291–316.

Arrhenius, G. (2000a). 'An Impossibility Theorem for Welfarist Axiology', *Economics and Philosophy*, 16: 247–66.

Arrhenius, G. (2000b). 'Future Generations: A Challenge for Moral Theory,' FD-Diss. Uppsala: University Printers.

Blackorby, C., Bossert, W., and Donaldson, D. (1997). 'Critical-Level Utilitarianism and the Population-Ethics Dilemma', *Economics and Philosophy*, 13(2): 197–230.

Blackorby, C., Bossert, W., and Donaldson, D. (2005). *Population Issues in Social Choice Theory, Welfare Economics, and Ethics*. Cambridge: Cambridge University Press.

Boserup, E. (1965). *The Conditions of Agricultural Growth: The Economics of Agrarian Change under Population Pressure*. London: Allen & Unwin.

Broome, J. (1992). *Counting the Cost of Global Warming*. Cambridge: The White Horse Press.

Broome, J. (2004). *Weighing Lives*. Oxford: Oxford University Press.

Ehrlich, P. R. (1968). *The Population Bomb*. New York: Buccaneer Books.

Evenson, R. E., and Gollin, D. (2003). 'Assessing the Impact of the Green Revolution 1960–2000', *Science*, 300(5620): 758–62.

Glover, J. (1977). *Causing Death and Saving Lives: The Moral Problems of Abortion, Infanticide, Suicide, Euthanasia, Capital Punishment, War, and Other Life-or-Death Choices*. Harmondsworth: Penguin.

Goldin, I. and Reinert, K. (2012). *Globalization for Development: Meeting New Challenges*, New Ed. Oxford: Oxford University Press.

Huemer, M. (2008). 'In Defence of Repugnance', *Mind*, 117(468): 899–933.

Narveson, J. (1967). 'Utilitarianism and New Generations', *Mind*, 76(301): 62–72.

Parfit, D. (1984). *Reasons and Persons*. Oxford: Clarendon Press.

Sen, A. K. (1981). *Poverty and Famines: An Essay on Entitlement and Deprivation*. Oxford: Oxford University Press.

Sidgwick, H. (1907). *The Methods of Ethics* (7th edn). London: Macmillan.

Simon, S. L. (1981). *The Ultimate Resource*. Princeton, NJ: Princeton University Press.

Tännsjö, T. (2002). 'Why We Ought to Accept the Repugnant Conclusion', *Utilitas*, 149(3): 339–59.

UN (2011). *World Population Prospects: The 2010 Revision*. New York: United Nations, Department of Economic and Social Affairs.

UN (2004). *World population to 2300*. New York: United Nations, Department of Economic and Social Affairs.

4

Demographic and Environmental Transitions

Sarah Harper

Human population started growing sometime between 100,000 and 50,000 years ago (Rogers and Harpending 1992; Di Rienzo et al. 1998; Stiner et al. 1999) during the Upper Paleolithic, and 12,000 years ago after the invention of agriculture (Wall and Przeworski 2000). At the end of the last ice age (last glacial maximum) some 20,000 years ago there were estimated to be around 1 million people, scattered across Europe, Africa, and Asia (Mithen 2006: 11). Humans had reached Australia, but probably not the Americas (see Mithen, 2006; Tamm et al. 2007). The next 15,000 years saw a dramatic evolution in human economy and society with the emergence of agriculture, settled dwellings, and civilizations. By 5,000 BC the world population had reached an estimated 5 million (Kremer, 1993: 683) and each continent was settled (see Mithen, 2006). It took a further 7,000 years for the human population to reach one billion, by around 1800 AD. This doubled to 2 billion by the early 1900s, (around 1930) doubled again to four billion within 50 years (1975), and had reached 6 billion by the millennium (see UN-DESA, 1999: table 1). The 21st century will probably see the global population grow from its current 7 billion to reach 10 billion by the middle of the century (UN-DESA, 2011), a threefold increase in just one hundred years, and then flatten. Indeed, this is the century in which the human population may stop increasing.

However, while the global population may stop growing this century, it will undergo considerable change in its defining characteristics; it will continue to increase its consumption of the Earth's resources, and it will need to adapt to an apparent rapid change in the Earth's climate. The first half of the 21st century will thus see unprecedented changes in the human population in terms of size—we are becoming larger; density—we are becoming more urban; distribution—we are increasingly mobile; and composition—we are becoming older. Alongside this is a change in the Earth's natural environment, in part a result of rapid population growth. It is increasingly being acknowledged that the growing numbers of people, and the industrialized, urbanized, high-consumption lives they lead, has contributed to—or even some would argue has caused—the planet's climate to change with rapid environmental effects.

Demographic Transition

Different regions of the world are experiencing different demographic transitions. Population increases will not be homogeneously spread across the globe. The less and least developed regions will account for 97 per cent of the growth to 2050. Asia will comprise 55 per cent of the world population by 2050 at 5 billion; Africa's population is projected to double in size by 2050 from 1.022 to 2.192 million, while Europe's will decline from 738 to 719 million (UN-DESA 2011: 2).

It is important, however, to consider not only changes in population size, but also other significant population changes of the 21st century: those of *density*, *distribution*, and *composition*. This century will see a continuous and rapid growth in the *density* of human population, as an increasing percentage live in cities and other urban areas, projected to reach 75 per cent by 2050. This will be reflected in the changing *distribution* of people, with a reduction in rural residents, alongside the overall increase in those living in Asia and Africa, and a fall in European and North American populations. The age *composition* of the population will also change as median ages rise and there is a proportionate shift from younger to older people across the globe.

This change in the size, density, distribution, and composition of the human population has arisen due to the *demographic transition*. This started in Europe sometime after 1750, in Asia and Latin America during the 20th century, and now there are indications that Africa will transition during the 21st century. Why the demographic transition occurred when it did, where it did, and how it did is strongly debated. However, as humans economically develop, mortality falls, sometime later fertility falls, and in the gap between the two trends population grows.

The classic demographic transition is typically associated with economic development, and is perceived as comprising four main stages (Bongaarts and Feeney 1998; Bucht 1996; Cliquet 1991; Lutz and Goldstein 2004; Van de Kaa 1987; Vaupel and Lundström 1996). In stage one populations experience high death rates from disease, famine, malnutrition, and lack of clean water and sanitation, and there is no impetus, or even thought, to reduce fertility. This phase is characterized by high birth and death rates, and a relatively small but often fluctuating population size—for example England pre-1780, and present-day Ethiopia. Stage two sees improvements in public heath, sanitation, clean water and food, and mortality rates; infant and child mortality, in particular, falls. There are, however, still high fertility rates, resulting in a rapidly expanding population size—for example, 19th-century England and present-day Sudan. In stage three rapidly falling fertility rates occur alongside low mortality rates. In this phase there is still expanding but slowing population size—for instance, England in the early 20th century and Uruguay today. Stage four sees low mortality and fertility and a high but relatively stable population—present-day United Kingdom and Canada, for example (Harper 2013).

Fertility Rates

Key to the demographic transition is changes in fertility rates. Generally described, the total fertility rate (TFR) is the number of live children born to women of child-bearing age. In technical terms the TFR of a population is the average number of children that would be born to a woman over her lifetime if she were to experience the exact current age-specific fertility rates across her lifetime, and if she were to survive to the end of her reproductive life.

The actual drivers of fertility fall have been long debated but broadly fall into three camps. One theory is that fertility falls in response to a fall in infant mortality. Economists describe this as the increase in child survival rates reducing the fertility required to achieve the desired number of surviving children. A second position is that high fertility is a response to an unmet need for family planning, and it is only through the introduction of modern family planning methods that women will start to reduce the number of births they have. The third broad hypothesis is that fertility fall is driven by education. Educating girls in particular, encourages later marriage and gives them access to the labour market, which reduces the number of births, but also and crucially, it changes the 'mindset' of the women and their communities and enables them to recognize the range of alternative choices they can make. Indeed one of the greatest contemporary demographers, Jack Caldwell, identified 'ideational change' as the biggest factor in falling fertility (Caldwell 1980). Within these broad trends lies a spectrum of factors such as urbanization, cultural change—in particular around family relationships and obligations, and labour market change.

Two-thirds of the world's countries are now at or below replacement level—crudely defined by a TFR of 2.1 children per woman.[1] These rates are diverse, including Hong Kong (the lowest at 0.99), Poland, Germany, Barbados,

---

[1] Strictly speaking, of course, TFRs will vary slightly across countries due to differences in nutrition, prevalence of disease, health care, and other factors that affect infant mortality rates.

Thailand, Viet Nam, Mauritius, Iran, Chile, Tunisia, the United States, and Myanmar (with a near-replacement rate of 2.08). A further 58 are low medium—that is with a TFR of 2.1–3—these include Ireland, New Zealand, Indonesia, Argentina, Sri Lanka, Bangladesh, Mexico, Venezuela, Botswana, Egypt, Samoa, and India. Eighteen are at high medium 3–4.1—including Zimbabwe, Bolivia, and Pakistan. Forty-eight remain high—4.1 and above—most but not all are in sub-Saharan Africa, and most are classified by the UN as Least Developed Countries (see UN-DESA 2011: 116–20).

The highest is Niger with 7.19 children per reproductive woman (UN-DESA 2011: 115). Although TFRs across the globe are mostly falling, the case of sub-Saharan Africa remains of concern. The medium UN scenario is that TFRs in Africa will approach replacement levels by 2100 (UN-DESA 2011: 11). If this occurs, the African population will increase from 1.0 billion now to 2.2 billion by 2050, and 3.6 billion by the end of the century (UN-DESA 2011: 2). However, TFRs still remain above 4 in many countries. As a consequence, if TFR reduction stalls and remains at its current 5.5 for the region, then sub-Saharan Africa's population will reach just under 3 billion (2.997 million) by 2050 and 15 billion (14.959 million) by 2100, leading to a maximum world population of over 26 billion by the century's end (UN-DESA 2011). It is thus important that the drivers of fertility reduction are understood so that African women can be able to choose the family size they desire. This is not only because a population of 26 billion would place considerable burden on the planet's resources, but because African governments increasingly recognize that such high birth rates are reducing the potential for development, and African women are themselves calling for measures which will improve their own well-being and those of their existing children (see, for example, Searchinger et al. 2013).

Fertility Stalling

Rapid population growth and high fertility threaten the well-being of individuals and communities in the poorest developing countries. While family planning and reproductive health programmes have made significant advances globally in helping women achieve the family size they desire, in some parts of the world, such as sub-Saharan Africa, fertility decline is slowing or even stalling (UN-DESA 2011: 31). Sub-Saharan Africa is not only the last region to initiate fertility transition, it has also experienced a weaker pace of decline in fertility compared to other regions, possibly due to the slower pace of socio-economic change in Africa as compared to elsewhere in the developing world (Shapiro et al. 2010). In addition, there is clear evidence of stalling in fertility decline in some African countries (Bongaarts 2008; Ezeh, Mberu, and

Emina 2009; Shapiro and Gebreselassie 2008). Kenya has stalled following a rapid fertility decline, and Benin, Rwanda, and Zambia have declined little in recent years and remained constant at above five children per woman, despite the fact that these countries are considered to have started fertility transitions (Machiyama 2010). There is currently a debate as to whether stalls in fertility decline in Africa are but a minor pause in the course of the fertility transition, or whether this is an indication of deeper processes (Bongaarts 2005, 2007; Westoff and Cross 2006). There is growing awareness that sustaining fertility decline will require continued improvements in female education, in infant and child mortality, and increased family planning initiatives (Shapiro et al. 2010). Other factors may also be intervening that are specific to the sub-Saharan case, or to the current African transition, which may be different from early time periods. There is interest, for example, in the role of social security and long-term care programmes as a spur to household decisions regarding fertility. Lack of such programmes may, for example, encourage women to continue child bearing to ensure their own old-age security. In a new development, Garenne (2011) reports that a study in the Pacific Islands indicates that stalling of fertility decline might occur as a result of deliberate reproductive strategies. Because couples might have an economic advantage to produce children who may later migrate and remit money to the family, they may choose to have more children.

The predominance of African countries with declining fertility combined with the number of countries that have experienced a stalling in fertilility decline elsewhere[2] (see Pantelides 1996) suggests the fertility transition will be ongoing in Africa and other parts of the world. However, if these stalls in fertility decline last for several years or even decades, they could have serious consequences for long-term demographic dynamics, especially when they occur at relatively high levels of fertility.

Tackling the Stalling of Fertility Decline

According to the UN-DESA (2011: 2), maximum world population will reach between 15 billion (high variant) and 6 billion (low variant), with 10 billion as the medium variant, by 2100. The high variant of 15 billion is generally thought to place significant strain on the Earth's resources, while the medium variant of 10 billion will require a significant increase in the requirement for food, water, energy, and minerals. Initial modelling suggests, for example,

---

[2] A typical case of fertility stall is that of Argentina, where fertility dropped from 7.0 children per woman in 1895 to 3.2 children per woman in 1947 and stayed at the same level for about 30 years before resuming its path in recent years towards replacement fertility.

that the difference between the high and low variants of the UN projections for sub-Saharan Africa is one child per woman by 2050, and achieving the low variant would result in a fall of half a billion people within sub-Saharan Africa. Furthermore, if it were possible to bring the TRF of sub-Saharan Africa down to the UN low variant of 1.66 rather than the medium prediction of 2.14 by 2100, then the world population would be potentially reduced by one billion people by the end of the century (Harper and Leeson 2012).

Of crucial importance here is female education. There is a strong association between those countries with a high level of educated women, with at least 80–100 per cent of the female population of reproductive age having completed at least junior secondary education, and those countries with below-replacement fertility levels. Similarly those countries with low female education rates of below 40 per cent of women of childbearing age having completed this level of education also have high TFRs. Girls' secondary education also dramatically affects fertility rates (see Searchinger et al. 2013: 8–9). A World Bank study found that, for every four years of education that girls attain, fertility rates drop by roughly one birth (Klasen 1999). Other research that focused on 65 countries suggests that doubling the proportion of women with a secondary education reduced average fertility rates from 5.3 to 3.9 children per woman (Subbarao and Raney 1995). The enrolment of all African girls in secondary school education would have a significant impact in enabling them to choose the numbers and timing of their childbirths, and would result in a significant fall in TFRs in the region.

As indicated earlier, broadly speaking, there are three major drivers behind fertility fall—reducing infant mortality, increasing family planning programmes, and empowering women. Education has a positive impact in all three. There is overwhelming evidence that education improves health and well-being and reduces levels of both mortality and fertility (Mlatsheni and Leibbrandt 2001; Palloni, Novak, and Rodrigues de Souza 2012). Girls and women not only face the challenges of high fertility and unwanted pregnancies; they are also primarily responsible for infant and child health, immunization, and nutrition. Indeed there is evidence that a mother's education is the most important determinant of child mortality, more important than household income or wealth, with each additional year of schooling being associated with a 5 to 10 per cent reduction in infant mortality (Schultz 1993a) and a 5 to 7 per cent reduction in child death (Mensch, Lentzner, and Preston 1985; Schultz 1993b).

In terms of empowerment, the effect of education on fertility is particularly strong in countries that still have relatively high overall fertility levels and hence are in the early phases of their demographic transitions (Skirbekk 2008). As a recent advocacy report noted, girls' secondary education is a tool for poverty alleviation and results in social benefits to the whole society; it equips women with critical thinking enabling civic participation and democratic change (Rihani 2005). Research has shown that while knowledge of modern family panning methods is now widespread throughout the region, those women with high levels of education are more likely to adopt family planning methods than those with low-level or no education (Searchinger et al. 2013).

Inequalities in Access to Education

It is now accepted by most societies that education is a fundamental human right—one that all individuals are entitled to, regardless of their personal characteristics or circumstances. Yet it is a right which is beset by inequalities; inequalities between countries and inequalities between genders. The Millennium Development Goals (MDGs) set the target of universal primary schooling by 2015. Yet little progress has been made in terms of reducing early school leaving rates—especially for girls (see UIS 2013). In 2011 the number of children leaving school before finishing primary school education (at least 34 million) in relation to those beginning primary school (137 million) stood at 25 per cent—the same proportion as at the beginning of the century (UIS 2013: 3). If trends continue, 58 out of the 86 countries that have not yet achieved universal primary enrolment will fail to do so by 2015 (UNESCO 2007: 2).

There is further inequality between the genders, despite the fact that the MDGs also set the target of eliminating gender disparities in primary and secondary education by 2005 and of achieving gender equality by 2015. There is thus considerable variation in differential gender access to education at both the primary and secondary levels. While there is parity in almost all the countries of Central and Eastern Europe, with Central Asia, North America, and Western Europe falling slightly behind, in contrast only three counties in the whole of sub-Saharan Africa and Central and West Asia have achieved this. Indeed, half the girls in Africa will not complete a primary education. These inequalities persist because traditionally, in terms of educational opportunities, all societies have privileged males over females. Thus disparities in educational attainment and literacy rates today reflect patterns which have been shaped by the policies and practices of the past (UNESCO 2012).

Worldwide, 90 per cent of primary-school-age children are enrolled in primary or secondary education, but this figure is only 76 per cent in sub-Saharan Africa (UN 2012: 16–17). Sub-Saharan Africa does not only have lower educational attainment than other regions, it is also the region with the greatest gender disparity against women (UIS 2011b: 11ff). The highest gender disparity in educational attainment exists in Benin, Burkina Faso, Chad,

Malawi, and Senegal. In these countries, less than half as many women as men have completed any formal education. In 47 countries, girls are less likely than boys to enter the last grade of primary education. The most extreme situations are found in the Central African Republic, Chad, the Democratic Republic of the Congo, and Yemen, where girls have around two-thirds of the participation rate of boys (UIS 2011b: 12). The region also has the lowest overall rate of participation in secondary education and the most severe gender disparities. In 2009, only 32 per cent of girls had any secondary school education, versus 41 per cent for boys (UIS 2011b: 19). Only 27 per cent of pupils completed upper secondary school programmes, falling as low as 6 per cent in the Central African Republic, Niger, Somalia, and Tanzania (UIS 2011b: 25–6).

A range of key barriers to universal education, and in particular universal secondary education, have been identified (UIS 2011a). These include inability of countries to meet the growing demand for education both financially and in terms of trained teachers, and inability of individual households to meet the direct and indirect costs of education (that is, tuition fees, school uniforms, and time away from household chores or external employment). Estimates of how much it would cost to achieve both universal primary and secondary education range from $33 billion to $69 billion per year (with primary education being $6 billion to $35 billion per year and secondary education from $27 billion to $34 billion per year) (Cohen and Bloom 2005: 9–10). There are considerable difficulties in producing accurate cost estimates, because of the uncertainties around estimating how to overcome the barriers, such as parents not enrolling their children in schools.

Population–Environment Interactions

The demographic transition not only leads to falling fertility and mortality and thus changes in population size, but also to associated developments in density (urbanization), distribution (migration), and composition (age structure or population ageing). While it is now apparent that it is important to consider these more complex aspects of population change together with environmental change in order to understand the reality of any mitigation that may be made (Harper 2013), and there is growing concern over the interaction of population with biodiversity, natural resource management, and ecosystems, most of the more complex population–environment interactions have focused on climate change (Young, Mogelgaard, and Hardee 2009; Jiang and Hardee 2011; McNeill 2006; Stephenson, Newman, and Mayhew 2010).

In terms of environmental interactions with population size, there is evidence that slowing population growth could provide over a quarter of the emissions reductions thought to be necessary by 2050 to avoid dangerous climate change (O'Neill 2009; O'Neill et al. 2010). In relation to distribution there is a clear renewal of interest in the contemporary migration–environment nexus (Piguet 2013). Research suggests that as environmental changes increase, migratory pressures will also increase (Solomon et al. 2007; Feng, Krueger, and Oppenheimer 2010). Recent papers, however, have emphasized that the environmental refugee scenario may be overstated and that environmentally related migration is complex and related to the temporality and kind of environmental change.[3] There is general agreement that the response to sudden climatic events will result in short-term temporary moves, as most people in environmentally disadvantaged regions will not have the resources to make permanent long-distance relocations. As Tacoli (2009) points out, much of the earlier literature following on from the IPCC (2007) report overlooked the fact that migration requires financial resources and social support, both of which may decline with climate change, which may thus result in fewer rather than more people being able to move. Environmental change has the potential to affect directly the hazardousness of place, and also affects migration indirectly, in particular through economic drivers, by changing livelihoods for example, and political drivers, through affecting conflicts over resources. Black et al. (2011) for example suggests that the environment drives migration through mechanisms characterized as the availability and reliability of ecosystem services and exposure to hazard. The impact of the environment is therefore highly dependent on economic, political, social, and demographic context. Harper (2013) takes a regional view and argues that the differential impact of climate change may rebalance the forecast distribution of economic growth, to the advantage of Europe and disadvantage of Asia. This will have a follow-on impact on the regional distribution of skilled migrant labour.

In terms of composition changes, there is evidence that the age structure of the population impacts upon consumption patterns and thus predicted carbon dioxide emissions (Zagheni 2011). O'Neill et al. (2012), for example, produce evidence for how carbon dioxide emissions from the use of fossil fuels are affected by demographic factors such as population growth or decline, ageing, urbanization, and changes in household size. Liddle (2011; 2013) and Liddle and Lung (2010) take the analysis a step further by analysing panels consisting of poor, middle, and rich countries, and show that the environmental impact relationships vary across development levels. Alternatively Menz and Welsch (2012) take a cohort approach suggesting that shifts

---

[3] See, for example, Adepoju. Noorloos, and Zoomers (2010), Warner (2010), Bardsley and Hugo (2010), Tacoli (2009), Barnett and Webber (2010), Skeldon (2009), Fielding (2011), Foresight (2011), Massey, Axinn, and Ghimire (2010), and Barbieri et al. (2010).

in both the age and the cohort composition have contributed to rising carbon emissions in OECD countries.

The question of density changes in population and climate converge around the city. It has been argued that many cities will need to adapt to mitigate the impact of short- and long-term climate change. However, most urban dwellers are left vulnerable in cities with limited infrastructure and services needed to mitigate climate change-related risks, and inadequate political and institutional systems. The existing vulnerability of African cities, for example, with their fast-growing populations and weak management, means any environmental change is likely to have significant consequences (Parnell and Walawege 2011). A further stream of research has considered the impact of urbanization on carbon dioxide emissions, concluding that there is a small but significant effect (Krey et al. 2012; O'Neill et al. 2012) which may be related to increased consumption (Satterthwaite 2009).

Population and Consumption—the Key

It is increasingly recognized that the central factor in the population–environment nexus is consumption. The Royal Society (2012) enquiry into population and the environment concludes that it is the combination of increasing population and increasing per capita consumption that is crucial. Considering both material and economic consumption (including the consumption of non-material goods and services), they acknowledge that consumption is critical to human development and contributes to enlarging people's capabilities without adversely affecting the well-being of others, supporting inter-generational fairness, respecting the carrying capacity of the planet, and encouraging the emergence of lively and creative communities. Furthermore, they argue that we need to acknowledge that material consumption does not necessarily lead to positive development, and is not always necessary for human development advances. It is, however, possible that economic consumption can contribute positively to human and economic development without causing environmental degradation.

Key here is the question of inequality. For the one billion people who live in extreme poverty and hunger, increased consumption is essential to raise their standard of living, and this includes increasing access to both goods and services.[4] Following the example of the Royal Society by considering the three main essentials—food, water, and energy—the extent of inequality is apparent.

---

[4] According to the FAO (2010), 925 million people were undernourished in 2010.

Around 884 million people are still without access to safe drinking water and 2.6 billion are without access to basic sanitation (Royal Society 2012: 49). Yet a child born in the developed world consumes 30 to 50 times more water than one born in the developing world (UNESCO 2003). In terms of food and calorific consumption, around one billion people do not receive sufficient calories to meet their minimum dietary requirements. Another billion people are chronically malnourished: they do not get the vitamins, minerals, essential fatty acids, and essential amino acids necessary for health (FAO 2010; Defra 2010). When we combine the predicted increases in population growth with the predicted increases in calorific intake, we see a rise in total demand for food of 40 per cent by 2030 and 70 per cent by 2050 (FAO 2006). The third factor, access to energy, is also very unequally divided, with energy insufficiency a major component of poverty. As countries develop, emissions levels increase. Currently per capita carbon dioxide emissions are up to 50 times higher in high-income countries than in those with low-incomes (EIA 2011). While global population increased fourfold during the 20th century, carbon dioxide emissions increased fifteen-fold; a fourfold increase per capita on average. However, a significant proportion of the population increase has been in the developing world, which is yet to increase emissions.

As the Royal Society (2012) concludes, in the short-term it is of the utmost urgency to reduce consumption and emissions that are already causing damage, for example greenhouse gases. However, 'it is [also] necessary to make space for those in poverty, especially the 1.3 billion people living in absolute poverty, to achieve an adequate standard of living' (Royal Society 2012: 101). Yet it is in these countries, which must increase both their material and economic consumption to attain the basics of human life, where the significant increases in population numbers will occur. Unless we can reduce the material consumption of the developed world, our finite planet will struggle to support the material and economic consumption demanded by the growth in living standards in the emerging, developing, and least-developed regions of the world.

Conclusion

The 21st century will see increasing tension between the demands of a growing population and the constraints imposed by climate change. Widespread warming of the planet is now evident according to the Fourth Assessment Report of the IPCC.[5] This commitment to certain levels of warming, and the

---

[5] See the IPCC (2007) synthesis report.

potential for much greater warming in the future, mean we need to consider localized impacts and think about adaptation to climate change, as well as mitigation. These population–environmental interactions will occur in the rural and urban environment, at local and regional levels. In terms of size, for example, there is the question of providing food for the growing world population. It is foreseen that climate change will have considerable impacts on the ability to produce food. These will stem from altered growing conditions, biodiversity loss, sea level rise, increased drought, and changes in disease patterns, weather pattern shifts, increased flooding, changes in fresh water supply, and an increase in extreme weather events. Food distribution will also be affected. However, one of the biggest factors will be the rapid and large increases in the demand for food brought on by an extra 3 billion people on the planet by 2050, and more importantly the growing consumption rates of this population. The IPCC highlight that Africa will be the continent hardest hit in this way, and in particular that this will make the demographic transition in Africa of a different quality and degree to that currently being experienced in Asia and Latin America.

In addressing the question 'is the planet full?' it is essential that we instate the demographic transition as part of the debate. First, the focus on global increase distracts us from the reality that fertility is falling in most countries and that we need to consider those where it is not. Second, the 21st century is not only seeing changes in global population size, the world's population is undergoing changes in its density—we are becoming more urban—due to our national and international mobility, and composition, especially age composition. The major shifts may all be related to the end stage of the demographic transition. Third, and importantly, the major question for the 21st century will probably not be size, but the relationship between population, consumption, and the environment, and the overwhelming need to develop governance and institutional frameworks that create and support economic and social systems which are not dependent on continued material consumption. Under these we might look forward to a population of 10 billion, drawing equitably on the natural resources of our finite planet, with a shared sense of well-being.

References

Adepoju, A., Van Noorloos, F., and Zoomers, A. (2010). 'Europe's Migration Agreements with Migrant-Sending Countries in the Global South: A Critical Review', *International Migration*, 48(3): 42–75.

Barbieri, A. F., Dominguez, E., Queiros, B. L., Ruiz, R. M., Rigotti, J. I., Carvalho, J. A. M., and Resende, M. F. (2010). 'Climate Change and Population Migration in Brazil's Northeast: Scenarios for 2025–2050', *Population and Environment,* 31: 344–70.

Bardsley, D. and Hugo, G. J. (2010). 'Migration and Climate Change: Examining Thresholds of Change to Guide Effective Adaptation Decision-Making', *Population and Environment,* 32(2–3): 238–62.

Barnett, J. and Webber, M. (2010). 'Accommodating Migration to Promote Adaptation to Climate Change', *Policy Research Working Paper 5270.* Washington, DC: World Bank. Last accessed 3 May 2013. <http://www-wds.worldbank.org/servlet/WDSContentServer/WDSP/IB/2010/04/13/000158349_20100413131732/Rendered/PDF/WPS5270.pdf>.

Black, R., Adger, W. N., Arnell, N. W., Dercon, S., Geddes, A., and Thomas, D. (2011). 'The Effect of Environmental Change on Human Migration', *Global Environmental Change,* 21(supplement 1): 3–11.

Bongaarts, J. (2008). 'Fertility Transitions in Developing Countries: Progress or Stagnation?' *Studies in Family Planning,* 39(2): 105–10.

Bongaarts, J. (2007). 'Fertility Transition in the Developing World: Progress or Stagnation?' Paper presented at the Annual Meeting of the Population Association of America, New York, 29–31 March. Last accessed 26 June 2013. <http://paa2007.princeton.edu/papers/71273>.

Bongaarts, J. (2005). 'The Causes of Stalling Fertility Transitions', *Working Paper 204.* New York: Population Council. Last accessed 26 June 2013. <http://www.popcouncil.org/pdfs/wp/204.pdf>.

Bongaarts, J. and Feeney, G. (1998). 'On the Quantum and Tempo of Fertility', *Population and Development Review,* 24(2): 271–91.

Bucht, B. (1996). 'Mortality Trends in Developing Countries: A Survey' in W. Lutz (ed.) *The Future Population of the World: What Can We Assume Today?* Revised Edition. London: Earthscan, pp. 133–48.

Caldwell, J. C. (1980). 'Mass Education as a Determinant of the Timing of Fertility Decline', *Population and Development Review,* 6(2): 225–55.

Cliquet, R. L. (1991). 'The Second Demographic Transition: Fact or Fiction?' Population Studies 23. Strasbourg: Council of Europe.

Cohen, J. E. and Bloom, D. E. (2005). 'Cultivating Minds', *Finance and Development,* 42(2): 9–14.

Defra (2010). *Food 2030,* London: UK Department for Environment, Food and Rural Affairs. Last accessed 26 June 2013. <http://archive.defra.gov.uk/foodfarm/food/pdf/food2030strategy.pdf>.

Di Rienzo, A., Donnelly, P., Toomajian, C., Sisk, B., Hill, A., Petzl-Erler, M. L., Haines, G. K., and Barch, D. H. (1998). 'Heterogeneity of Microsatellite Mutations Within and Between Loci, and Implications for Human Demographic Histories', *Genetics,* 148(3): 1269–84.

EIA (2011). 'International Energy Statistics: CO2 Emissions', US Energy Information Administration. Last accessed 26 June 2013. <http://www.eia.gov/cfapps/ipdbproject/IEDIndex3.cfm?tid=90&pid=44&aid=8>.

Ezeh, A. C., Mberu, B. U., and Emina, J. O. (2009). 'Stall in Fertility Decline in Eastern African Countries: Regional Analysis of Patterns, Determinants and Implications', *Philosophical Transactions of the Royal Society B*, 364(1532): 2991–3007.

FAO (2010). 'Global Hunger Declining, But Still Unacceptably High', *Policy Brief*, September. Rome: Food and Agricultural Organization. Last accessed 26 June 2013. <http://www.fao.org/docrep/012/al390e/al390e00.pdf>.

FAO (2006). *Prospects for Food, Nutrition, Agriculture and Major Commodity Groups: World Agriculture Towards 2030/2050*, Interim Report. Rome: Global Perspectives Studies Unit, Food and Agriculture Organization of the United Nations. Last accessed 26 June 2013. <http://www.fao.org/fileadmin/user_upload/esag/docs/Interim_report_AT2050web.pdf>.

Feng, S., Krueger, A. B., and Oppenheimer, M. (2010). 'Linkages Among Climate Change, Crop Yields, and Mexico-US Cross-Border Migration', *Proceedings of the National Academy of Sciences*, 107, 14257–62.

Fielding, A. J. (2011). 'The Impacts of Environmental Change on UK Internal Migration', *Global Environmental Change*, 21(supplement 1): 121–30.

Foresight (2011). *Migration and Global Environmental Change: Future Challenges and Opportunities*, Final Project Report. London: Government Office for Science. Last accessed 10 October 2013. <http://www.bis.gov.uk/foresight/our-work/projects/published-projects/global-migration/reports-publications>.

Garenne, M. L. (2011). 'Testing for Fertility Stalls in Demographic and Health Surveys', *Population Health Metrics*, 9. <http://www.pophealthmetrics.com/content/9/1/59>.

Harper, S. (2013). 'Population–Environment Interactions: European Migration, Population Composition, and Climate Change', *Environmental and Resource Economics*, 55(4): 525–41.

Harper, S. and Leeson, G. (2012). 'The Role of Education in Reducing Maximum World Population', *OIPA Working Paper*. Oxford: Oxford Institute for Population and Ageing, Oxford Martin School.

IPCC (2007). *Climate Change 2007: Synthesis Report*. (Contribution of Working Groups I, II and III to the Fourth Assessment Report of the IPCC). Geneva, Switzerland: Intergovernmental Panel on Climate Change. Last accessed 10 May 2013. <http://www.ipcc.ch/publications_and_data/publications_ipcc_fourth_assessment_report_synthesis_report.htm>.

Jiang, L. and Hardee, K. (2011). 'How do Recent Population Trends Matter to Climate Change?' *Population Research and Policy Review*, 30: 287–312.

Klasen, S. (1999). 'Does Gender Inequality Reduce Growth and Development? Evidence from Cross-Country Regressions', *Policy Research Report on Gender and Development Working Paper 7*. Washington, DC: World Bank. Last accessed 5 May 2013. <http://siteresources.worldbank.org/INTGENDER/Resources/wp7.pdf>.

Kremer, M. (1993). 'Population Growth and Technological Change: One Million B.C. to 1990', *Quarterly Journal of Economics*, 108(3): 681–716.

Krey, V., O'Neill, B. C., van Ruijven, B., Chaturvedi, V., Daioglou, D., Eom, J., Jiang, L., Nagai, Y., Pachauri, S., and Ren, X. (2012). 'Urban and Rural Energy Use and Carbon Dioxide Emissions in Asia', *Energy Economics*, 34(Supplement 3): 272–83.

Liddle, B. (2013). 'Population, Affluence, and Environmental Impact Across Development: Evidence from Panel Cointegration Modeling', *Environmental Modelling and Software*, 40: 255–66.

Liddle, B. (2011). 'Consumption-Driven Environmental Impact and Age Structure Change in OECD Countries: A Cointegration-STIRPAT Analysis', *Demographic Research*, 24: 749–70.

Liddle, B. and Lung, S. (2010). 'Age-structure, Urbanization, and Climate Change in Developed Countries: Revisiting STIRPAT for Disaggregated Population and Consumption-related Environmental Impacts', *Population and Environment*, 31: 317–43.

Lutz, W. and Goldstein, J. (2004). 'How to Deal with Uncertainty in Population Forecasting?' *International Statistical Review*, 72(1): 1–4.

Machiyama, K. (2010). 'A Re-examination of Recent Fertility Declines in Sub-Saharan Africa', *DHS Working Paper 68*. Washington, DC: United States Agency for International Development. Last accessed 3 May 2013. <http://pdf.usaid.gov/pdf_docs/PNADT374.pdf>.

Massey, D. S., Axinn, W. G., and Ghimire, D. J. (2010). 'Environmental Change and Out-Migration: Evidence from Nepal', *Population and Environment*, 32(2–3): 109–36.

McNeill, J. R. (2006). 'Population and the Natural Environment: Trends and Challenges', *Population and Development Review*, 32: 183–201.

Mensch, B., Lentzner, H., and Preston, S. H. (1985). *Child Mortality Differentials in Developing Countries* (United Nations Population Studies 97). New York: United Nations.

Menz, T. and Welsch, H. (2012). 'Population Aging and Carbon Emissions in OECD Countries: Accounting for Life-Cycle and Cohort Effects', *Energy Economics*, 34(3): 842–9.

Mithen, S. (2006). *After the Ice: A Global Human History 20,000–5000 BC*. London: Phoenix.

Mlatsheni, C. and Leibbrandt, M. (2001). 'The Role of Education and Fertility in the Participation and Employment of African Women in South Africa', *DPRU Working Paper 01/54*. Cape Town: Development Policy Research Unit, University of Cape Town.

O'Neill, B. C. (2009). 'Climate Change and Population Growth' in L. Mazur (ed.) *A Pivotal Moment: Population, Justice and the Environmental Challenge*. New York: Island Press, pp. 81–94.

O'Neill, B. C., Dalton, M., Fuchs, R., Jiang, L., Pachauri, S., and Zigova, K. (2010). 'Global Demographic Trends and Future Carbon Emissions', *Proceedings of the National Academy of Sciences*, 107: 17521–6.

O'Neill, B. C., Ren, X., Jiang, L., and Dalton, M. (2012). 'The Effect of Urbanization on Energy Use in India and China in the iPETS Model', *Energy Economics*, 34 (Supplement 3): 339–45.

Palloni, A., Novak, B., and Rodrigues de Souza, L. (2012). 'Female Education, Low Fertility, and Economic Development', *CDE Working Paper No. 2012–03*. Madison, WI: Center for Demography and Ecology, University of Wisconsin-Madison. Last accessed 5 May 2013. <http://www.ssc.wisc.edu/cde/cdewp/2012-03.pdf>.

Pantelides, E. A. (1996). 'A Century and a Quarter of Fertility Change in Argentina: 1869 to the Present' in J. M. Guzmán, S. Singh, G. Rodríguez and E. A. Pantelides (eds), *The Fertility Transition in Latin America*. Oxford: Clarendon Press, pp. 345–58.

Parnell, S. and Walawege, R. (2011). 'Sub-Saharan African Urbanisation and Global Environmental Change', *Global Environmental Change*, 21(Supplement 1): 12–20.

Piguet, E. (2013). 'From "Primitive Migration" to "Climate Refugees": The Curious Fate of the Natural Environment in Migration Studies', *Annals of the Association of American Geographers*, 103: 148–62.

Rihani, M. A. (2005). *Keeping the Promise: Five Benefits of Girls' Secondary Education*. Washington, DC: Academy for Educational Development (AED), Global Learning Group.

Rogers, A. R. and Harpending, H. (1992). 'Population Growth Makes Waves in the Distribution of Pairwise Genetic Differences', *Molecular Biology and Evolution*, 9(3): 552–69.

Royal Society (2012). *People and the Planet*. (The Royal Society Science Policy Report 01/12). London: The Royal Society. Last accessed 10 May 2013. <http://royalsociety.org/uploadedFiles/Royal_Society_Content/policy/projects/people-planet/2012-04-25-PeoplePlanet.pdf>.

Satterthwaite, D. (2009). 'The Implications of Population Growth and Urbanization for Climate Change', *Environment and Urbanization*, 21(2): 545–67.

Schultz, T. P. (1993a). 'Investments in the Schooling and Health of Women and Men: Quantities and Returns', *The Journal of Human Resources*, 28(4): 694–734.

Schultz, T. P. (1993b). Mortality Decline in the Low-Income World: Causes and Consequences. *The American Economic Review*, 83(2): 337–42.

Searchinger, T., Hanson, C., Waite, R., Harper, S., Leeson, G., and Lipinski, B. (2013). 'Achieving Replacement Fertility', *Working Paper* (Installment 3 of Creating a Sustainable Food Future) in T. Searchinger (ed.) *Framing Paper: The Challenge of Feeding the World Sustainably by 2050*. Washington, DC: World Resources Institute, World Bank. <http://www.wri.org/sites/default/files/achieving_replacement_level_fertility_0.pdf>.

Shapiro D. and Gebreselassie, T. (2008). 'Fertility Transition in Sub-Saharan Africa: Falling and Stalling', *African Population Studies*, 23(1): 3–23.

Shapiro, D., Kreider, A., Varner, C., and Sinha, M. (2010). 'Stalling of Fertility Transitions and Socioeconomic Change in the Developing World: Evidence from the Demographic and Health Surveys', paper prepared for the 36th Chaire Quetelet symposium in demography, Catholic University of Louvain, Belgium, November. Last accessed 26 June 2013. <http://economics.buffalo.edu/documents/DavidShapiro StallingofFertilityTransitionsSocioecoChange.pdf>.

Skeldon, R. (2009). 'Of Skilled Migration, Brain Drains and Policy Responses', *International Migration* 47(4): 3–29.

Skirbekk, V. (2008). 'Fertility Trends by Social Status', *Demographic Research*, 18: 145–80.

Solomon, S., Qin, D., Manning, M., Chen, Z., Marquis, M. Averyt, K. B., Tignor, M., and Miller, H. L. (eds) (2007). *Climate Change 2007: The Physical Science Basis* (Contribution of Working Group I to the Fourth Assessment Report of the Intergovernmental Panel on Climate Change, 2007). Cambridge and New York: Cambridge University Press.

Stephenson, J., Newman, K., and Mayhew, S. (2010). 'Population Dynamics and Climate Change: What Are the Links?' *Journal of Public Health*, 32(2): 150–6.

Stiner, M. C., Munro, N. D., Surovell, T. A., Tchernov, E., and Bar-Yosef, O. (1999). 'Paleolithic Population Growth Pulses Evidenced by Small Animal Exploitation', *Science*, 283(5399): 190–4.

Subbarao, K. and Raney, L. (1995). 'Social Gains from Female Education: A Cross-National Study', *Economic Development and Cultural Change*, 44(1): 105–28.

Tacoli, C. (2009). 'Crisis or Adaptation? Migration and Climate Change in a Context of High Mobility', *Environment and Urbanization*, 21(2): 513–22.

Tamm, E., Kivisild, T., Reidla, M., Metspalu, M., Smith D. G. et al., (2007). 'Beringian Standstill and Spread of Native American Founders', *PLoS ONE*, 2(9): e829.

UIS (2013). 'Schooling for Millions of Children Jeopardized by Reductions in Aid', *UIS Fact Sheet 25*. Montreal: Institute for Statistics, United Nations Educational, Scientific and Cultural Organization. <http://reliefweb.int/sites/reliefweb.int/files/resources/fs-25-out-of-school-children-en.pdf>.

UIS (2011a). *Financing Education in Sub-Saharan Africa: Meeting the Challenges of Expansion, Equity and Quality*. Montreal: Institute for Statistics, United Nations Educational, Scientific and Cultural Organization. Last accessed 5 May 2013. <http://www.uis.unesco.org/Library/Documents/Finance_EN_web.pdf>.

UIS (2011b). *Global Education Digest 2011: Comparing Education Statistics Across the World*. Montreal: Institute for Statistics, United Nations Educational, Scientific and Cultural Organization. Last accessed 5 September 2013. <http://www.uis.unesco.org/Library/Documents/global_education_digest_2011_en.pdf>.

UN (2012). *The Millennium Development Goals Report 2012*. New York: United Nations.

UN-DESA (2011). *World Population Prospects: The 2010 Revision, Volume I: Comprehensive Tables* (ST/ESA/SER.A/313). New York: United Nations, Department of Economic and Social Affairs, Population Division. Last accessed 10 May 2013. <http://esa.un.org/wpp/Documentation/pdf/WPP2010_Volume-I_Comprehensive-Tables.pdf>.

UN-DESA (1999). *The World at Six Billion*. New York: United Nations, Department of Economic and Social Affairs, Population Division. Last accessed 10 October 2013. <http://www.un.org/esa/population/publications/sixbillion/sixbillion.htm>.

UNESCO (2012). *World Atlas of Gender Inequality in Education*. Paris: United Nations Educational, Scientific and Cultural Organization. Last accessed 5 May 2013. <http://www.uis.unesco.org/Education/Documents/unesco-world-atlas-gender-education-2012.pdf>.

UNESCO (2007). *Education for All by 2015: Will We Make A Difference?* United Nations Educational, Scientific and Cultural Organization. Oxford: Oxford University Press. Last accessed 5 September 2013. <http://unesdoc.unesco.org/images/0015/001547/154743e.pdf>.

UNESCO (2003). 'Political Inertia Exacerbates Water Crisis, Says World Water Development Report First UN System-Wide Evaluation of Global Water Resources', *Press Release No 2013–16*, 5 March. Paris: United Nations Educational, Scientific and Cultural Organization. Last accessed 26 June 2013. <http://portal.unesco.org/en/ev.php-URL_ID=10064&URL_DO=DO_TOPIC&URL_SECTION=201.html>.

Van de Kaa, D. J. (1987). 'Europe's Second Demographic Transition', *Population Bulletin*, 42: 1–59.

Vaupel, J. W. and Lundström, H. (1996). 'The Future of Mortality at Older Ages in Developed Countries' in W. Lutz (ed.), *The Future Population of the World: What Can We Assume Today?* (Rev. ed.). London: Earthscan, pp. 278–95.

Wall, J. D. and Przeworski, M. (2000). 'When Did the Human Population Size Start Increasing?' *Genetics*, 155: 1865–74.

Warner, K. (2010). 'Global Environmental Change and Migration: Governance Challenges', *Global Environmental Change*, 20(3): 402–13.

Westoff, C. F. and Cross, A. R. (2006). 'The Stall in the Fertility Transition in Kenya', *DHS Analytical Studies 9*. Calverton, Maryland: ORC Macro. Last accessed 29 August 2013. <http://www.measuredhs.com/pubs/pdf/AS9/AS9.pdf>.

Young, M. H., Mogelgaard, K., and Hardee, K. (2009). 'Projecting Population, Projecting Climate Change: Population in IPCC Scenarios', *PAI Working Paper WP09-02*. Washington, DC: Population Action International. Last accessed 5 May 2013. <http://populationaction.org/reports/projecting-population-projecting-climate-change-population-in-ipcc-scenarios/>.

Zagheni, E. (2011). 'The Leverage of Demographic Dynamics on Carbon Dioxide Emissions: Does Age Structure Matter?' *Demography*, 48(1): 371–99.

5

Towards a Contemporary Understanding of *The Limits to Growth*

Ian Johnson

The Limits to Growth, first published over forty years ago by Meadows et al. (1972), unleashed a major intellectual storm while simultaneously helping to create a new generation of ecologists, scientists, and economists devoted to better understanding the role that the environment would play in affecting economic growth and social welfare.[1] To the general reader *The Limits to Growth* introduced concepts of exponential growth, of how systems interact and the importance of systems thinking, and of how, within a finite planet, that interaction could become a binding constraint on economic growth. It introduced the casual reader to the concept of 'overshoot', what we would today describe as unsustainable development. Despite its seemingly obvious message—that if we live on a finite planet, a statement that is hard to disagree with, exponential growth of goods and services that deplete our planet must logically reach a point of limits—when published, *The Limits to Growth* unleashed a major war amongst intellectuals and policy analysts. To some it was a totally worthless exercise based upon highly flawed assumptions and a misplaced pessimism in technological change. To others it represented a genuine breakthrough in thinking holistically about the interconnected world we lived in.[2] Many critics believed that the combination of techno-logical progress and technical substitution would render the concept of limits

---

[1] It came on the heels of other books describing the impacts of global phenomena such as Rachel Carson's *Silent Spring* (1962) which assessed the impact of indiscriminate use of pesticides; Paul Ehrlich's *The Population Bomb* (1968) which identified potential concerns over widespread famine; and early pioneers such as Bert Bolin (1970), who brought attention to the issue of climate change and the carbon cycle, and Herman E. Daly, already writing on the economics of a steady state with limited resources (for example, Daly 1968).

[2] See Bardi (2011) for a description of the intellectual debate of the time.

meaningless. Others disagreed with what they viewed as a 'doom and gloom' prediction. A book designed to address the predicament of mankind had quickly become a book about the prediction of the future of mankind. Nothing could have been further from the truth. *The Limits to Growth* offered a set of simulated scenarios which allowed the reader to gauge a series of potential outcomes on the basis of reasonable and plausible assumptions. Only one prediction was made in the report: it argued that at the then-present resource consumption rates the 'great majority of the currently important nonrenewable resources will be extremely costly 100 years from now' (Meadows et al.: 66). Only the most sceptical would find this statement anything but an integral part of today's conventional wisdom.

The Limits to Growth in Historical Perspective

But how did *The Limits to Growth* fare in retrospect? The answer is, quite well. A number of scenarios of resource use stand the test of time pretty well. The report's estimates on population, industrial output, non-renewable resources, and pollution are essentially on track (see Figure 5.1).

Evidence that the world may be moving into overshoot increases with each new scientific report: our global fisheries are certainly unsustainable at present rates of depletion and climate change concerns increase with each new finding (for example, see Figure 5.2). A noteworthy study by Graham Turner (2008) analysed data for the period 1970 to 2000 on the five key factors simulated by the original *The Limits to Growth* team (population, food production, industrial production, pollution, and non-renewable resources).[3] Turner found that the standard scenario base case created by *The Limits to Growth* team in the 1970s closely approximated the empirical observations over the 1970-to-2000 period. This confirmed the concerns expressed in the 1970s that continued economic expansion under existing economic models of growth in consumption and production were on track towards a global collapse or what the team called 'overshoot' sometime around the middle of the 21st century. A more recent concern with regard to climate change is the potential for non-linear effects—the so-called 'tipping points'; across the globe, a single event would result in significant economic damage and social disruption. Evidence suggests that as greenhouse gases accumulate the probability of such events increases, causing large-scale damage and social and economic dislocation. Dunlop (2012) has identified over ten potential 'tipping points' that may occur once we exceed the current 'political' target of 2C (intended to limit

---

[3] Turner (2012) updates the statistical analysis to cover a 40-year period spanning 1970–2010.

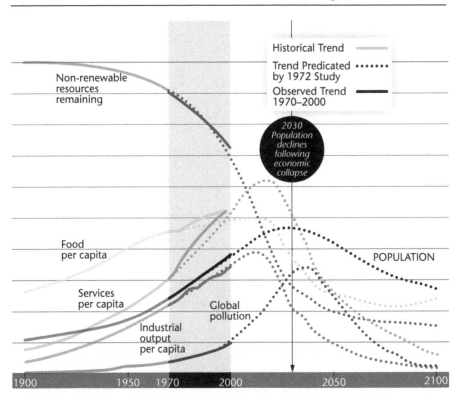

Figure 5.1. *The Limits to Growth*—historical, predicated, and observed trends
Source: Strauss (2012) based on Meadows et al. (1972).

average global temperature rises to no more than 2 degrees Celsius). Apocalyptic, possibly, but a call to action that today is being expressed, at least with respect to the potential impact of global pollution caused by the emissions of greenhouse gases. As Turner (2008: 38) notes, 'the data . . . presented . . . lends support to the conclusion . . . that the global system is on an unsustainable trajectory unless there is substantial and rapid reduction in consumptive behaviour, in combination with technological progress'. Yet *The Limits to Growth* was not a doom-and-gloom book with apocalyptic messages. It made the important point that the paths we were on were chosen; they were anthropogenic in nature, and they could be changed. The pathway towards an unsustainable world is not preordained; it is set by the deliberate policies and actions we take. In that sense, while it was (and has been shown) to be realistic, it was also a plea for action to promote hope. Sadly, its critics were short-sighted and uncomprehending.

The stirrings of debate had already begun even before the publication of Turner's work. System planning, indeed any form of planning, had been roundly rejected by the new neo-conservatives and the so-called Washington

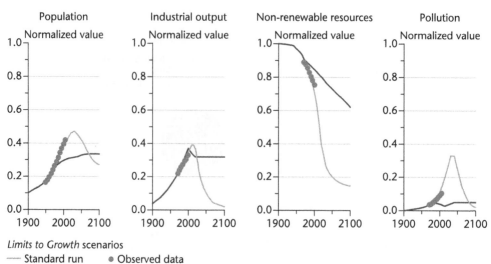

Figure 5.2. Comparison between base case scenario and actual observations
Source: van Vuuren and Faber (2009: 23).

Consensus which made the ideological case that free and unregulated markets would provide *all* the goods and the services required for humankind to prosper. Central planning of any kind was antithetical; market solutions were *de rigueur*. I recall as a young World Bank energy economist the dramatic change during the Reagan–Thatcher free market years where our focus on the energy and electric power sector shifted from the careful and prudent analysis of least-cost system planning as a basis for investment and policy reform to the idea that the free market would provide all the answers. It didn't. It couldn't. The early reactions to *The Limits to Growth* were similar. Why plan? Why worry about feedback loops, interconnections, and systems effects when the market is all-seeing and all-powerful? This loosely held philosophy has potentially lost us thirty years of prudently managed sustainable development. Voices in the wilderness were there but were largely ignored.[4]

The Role of Technology and *The Limits to Growth*

The Limits to Growth was born during a period of great technological optimism. The world had only recently witnessed the landing of the first human on the moon; breakthroughs in medicine were extending life by years; computers

---

[4] See for example Simmons (2000).

were in their infancy but promised great hope for analytical and computational speed (indeed the researchers themselves were early pioneers of dynamic programming and systems analysis made possible by computer breakthroughs); and the developing world was living off the end of the 'green revolution' which had increased crop yields by significant margins, staving off the fears of mass famine (see Goldin and Reinert 2012: 141–3). It is little wonder that 'technology as saviour' was a hotly debated topic then as, indeed, it is today.

The Limits to Growth research team were unfairly perceived to be rather neutral in regards to technology. It was assumed to be a largely linear phenomenon, and the early criticism was that of comparing the pessimism of resource limits with the seemingly misplaced pessimism of technological progress.[5] Some argued that rapid and sustained growth in technical progress would always offset any negative impacts of resource use, population growth, and pollution, and that technical progress would, in fact, be the driver for gains in productivity. Furthermore, many of the technological optimists implicitly made assumptions that ultimately everything was substitutable: once resources were depleted or close to depletion perfect substitutes would somehow appear. Others argued the case that there was considerable evidence of diminishing returns to technology investment (Ayres 1998 cited in Bardi 2011: 77ff). Daly (1991) made the case that technological change is systematically overestimated in terms of its impact on total factor productivity. He noted that '[s]uch findings cast doubt on the notion that technology, unaided by increased resource flows, can give us enormous increases in output' (Daly 1991: 106). Still others made the case for 'great leaps forward'—sporadic technological quantum jumps driven by exogenous factors related to events such as war, energy crises, and deliberate political aspirations (such as the space race of the 1960s). The truth is that evidence can be found to fit all theories of linear and non-linear shifts in technological progress. In the final analysis it is blind faith that leads us to be technological optimists or pessimists: our views are coloured by what we want to see. The models such as those used to simulate limits to growth can demonstrate the positive and negative roles of technology in limiting the impacts of resource use or in delaying the impacts until well into the future.

The more important point is that technological progress is only of real value if it can demonstrate a clear improvement in the human condition sustained well into the future and hence within the boundaries that natural limits impose. The overwhelming bulk of investment in emerging technology is financed through private sources and, as such, technology returns must

---

[5] In fact this was an unfair criticism of the Report. See Bardi (2011) and Turner (2008).

meet the financial requirements of due diligence; largely those of short-term financial gain. To those concerned with the long-term future of planet Earth this seems anathema. Increasingly the application of technology provides both a public-good and a private-good return and, all too often, these are in conflict. Ensuring that financial returns are consistent with economic or societal gains remains a significant challenge for public policy. Two examples come to mind. The first is the decreasing financial costs of exploration and development of so-called 'non-conventional oil' compared with the increasing costs to society and the planet of that exploitation—discussed later in this chapter. As financial costs induce increased exploitation the societal costs increase also, especially when allowance is made for the cost of the impact of climate change. A second example relates to the financial sector. The recent dramatic advances in computer speed have encouraged the development of mathematical algorithms that can compute, in nanoseconds, financial currency trades. What value such trades have other than to make a few casino bankers extraordinarily rich is questionable but recent evidence suggests that it has had little positive impact on the real economy or on welfare gains (Henderson, 2009; Foresight, 2011, 2012a, b).

If technological developments are to be harnessed for the common good of humanity it will likely only come about if enlightened public policy sets both a direction and a vision. The public-good content of technical change is increasing in importance and hence public policies must become more pro-active on a number of fronts by:

- *Increasing* investment in long-term global public goods aimed at increasing human welfare, sustained well into the future. Investment can be stand-alone or within the framework of new joint ventures and partnerships.

- *Maintaining* a watchful eye on the implementation of new and emerging technologies to ensure that they do not suffer unduly from unintended negative consequences. The case of technological innovation in energy efficiency is instructive, whereby unit efficiency is improved but, in aggregate, overall use increases (the so-called 'Jevons effect');[6] or the case for a 'Tobin-style' tax on financial speculation and currency trading which would help reduce the negative 'public-goods' impact of casino-style speculation. Prudent and complementary public policy is often also required.

- *Maintaining* a watchful eye on the potential substitutability of technical innovation. Not everything is substitutable. At least not yet. For example,

[6] See Giampietro and Mayumi (2008).

while humanity has created the means by which some species can be replicated or sustained (through cloning, genetic management, and *in situ* conservation) there are questions about how ecosystems, composed of an intricate network of life-sustaining systems, can be replicated other than by conservation. The value of ecosystem services to the functioning of the planet and the survival of the human species remains underappreciated. The planet's major ecosystems are of crucial value, and their preservation has many advantages, from recreational to climate regulation, but perhaps it is their complexity and fundamental diversity that is critical. At the present moment there are no known viable substitutes for 'biodiversity', even though scientists are beginning to recognize its importance to our survival. Public policy is needed to defend and protect systems for which no acceptable substitute exists; a clear plea to protect our last wildernesses, natural habitats, and ecosystems. Valuing ecosystem services and reflecting these values in public policy decisions and, where possible, in markets, is essential.

- *Encouraging* technological innovation that reinforces all the positive externalities in application and discourages negative use by taking into account the full cycle costs of its deployment over time. Nuclear waste disposal is a classic case in point: with positive discount rates the costs of waste disposal were treated as almost zero in the initial calculus of building nuclear power stations; a short-sighted policy which has now come home to roost.

More recently there has been a great deal of optimism in a new form of technological progress, that which emulates the rhythms of nature (Pauli, 2010). Biomimicry research is in its infancy but it promises much in the way of benign technologies that are at one with the natural ebbs and flows of nature. They are deemed to be not only sustainable and economic but also employment generating on a significant scale. Their promise is yet to be realized.

The Limits to Growth stimulated a debate on the role of technical progress in managing the Earth's limited resources. We now more fully recognize that technological innovation can support or destroy life on Earth. A real and lasting contribution of *The Limits to Growth* is that it started an intellectual journey that continues to this day. The debate on how, by the middle to the end of this century, nine to ten billion humans will live off a fixed stock of natural capital; on whether we are able to make major adjustments to consumption behaviours; introduce less polluting production patterns; and meet the social and moral obligation to lift one quarter of our global population out of poverty, continues.

Conceptualizing the Limits to Growth

The Limits to Growth also introduced the then-unheralded concepts of systems modelling and modelling on a global scale. Holistic thinking in scientific circles was rare at that time. The understanding of systems and our ability to model them was in its infancy. The Executive Committee of the Club of Rome noted at the time: '. . . the essential significance of the project lies in its global concept, for it is through knowledge of wholes that we gain understanding of components, and not vice versa' (Meadows et al. 1972: 188).

That the concepts underlying *The Limits to Growth* have an enduring quality is as important as recognizing that it is now necessary to place them within a contemporary framework. Forty years ago *The Limits to Growth* promoted a major debate dedicated to better understanding our global humanity, its place in the natural world, and the pressures it was likely to come under. The United Nations Environment Programme (UNEP) was born in the same year as *The Limits to Growth*. It would be ten years before the international financial community, especially the World Bank, would begin to embrace environmental factors and a further ten years before the corporate and private sector would follow suit. But times have changed; knowledge and understanding of environmental factors have dramatically increased and broadened across society.

The natural limits of growth

Much of the debate over the past decades has been centred on the issues of geo- or biophysical depletion of the planet's natural capital. Of course, this is not unreasonable given the obvious fact that the planet has a fixed stock of natural capital. We only have one Earth and, to a broad approximation, its natural assets are fixed. Physical depletion, by definition, has limits. Of course, as already noted, technological innovation and progress, technical substitution, and prudent management can extend the lifespan of that stock but, fundamentally, it is fixed. Recent attempts have been made to assess the limits of our biophysical capacity in terms of providing guidance to where the boundaries of a safe operating space might be for humanity. Rockström et al. (2009), for example, provide a compelling case by identifying what they term 'a safe operating space' for humanity. They identify nine biophysical issues that operate at global and regional levels. On the global scale they identify climate change, ocean acidification, and stratospheric ozone depletion as key global commons issues; the remainder are largely regional and local issues— namely, global phosphorous and nitrogen cycles, atmospheric aerosol loading, fresh water use, land use change, biodiversity loss, and chemical pollution. The boundaries are described in physical terms, although, as the author explains, feedback loops and the complexities of interconnected processes provide uncertainty with respect to potential impact; a useful reminder of the importance of resilience and risk management.

The economic limits of growth: oil and water

Yet, long before the world has reached the physical limits of depleting its natural capital or decreasing its biospheric resilience, it will reach its economic limits. Daly (2008) has written eloquently about the plausible case of reaching a point of 'uneconomic growth': where the costs to society of a unit of growth (as conventionally measured by GDP) are greater than the societal benefits of that growth.[7] Hotelling (1931), to a large extent, founded the intellectual underpinnings of how to better understand the economics of depletion of natural capital.

Two examples are worth considering: oil and water. The first is an essential requirement for the kind of economic and industrial growth we have witnessed for close to one hundred years; where economic growth goes, so follows oil consumption. And water, the central requirement for the existence of life as we know it on the planet.

The first example is oil. Total oil consumption in the world to date has been variously estimated at around 10 per cent of total global oil reserves, most of which, under today's prices and technical knowledge, are non-exploitable.[8] In theory, there is sufficient oil to last another century or beyond. So why worry? Of course the answer lies in the fact that the cost to society is growing. If we have entered, as Daly suggests, an era of uneconomic growth, we have simultaneously almost certainly entered a period of uneconomic oil. To the oil companies, the cost of oil is driven by the long-run marginal financial cost of exploration, development, production, and transportation. But to society at large, it is also driven by any additional costs that occur, especially those costs due to local and global environmental damage. And these are rising—and rising fast.

Future oil exploration has been driven by two factors. The first is the identification of new sources of fossil fuels, often in remote or environmentally fragile 'hot spots'. The coastal waters around the Gulf of Mexico; the Amazon and adjacent coastal zones of Brazil; the Mediterranean; and more

---

[7] For an overview see Daly (2006).

[8] Estimates are difficult to come by. Proven estimates of oil reserves (that exclude next generation oil production from bitumen and tar sands) are estimated at between 900 billion barrels and 1,300 billion barrels (for example Mason 2010). Thus a large volume of oil is not yet considered proven until it can be technically and economically exploited. Twenty years ago tar sands were not considered viable. Today technological development is reducing the financial costs of exploration dramatically.

recently the Arctic have all been targeted for expanded exploration and production. All these are fragile and could result in potential human and ecological damage as a result of leakage, poor management, and other largely unintended risks. The damage caused by the 2010 oil spill in the Gulf of Mexico has been estimated variously at between US$13 billion and US$100 billion.[9] The Arctic has been estimated to contain around 90 billion barrels of oil, 1,669 trillion cubic feet of natural gas, and 44 billion barrels of natural liquid gas (USGS 2008), sufficient to add about three years and twenty-five years respectively to world supplies. But it is contained in an inhospitable environment which adds to costs and increases the risks of leakage. Not only could this decimate one of the world's last remaining undisturbed environments on Earth, but recent evidence also suggests that, in addition, there is the increased possibility of the thawing of the permafrost which could release highly potent methane into the atmosphere (UNEP 2011b; Wijkman and Rockström 2012).

The second factor is that recently developed techniques have opened up vast areas for new exploration. Hydraulic fracturing, more commonly known as 'fracking', is a process by which water mixed with chemicals is pumped at high pressure into rock formations that contain highly distributed pockets of oil and gas, often in lateral rock formations.[10] The chemicals emulsify the oil and gas which can then be pumped to the surface for treatment and onward distribution to refineries. Investment in fracking has caused a mini-energy boom in some parts of the world, notably in North America. In Canada, new techniques for securing hitherto unobtainable oil from tar sands has caused a similar boom. Oil secured with these new techniques might add only some three to five years or so of additional global oil and gas supply, but could create a technological fossil fuel 'lock-in' that would result in a long-term high cost in terms of its impact on the global climate (Dangerman and Schellnhuber 2013; Pearce 2013). This, in turn, promotes next-generation exploration at even higher social costs and with potentially greater damage. Many of us can recall that the very notion that tar sands could be considered a new source of oil and gas was looked on as a complete non-starter; it was an energy source that could never be exploited. To some this seemed implausible even twenty years ago (Gillespie 2008; Hoffmans 2012). It is a reality today. A deeper understanding of path dependency with regard to incremental oil production

---

[9] Estimates are largely in the media rather than from scientific investigation. See, for example, Haq (2010). Other estimates have placed the figures at closer to $100 billion when all costs and damages are assessed including environmental and livelihood loss (Spillius 2010). All agree that this is the most expensive oil spill in history.

[10] The technique was originally developed in the 1940s. However, in the 1990s, when oil prices continued at a high level, incentives to develop more sophisticated techniques, known as 'horizontal slickwater fracturing', were developed which require the high-pressure injection of chemicals into rock formations.

is an area requiring further investigation. It may represent one of the greater risks facing humanity. If a three- to five-year increment in fossil fuel use results in, let's say, a 30-year technological 'lock-in'[11] and this drives a new generation of exploration and development, the notion of maintaining the planet below a 2°C or 3°C level will be lost. One major oilfield, the Athabasca tar sands in Western Canada, alone, could contribute significantly to global supplies,[12] and the region is already gearing up for a Middle East style oil boom, with new fossil-fuel-based industries planned for expansion.

It is worth considering the full range of costs associated with the drive for 'new and unconventional' oil supplies. The tar sands are instructive. A value can be assessed for the land damaged; for the water and energy used; for the use and long-term storage of harmful chemicals;[13] for the obvious and sometimes irreversible damage to ecosystems; and for the health, social, and cultural impacts on local residents. But to this must be added the cost of carbon emissions, variously estimated in ranges of $20 to over $40 per tonne of carbon.[14] The external cost effects are now starting to outpace the internal costs of resource management. It is likely that in many circumstances the real societal cost of oil is closer to $250 per barrel than the current market price of around $104 per barrel (Bloomberg 2013). Some studies have gone further. One study commissioned in the United States determined that if all the costs of securing oil supplies to the United States were taken into account, the real cost of oil to the United States consumer would be closer to $400 per barrel (Nelder 2007).[15] No matter where the correct price level lies, it is substantially above the current market price. The cost of securing new liquid fossil fuels is likely higher than the benefits to society. And, as more oil is consumed, the potential damage and impact costs of addressing climate change increase.

---

[11] Metz et al. (2007: 662–3) suggests a 30 year 'lock-in'.

[12] 'According to *Petroleum Economist*: "Although tar sands occur in more than 70 countries, the bulk is found in Canada in four regions: Athabasca, Wabasca, Cold Lake, and Peace River; together covering an area of some 77,000 km². In fact, the reserve considered to be technically recoverable is estimated at 280–300 Gb (billions of barrels), larger than the Saudi Arabia oil reserves [optimistically] estimated at 240 Gb. The total reserves for Alberta, including oil not recoverable using current technology, are estimated at 1,700–2,500 Gb"' (Premium Petroleum Corp. 2007).

[13] The chemicals used represent a potent cocktail of harmful and less harmful compounds. These include hydrochloric acid, sodium chloride, polyacrylamide and other friction reducers, ethylene glycol, borate salts, sodium, potassium, glutaraldehyde and other disinfectants, guar gum and other water-soluble agents, citric acid, isopropanol, methanol, isopropyl alcohol, 2-butoxyethanol, and ethylene glycol.

[14] These figures are taken from the UN (2010) and Price, Thornton, and Nelson (2007) respectively. Stern (2007) calculates that this implies a social cost of carbon of $30/tCO2e in 2000. This would be well over $40 in 2012 prices. In addition, Stern also notes that any delay in addressing climate change increases the social cost of carbon.

[15] Nelder quotes Milton Copulus, head of the National Defense Council Foundation, who has assessed the total cost of oil to the United States at $480 a barrel by taking into account military and security costs as well as those associated with exploration and development.

The second example is that of fresh water resources. Contrary to conventional wisdom, water resources are not scarce. On a global scale, fresh water availability could meet demand for thousands of years. Even as fresh water is depleted we could then rely upon technological innovation to transform sea water to fresh water (although this is potentially energy intensive). In land-locked countries, access to fresh water can be secured through expensive infrastructure carrying water long distances through canals and pipelines; mining aquifers, and managing the collection of rainwater. More expensive technologies include energy-intensive desalination of sea and brackish water as is practiced in some Middle Eastern and Mediterranean countries. All of this is possible; it only requires money. Indeed, the issue of water scarcity is really one of cost for capital investments and, in many cases, improved water management. Many parts of the world suffer from periodic droughts, from low and depleting local water supplies, and from low-quality water supplies. Yet one way to consider water scarcity is to understand it as economic scarcity: it is the cost of securing water that is the binding constraint. Water resources remain the most subsidized of the planet's natural capital. Few countries price water at anything close to its economic value, the net result of which is that the global water subsidy is in the order of $400 billion per annum.[16]

Understanding the economic limits of water use is valuable in being able to determine rational policies for water use and management and for placing a real value on 'water scarcity'. As in the case of oil, it is important to reflect all the costs associated with exploration, development, and delivery of water resources. An understanding of the scarcity of water derives from the economic cost of delivering water to the consumer; largely the farmer (agriculture is responsible for 75 per cent of water use), the household, or industry.

One way to explain scarcity is to study the cost of meeting the future demand for water. By constructing a hierarchy of potential projects and investments to meet demand—whether drilling, or building dams, transmission canals, and urban networks—it is possible to understand the future costs of harnessing water. To this must be added any potential environmental damage estimates and also, especially in the case of major infrastructure, any potential social costs due to relocating communities from the site. As is the case for oil exploration, future water resources are now to be found in more

---

[16] This is a rough 'guesstimate' thought to be correct in terms of order of magnitude. It is informed by work currently underway with a colleague intended to estimate the real resource cost of water subsidies. Most existing estimates of water subsidies are considerably lower, but only take account of the direct financial subsidy. The above figure moves beyond this narrow and incomplete view of water subsidies by allowing for the full economic costs. These include the cost of exploration, capital development, and operation and maintenance, as well as environmental and social costs, and the cost of managing the disposal of water in an environmentally sustainable manner (removal of heavy metals, pollutants, waste and sewerage, etc) that meet public health standards (amongst other things).

remote and more ecologically fragile areas of the world. In some countries, especially in Asia, the dislocation of residents and communities imposes a high financial and social cost. What is clear in almost all countries is that these costs are rising rapidly and, in some cases, discontinuously, with major leaps in costs as investments move from local supplies to large intra-basin transfers to desalination; as more and more resources must be provided for capital investment; and as recurrent costs rise. There is significant evidence that the introduction of improved demand management, realistic pricing to reflect the real costs of water delivery, and improved management in water utilities can play a significant role in reducing overall costs. Nevertheless, the increasing demand for water will require new levels of investment in the future and this will rise over time. Analysing the rising cost of capital investment in water resource facilities also has the advantage of highlighting the opportunities for (and level of investment resources saved) in applying demand management policies.

The point at which managing our natural resources become a brake on economic growth is difficult to assess. Much depends upon the domestic costs of minerals and natural resources development and whether income opportunities exist for the export of minerals. The implications of rising energy prices on economic growth are well documented (Hall and Klitgaard 2012; Kümmel 2011; Ayres and Warr 2010), although the impact of rising water resource management costs is somewhat less well documented. Climate change is likely to place greater pressure on the rising costs of water management as reserve margin requirements, flood control, and drought management will all require additional investment.

Financial costs versus economic costs

It is important to understand the key differences between financial costs (the immediate costs to the oil company or the water utility) and the economic costs (the real costs borne by society). The cases of oil and water are instructive of the challenges ahead. In the case of oil, the financial costs of exploration and development appear to be decreasing. New developments in 'fracking' technologies, the lack of an adequate carbon price, and the likely subsidies embedded in the water and land used for exploration all contribute to a low and falling price curve. The very factors not counted in the financial calculus, of course, contribute to a rising (and potentially rapidly rising) economic or societal cost curve. In the case of water resources, the financial and economic or societal cost curves are rising but in tandem. The additional costs of meeting new demands are very real, require new and expensive investment, and involve higher recurrent costs. In time there will be a convergence of financial and economic costs with price signals to the market place that will reflect the full cost of delivery. The danger we face is the widening gap in fossil fuels exploration as the societal cost, in terms especially of climate risk, is rising rapidly.

The Limits of Economic Theory

The flip side to a contemporary understanding of *The Limits to Growth* is to assess the kind of growth we have witnessed over the past decades and to question its efficacy. Forty years ago economic growth was predicated upon vastly increased consumption, the draw-down of natural capital stocks as a means of increasing income at a low cost, and the trickle-down effects of rising aggregate GDP. These were treated as conventional wisdom: economic growth was good irrespective of how it was distributed or how it was produced. Over the past few decades a number of economists have begun questioning the conventional wisdom of the classical definitions of economic growth.[17]

The foundations for modern economics were built when the world was dramatically different from how it is today. Current economic theory of growth and wealth creation rests largely on assumptions that were made over two hundred years ago but many are no longer valid for today's world. Shifts in lifestyles, communications, and changes in the patterns of production and consumption have been sufficiently large as to call into question the validity of current economic growth theory. The dramatic rise in economic growth in the emerging world, especially in Asia and Latin America, has also called into question the sustainability of lifestyles afforded to rich countries across the globe.

The limits of the classical measurements of national wealth (and the growth in such wealth) have been well documented ever since the creation of national accounts and their use in determining relative wealth. GDP has long been the most quoted and least understood metric of economics. In particular, it excludes a great many factors that are of vital importance to the full functioning of society (such as protection of natural habitats and improved well-being, and happiness) and yet manages simultaneously to include factors that most of us would deem undesirable (such as crime, social unrest, and war). And yet, for all its flaws, it remains stubbornly the most quoted metric of economic achievement and of measuring relative economic performance. Despite these criticisms, changes in GDP continue to be the most common definition of 'economic growth' and such growth is politically accepted as the metric for 'progress'.

---

[17] See, for example, Daly (1991), Dasgupta and Mäler (2000), Nordhaus and Tobin (1973), Sen (1976), Sarkozy Report (2009), Korten (2010), and Johnson and Jacobs (2012).

Economic growth has been used as a measure of how wealth was changing and as a measure of social progress. It is neither. Economic growth was expected to be linear and non-binding: technology and human ingenuity would provide the buffer against any limits. Yet economic growth, as classically defined, and often as not prescribed, has not produced wealth and social progress for most people on our planet.

From Growth to the 'Steady-State' Economy

These facts have been recognized by several leading thinkers and economists, and there is now a nascent movement to review the underpinning of economic theory as well as to begin using economics to measure many goods and services that have hitherto remained unmeasured, including natural resources.[18] Much of the initial questioning of economic growth theory and its relationship with the environment can be traced back to the 1960s through two broad strands of intellectual reasoning. The first was the growth in ecological economics, and the second the growth in environmental economics (see Runnalls 2011). The former typically emphasized the economy as a subset of ecology and had its roots in the concerns of natural systems and their carrying capacity. The latter has grown out of welfare economics and concerns itself with the valuation of natural assets and the economic cost of environmental damage. Foremost amongst the ecological economists was Herman Daly, an academic and former senior economist at the World Bank, and protégé of Nicholas Georgescu-Roegen. Daly and Cobb (1989) promoted the concepts of ecological economics and the need to balance economy with ecology (see also Daly 2008). The second stream of economic thinking that emerged is exemplified by the work of David Pearce and associates;[19] those at the micro and sector level who, through a welfare economics lens, analysed the economic cost of environmental externalities and promoted new concepts such as the 'polluter pays principle' and the application of cost–benefit analysis to activities involving environmental and social goods, as well as more macro-oriented economists who began to see the impact that correct pricing and good microeconomic analysis would have on macroeconomic balance sheets and growth. More recently, the two streams have merged, creating a broader alliance around issues of the nature and quality of economic growth and its prospects (Jackson 2009).

[18] See, for example, the European Commission's 'Beyond GDP' initiative (<http://www.beyond-gdp.eu/>) or the French Government's Commission on the Measurement of Economic Performance and Social Progress (<http://www.stiglitz-sen-fitoussi.fr/en/index.htm>).
[19] See for example Pearce, Markandya, and Barbier (1989) and Pearce and Barbier (2000). See also K. Turner (2005), WCED (1987), and Sukhdev et al. (2010).

The promotion of economic growth has, in particular, come under attack. Today's economic growth perpetuates overconsumption (in part to revitalize ailing companies and to fill government coffers). The fact that more consumption is part of the problem and not part of the solution escapes all but the clear minded. Intuition and common sense tell us that it makes no sense for governments, trying to revive the holy grail of quarterly economic growth figures, to implore their citizens to go out on the 'High Street' and buy more goods (they don't need) with money (they don't have). In simple terms, we grow our economies through increased consumption (and waste) fuelled by increased debt (Williams 2009; Lee 2008). Daly and others have argued for a new concept in economics; that of the 'steady state'. Once a certain level of adequate economic and social progress is achieved, moving towards a steady-state economy reduces the requirement for massive, consumption-led growth. In place of such growth Daly (1991: 17) defines a steady-state economy as one that ensures: '...constant stocks of people and artifacts, maintained at some desired, sufficient levels by low rates of maintenance "throughput", that is, by the lowest feasible flows of matter and energy from the first stage of production to the last stage of consumption'. Once basic needs and requirements are met, a steady-state economy would be aligned with the human needs of the planet and with its physical limits. Such approaches must, of course, recognize that perhaps one third of humanity on our planet still needs to see conventional growth to achieve a morally decent standard of living. Inherent in Daly's approach is the need to uplift those in absolute poverty. A steady-state economy would, in the broadest sense, conform to the general understanding of sustainability: it would aim to meet humanity's needs while also maintaining the life-support systems of the planet.

The extent to which a steady-state economy would build the bridge between physical ecological limits on one hand and real economic progress ('new growth?') on the other would depend upon a number of actions. These include:

- An emphasis on the conservation of natural capital at a minimum maintenance level consistent with the life-support services it provides.

- The depletion of nonrenewable resources at a rate no faster than they can be regenerated.

- The consumption of nonrenewable resources (such as fossil fuels) at a rate they can be replaced by the discovery of renewable substitutes but taking into account the full range of negative external costs associated with such consumption. In particular with regard to harmful environmental effects such as climate change.

- The reduction of waste and the addition of waste products back into the economy only at a rate less than they can be safely assimilated.

- The need to be aware of intergenerational responsibilities by avoiding technologies that obviously include unreasonable risks or high costs for more than one generation.

In addition, new economic growth to meet human needs must also:

- Reduce the level of inequality within and between societies in order to promote stability and eliminate the obscene 'tail ends' of wealth and poverty.
- Increase the level of remunerative work and employment.
- Make markets work for the real economy.

The range of technical, economic, and institutional means to achieve these goals is well beyond the scope of this chapter, although the knowledge, on a number of fronts, certainly exists. Technological knowledge is available to meet the objectives of waste minimization and fuel substitution towards renewable energy sources and water savings.[20] Cutting the umbilical cord between resource use and economic growth appears feasible and highly desirable (UNEP 2011a). There is a growing knowledge of reverse engineering of our tax systems, which currently subsidize the things we don't want such as fossil fuels and tax the things we do want such as more jobs (Johnson and Jacobs 2012). We have experience of making markets work for public goods and for environmental services (Sukhdev et al. 2010; Broekhoff 2007; Linacre, Kossoy, and Ambrosi 2011). Our knowledge has never been greater in terms of knowing what to do and our politics has never been weaker. Our experience has taught us to understand that the planet's biophysical limits do impose real economic costs, including the impact of rapid oil price rises on economic growth (Bacon and Kojima 2008), and the potential costs of adjusting to a new era of climate change adaptation and mitigation (Stern 2007). Our economic understanding of how we can simultaneously reduce resource use in the production of wealth while also creating employment opportunities remains incomplete: a major challenge lies ahead.

Current Limits, Future Challenges, and Potential Scenarios

The Limits to Growth produced a major and timely debate that now questions some of the fundamentals of our economic growth paradigms. We now have a clear understanding of our limits in terms that are not only biophysical but also include the real cost to our economic and social systems. The rapid

---

[20] von Weizsäcker et al. (2009) identify pragmatic ways in which a fivefold increase in efficiency can be achieved.

draw-down of our natural capital that has occurred in the past century may well be increased even further in the next century, unless actions are taken.

The link between biophysical assets and human welfare has spawned concerns over the Earth's carrying capacity that go well into the future. Demographic projections and income requirements to move the poor out of absolute poverty, combined with a rapidly growing middle class (with more than 70 million added to the middle class each year) have reinforced these concerns (see Wilson and Dragusanu 2008). Under present per capita growth scenarios and assuming that, as a reasonable normative goal, we should eliminate the worst forms of poverty by the middle of the century, the planet could conservatively witness a non-linear shift from the current $35 trillion GDP to at least $135 trillion by 2050 (Hamilton and Johnson 2004: 34); a threefold increase in infrastructure, energy use, and food consumption, plus all of the lifestyle demands of an emerging world requiring and potentially demanding a material lifestyle for all which approximates to that of the United States. Indeed, while the planet may need to absorb an additional 2 billion people by the middle of the century, it is important not to forget that it will also be absorbing more than 4 billion people with new middle-class lifestyles, consumption habits, and aspirations.[21] Managing this transformation may be a significantly larger challenge than managing the additional population increase per se.

Can this be achieved in a harmonious and progressive manner? The likelihood is that it cannot, unless major accommodations are made. A tripling of energy demand on the basis of fossil fuel dependency hardly seems conducive to a sustainable future.

The larger question is whether there are new growth paths that can accommodate simultaneously a decrease in resource use and an increase in living standards (including for people currently living in the developing world). Efforts have been made to calculate the 'footprint' or carrying capacity of Earth as a result of rising economic growth (GFN 2012). Estimates are highly aggregative but indicate that today humanity uses the equivalent of 1.5 planets to provide the resources that are used and to absorb the waste, meaning that the planet now requires eighteen months to regenerate one year's worth of consumption. Using United Nations scenarios of population and consumption patterns reveals that, by 2030, the planet will have increased its resource depletion to an equivalent of two Earths, and by 2050 to three: a new but no less clear definition of 'overshoot'.

---

[21] Estimates of those joining the middle classes are somewhat vaguely defined. Most are in Asia and the higher-income developing countries. The estimates may well be conservative. Lifestyles and not numbers will largely define sustainability concerns (Wilson and Dragusanu 2008).

What then might be done? The first step is to reject the current tendency to view economic theory as a Newtonian concept based on intractable laws of nature. We need to bring a more human-centred economics into focus that goes back to the original roots of the first economists (such as Adam Smith) who were, to a large degree, moral philosophers. We need to re-examine current economic theory to see where it fails to promote optimum human welfare and how it can be altered to better suit humanity's needs within an understanding of the fragility of our global stock of natural capital. A triple divorce has occurred which has disconnected our economies from the fundamental role they were intended to fulfil. The first is the widening rift between production and employment. The aim of raising labour productivity has given way to the obsession with eliminating labour altogether from the production process. Second is the rift between finance and economy, a divorce of financial markets from the real economy. Money and financial markets have become ends in themselves, undermining the essential understanding that markets were to be an efficient means to support social and economic progress. The last is the rift between economy and ecology where the blind pursuit of consumption-led economic growth is rapidly destroying the ecological foundations upon which human life depends.

Yet recourse to economics, finance, and ecology are an insufficient mix to address the emerging concerns of a new global humanity. More must be done to align our values, beliefs, and value system to a new global reality.

It is becoming increasingly obvious that a new paradigm is needed which brings together the various dimensions of the human experience and our ability to sustain life on Earth. This embraces, and yet goes well beyond, notions of resource limitations and the nature of economic wealth creation. It goes to the heart of how we function as a species and how we can survive peacefully and sustainably on our planet. In many respects it represents a continuation of an intellectual journey initiated by the Club of Rome and *The Limits to Growth*, and expanded upon by the ecological movement and new thinking on economics to a more holistic and comprehensive view. Ben Eli (2012), a disciple of Buckminster Fuller, has taken the definition of sustainability further, noting that there are many factors that shape the equilibrium of a population and the capacity of its environment to carry it. In Eli's view, sustainability has lost its true meaning. Rather, he looks at it from a systems viewpoint as 'a dynamic equilibrium in the process of interaction between a population and the carrying capacity of its environment such that the population develops to express its full potential without producing irreversible adverse effects on the carrying capacity of the environment upon which it depends' (Eli 2012: 4). Once systems thinking is invoked, complexity increases, and the search for a new paradigm that adequately covers all factors, their interactions, and feedback loops is required. Eli identifies five domains that interact: the *material* domain, regulating the flows of materials and energy; the *economic* domain, for creating lasting wealth; the domain of *life*, providing the basis for appropriate behaviour in the biosphere; the *social* domain, which provides the basis for social and human interaction; and the *spiritual* domain, which identifies the necessary attitudinal and value orientations, and acts as a basis for a universal code of values and ethics.

Understanding life on Earth in all its manifestations and the changes that will unfold during the 21st century remains a challenge for humanity. The simple question of 'is the planet full?' unfolds its answers along many dimensions. To find a satisfactory and intellectually rigorous understanding of sustainability in the light of increasing human pressures on a finite planet will demand new approaches, new ways of thinking, and new values. The current trajectory of unbridled economic growth unevenly distributed and based upon a rapid draw-down of our fixed natural capital assets is a course for certain disaster. Long before the Earth fills up we will see unparalleled environmental problems, human misery, and the depletion of the key elements that sustain us. Fortunately, the problems created are all anthropogenic: what humanity has done can be undone. We can set course using more enlightened growth strategies that create real and lasting wealth for all; we can bring our natural capital back to a state of positive regenerative capacity, and we can recalibrate our values and ethics to serve all of humanity.

The time is ripe for a new narrative, new metaphors, and a new storyline for humanity. A new renaissance with new possibilities and new frontiers must take hold. The remedies lie not only in technological fixes or in marginal changes to our economic, social, and financial systems, but to a re-examination of the fundamental ideas and values on which the current system is based. Refining our understanding of 'limits' and redefining 'growth' are a good start. Yet the limits we confront are mental limits—limits to our perception, understanding, imagination, idealism, and values. That *The Limits to Growth* started us on a journey is to its credit. That we are far from realizing a new world, managed by the limitless stock of human ingenuity but within the limited stock of natural life-support systems, is the challenge before us. Whether we will confront those limits remains an open question.

References

Ayres, R. U. (1998). 'Technological Progress: A Proposed Measure', *Technological Forecasting and Social Change*, 59(3): 213–33.

Ayres, R. U. and Warr, B. (2010). *The Economic Growth Engine: How Energy and Work Drive Material Prosperity*. Cheltenham: Edward Elgar.

Bacon, R. and Kojima, M. (2008). *Vulnerability to Oil Price Increases: A Decomposition Analysis of 161 Countries* (Extractive Industries and Development Series #1). Washington, DC: World Bank.

Bardi, U. (2011). *The Limits to Growth Revisited* (Springer Briefs in Energy). New York: Springer.

Bloomberg (2013). 'Energy and Oil Prices [Crude Oil (Brent), USD/bbl]'. Last accessed 28 May 2013. <http://www.bloomberg.com/energy/>.

Bolin, B. (1970). 'The Carbon Cycle', *Scientific American*, 223: 125–32.

Broekhoff, D. (2007). 'Voluntary Carbon Offsets—Getting What You Paid For', Testimony Before the House Select Committee on Energy Independence and Global Warming, United States House of Representatives, 18 July. Last accessed 30 May 2013. <http://www.gpo.gov/fdsys/pkg/CHRG-110hhrg58085/html/CHRG-110hhrg58085.htm>.

Carson, R. (1962). *Silent Spring*. Boston: Houghton Mifflin.

Daly, H. (2008). *A Steady-State Economy: A Failed Growth Economy and A Steady-State Economy are not the Same Thing; They are the Very Different Alternatives We Face*. UK Sustainable Development Commission, 28 April. Last accessed 30 May 2013. <http://www.sd-commission.org.uk/data/files/publications/Herman_Daly_thinkpiece.pdf>.

Daly, H. (2006). 'Uneconomic Growth' in D. A. Clark (ed.), *The Elgar Companion to Development Studies*. Cheltenham: Edward Elgar, pp. 654–8.

Daly, H. (1991). *Steady-State Economics*, 2nd ed. Washington, DC: Island Press.

Daly, H. (1968). 'On Economics as a Life Science', *Journal of Political Economy*, 76(3): 392–406.

Daly, H. and Cobb, J. B. Jr (1989). *For the Common Goods: Redirecting the Economy Toward Community, Environment and a Sustainable Future*. Boston: Beacon Press.

Dangerman, A. T. C. J. and Schellnhuber, H. J. (2013). 'Energy Systems Transformation', *Proceedings of the National Academy of Sciences (PNAS)*, 110(7): 2436–7.

Dasgupta P. and Mäler, K. G. (2000). 'Net National Product, Wealth, and Social Well-Being', *Environment and Development Economics*, 5: 69–93.

Dunlop, I. T. (2012). 'The Future of Energy: The Most Likely Scenario—Emergency Action', *DRET Draft Energy White Paper*, March. Canberra: Department of Resources, Energy and Tourism, Australian Government. Last accessed 30 May 2013. <http://cpd.org.au/wp-content/uploads/2012/03/ITD-Submission-on-EWP-March-2012.pdf>.

Eli, M. B. (2012). 'The Cybernetics of Sustainability: Definition and Underlying Principles', in J. Murray, G. Cawthorne, C. Day, and C. Andrew (eds), *Enough for all Forever: A Handbook for Learning About Sustainability*. Illinois: Common Ground Publishers.

Ehrlich, P. (1968). *The Population Bomb*. New York: Ballantine Books.

Foresight (2012a). 'Algorithmic Trading and Changes in Firms' Equity Capital', Driver Review DR23, 23 October. London: Government Office for Science. Last accessed 3 June 2013. <http://www.bis.gov.uk/assets/foresight/docs/computer-trading/12-1056-dr23-algorithmic-trading-and-changes-in-firms-equity-capital>.

Foresight (2012b). 'Computer-Based Trading and Market Abuse', Driver Review DR20, 23 October. London: Government Office for Science. Last accessed 3 June 2013. <http://www.bis.gov.uk/assets/foresight/docs/computer-trading/12-1053-dr20-computer-based-trading-and-market-abuse>.

Foresight (2011). 'The Future of Computer Trading in Financial Markets', *Working Paper 11/1276*, 8 September. London: Government Office for Science. Last accessed 3 June 2013. <http://www.bis.gov.uk/assets/foresight/docs/computer-trading/12-1053-dr20-computer-based-trading-and-market-abuse>.

GFN (2012). 'World Footprint—Do We Fit on the Planet?', *Global Footprint Network* (webpage last updated 14 May 2012). Last accessed 26 February 2013. <http://www.footprintnetwork.org/en/index.php/GFN/page/world_footprint/>.

Giampietro, M. and Mayumi, K. (2008). 'The Jevons Paradox: The Evolution of Complex Adaptive Systems and the Challenge for Scientific Analysis' in J. M. Polimeni, K. Mayumi, M. Giampietro, and B. Alcott (eds), *The Jevons Paradox and the Myth of Resource Efficiency Improvements*. London: Earthscan, pp. 79–140.

Gillespie, C. (2008). 'Alberta's Oil-Sands: Scar Sands', *Canadian Geographic*, 128(3): 64.

Goldin, I. and Reinert, K. (2012). *Globalization for Development: Meeting New Challenges*, New Edn. Oxford: Oxford University Press.

Hall, C. and Klitgaard, K. (2012). *Energy and the Wealth of Nations: Understanding the Biophysical Economy*. London: Springer.

Hamilton, K. and Johnson, I. (2004). 'Responsible Growth to 2050', *World Economics*, 5(4): 33–51.

Haq, H. (2010). 'The BP Oil Spill 2010: How Much Will It Cost?' *The Christian Science Monitor*, 3 May. Last accessed 3 June 2013. <http://www.csmonitor.com/Business/new-economy/2010/0503/BP-oil-spill-2010-How-much-will-it-cost>.

Henderson, H. (2009). 'Changing the Game of Finance', Paper presented at *'The World As We Want to Be' SRI in the Rockies 21st Anniversary conference*, 25–28 October. Last accessed 3 June 2013. <http://www.policyinnovations.org/ideas/policy_library/data/01551/_res/id=sa_File1/changing_the_game_of_finance.pdf>.

Hoffmans, L. (2012). 'America's (Un)Peak Oil', *Forbes* (web post), 26 October. Last accessed 3 June 2013. <http://www.forbes.com/sites/larahoffmans/2012/10/26/americas-unpeak-oil/>.

Hotelling, H. (1931). 'The Economics of Exhaustible Resources', *The Journal of Political Economy*, 39(2): 137–75.

Jackson, T. (2009). *Prosperity without Growth? The Transition to a Stable Economy*. UK Sustainable Development Commission, March. Last accessed 28 May 2013. <http://www.sd-commission.org.uk/data/files/publications/prosperity_without_growth_report.pdf>.

Johnson, I. and Jacobs, G. (2012). 'Crises and Opportunities: A Manifesto for Change', *Cadmus*, 1(5): 11–25.

Korten, D. (2010). *Agenda for A New Economy: From Phantom Wealth to Real Wealth*, 2nd Ed. San Fransico, CA: Beret Koehler Publishers.

Kümmel, R. (2011). *The Second Law of Economics: Energy, Entropy, and the Origins of Wealth*, London: Springer.

Lee, Y. H. (2008), 'Waste Management and Economic Growth', *ETHOS: World Cities Summit Issue*, June. Singapore: Civil Service College, pp. 51–61. Last accessed 3 June 2013. <http://www.cscollege.gov.sg/Knowledge/Ethos/Lists/issues/Attachments/34/ETHOS_WCS.pdf>.

Linacre, N., Kossoy, A., and Ambrosi, P. (2011). *State and Trends of the Carbon Market*. Washington, DC: World Bank. Last accessed 3 June 2013. <http://siteresources. worldbank.org/INTCARBONFINANCE/Resources/State_and_Trends_Updated_June_2011.pdf>.

Mason, R. (2010). 'Oil Reserves "Exaggerated by one-third"', *The Telegraph*, 22 March. Last accessed 4 June 2013. <http://www.telegraph.co.uk/finance/newsbysector/energy/oilandgas/7500669/Oil-reserves-exaggerated-by-one-third.html>.

Meadows, D. H., Meadows, D. L., Randers, J., and Behrens, W. W. III. (1972). *The Limits to Growth: A Report to the Club of Rome's Project on the Predicament of Mankind*. Washington, DC: Potomac Associates.

Metz, B., Davidson, O. R., Bosch, P. R., Dave, R., and Meyer, L. A. (eds) (2007). *Climate Change 2007: Mitigation of Climate Change*. (Contribution of Working Group III to the Fourth Assessment Report of the Intergovernmental Panel on Climate Change, 2007). Cambridge: Cambridge University Press.

Nelder, N. (2007). 'The True Cost of Oil: $65 Trillion per year?', Energy & Capital, 29th June. Last accessed 3 June 2013. <http://www.energyandcapital.com/articles/oil-gas-crude/461>.

Nordhaus, W. and Tobin, J. (1973). 'Is Growth Obsolete?' in M. Moss (ed.) *The Measurement of Economic and Social Performance*. New York: Colombia University Press, pp. 509–64.

Pauli, G. A. (2010). *The Blue Economy: A Report to the Club of Rome*, Cambridge, MA: Paradigm Publications.

Pearce, D. W. and Barbier, E. B. (2000). *Blueprint 6: For a Sustainable Economy*. London: Earthscan.

Pearce, D. W., Markandya, A., and Barbier, E. B. (1989). *Blueprint for a Green Economy*. London: Earthscan.

Pearce, F. (2013). 'Is Obama About to Blow his Climate Credentials?', *New Scientist*, 2901, 28 January. Last accessed 7 August 2013. <http://www.newscientist.com/article/mg21729010.200-is-obama-about-to-blow-his-climate-credentials.html>.

Premium Petroleum Corp. (2007). 'Premium Petroleum Corp. Increases Lands Position to 11,520 Acres', *Market Wired*, 19 September. Last accessed 19 Martch 2013. <http://www.marketwire.com/press-release/Premium-Petroleum-Corp-Increases-Lands-Position-to-11520-Acres-PINK-SHEETS-PPTL-771517.htm>.

Price, R., Thornton, S., and Nelson S. (2007). 'The Social Cost of Carbon and the Shadow Price of Carbon: What They Are, and How to Use Them in Economic Appraisal', *DEFRA Evidence and Analysis Series*, December. London: UK Department of Environment, Food and Rural Affairs. Last accessed 3 June 2013. <http://archive.defra.gov.uk/evidence/series/documents/shadowpriceofcarbondec-0712.pdf>.

Rockström, J. et al. (2009). 'Planetary Boundaries: Exploring the Safe Operating Space for Humanity', *Ecology and Society*, 14(2): online. Last accessed 29 May 2013. <http://www.ecologyandsociety.org/vol14/iss2/art32/>.

Runnalls, D. (2011). 'Environment and Economy: Joined at the Hip or Just Strange Bedfellows', *SAPIENS (Surveys and Perspectives Integrating Environment and Society)*, 4(2): online. Last accessed 3 June 2013. <http://sapiens.revues.org/1150>.

Sarkozy, N. (2009). *Report by the Commission on the Measurement of Economic Performance and Social Progress*. Last accessed 8 August 2013. <http://www.stiglitz-sen-fitoussi.fr/documents/rapport_anglais.pdf>.

Sen, A. K. (1976). 'Real National Income', *Review of Economic Studies*, 43: 19–39.

Simmons, M. R. (2000). 'Revisiting The Limits to Growth: Could The Club of Rome Have Been Correct, After All?', An Energy White Paper. Simmons and Company International. Last accessed 3 June 2013. <http://www.simmonsco-intl.com/content/documents/whitepapers/172.pdf>.

Spillius, A. (2010). 'BP Oil Spill Could Cost $100bn', *The Telegraph*, 18 June. Last accessed 6 June 2013. <http://www.telegraph.co.uk/finance/newsbysector/energy/oilandgas/7836982/BP-oil-spill-could-cost-100bn.html>.

Stern, N. (2007). *The Economics of Climate Change: The Stern Review*. Cambridge: Cambridge University Press and London: UK Cabinet Office and HM Treasury.

Strauss, M. (2012). 'Looking Back on the Limits of Growth', *Smithsonian Magazine*, April. Last accessed 3 June 2013. <http://www.smithsonianmag.com/science-nature/Looking-Back-on-the-Limits-of-Growth.html>.

Sukhdev, P., Wittmer, H., Schröter-Schlaack, C., Nesshöver, C., Bishop, J., Ten Brink, P., Gundimeda, H., Kumar, P., and Simmons, B. (2010). *The Economics of Ecosystems and Biodiversity: Mainstreaming the Economics of Nature: A Synthesis of the Approach, Conclusions and Recommendations of TEEB*. Malta: Progress Press.

Turner, G. (2012). 'On the Cusp of Global Collapse: Updated Comparison of *The Limits to Growth* with Historical Data', *GAIA*, 21(2): 116–24.

Turner, G. (2008). 'A Comparison of the Limits to Growth with Thirty Years of Reality', *CSIRO Working Paper 2008–09*, June. Canberra: CRISO Sustainable Ecosystems. Last accessed 29 May 2013. <http://www.fraw.org.uk/files/limits/csiro_2008.pdf>.

Turner, K. (2005). 'Blueprint Legacy: A Review of Professor David Pearce's Contribution to Environmental Economics and Policy', *CSERGE Working Paper PA 05-01*. Norwich: Centre for Social and Economic Research on the Global Environment, University of East Anglia. Last accessed 29 May 2013. <http://www.cserge.ac.uk/sites/default/files/pa_2005_01.pdf>.

UN (2010). *Report of the Secretary-General's High-Level Advisory Group on Climate Change Financing*, 5 November, United Nations. Last accessed 3 June 2013. <http://www.un.org/wcm/webdav/site/climatechange/shared/Documents/AGF_reports/AGF%20Report.pdf>.

UNEP (2011a). *Decoupling Natural Resource Use and Environmental Impacts from Economic Growth*. Switzerland: United Nations Environment Programme. Last accessed 30 May 2013. <http://www.unep.org/resourcepanel/decoupling/files/pdf/decoupling_report_english.pdf>.

UNEP (2011b). *Policy Implications of Warming Permafrost*. Nairobi: United Nations Environment Programme. Last accessed 28 May 2013. <http://www.unep.org/pdf/permafrost.pdf>.

USGS (2008). 'Circum-Arctic Resource Appraisal: Estimates of Undiscovered Oil and Gas North of the Arctic Circle', *USGS Fact Sheet 2008–3049*. US Geological Survey. Last accessed 7 August 2013. <http://pubs.usgs.gov/fs/2008/3049/fs2008-3049.pdf>.

van Vuuren, D. P. and Faber, A. (2009). *Growing Within Limits: Report to the Global Assembly 2009 of the Club of Rome*. Bilthoven, The Netherlands: Netherlands Environmental Assessment Agency. Last accessed 3 June 2013. <http://www.rivm.nl/bibliotheek/rapporten/500201001.pdf>.

von Weizsäcker, E., Hargroves, K., Smith, M., Desha, C., and Stasinopoulos, P. (2009). *Factor Five: Transforming the Global Economy Through 80% Improvements in Resource Productivity*. London: Earthscan.

WCED (1987), *Our Common Future: Report of the Commission on Environment and Development* (UN document GA A/42/427). New York: United Nations.

Wijkman, A. and Rockström, J. (2012). *Bankrupting Nature*. London: Earthscan.

Williams, I. (2009). 'Waste—The Global Challenge', Future Agenda website, 12 September. Last accessed 8 August 2013. <http://www.futureagenda.org/?cat=16>.

Wilson, D. and Dragusanu, R. (2008). 'The Expanding Middle: The Exploding World Middle Class and Falling Global Inequality', *Global Economic Papers 170*. New York: Goldman Sachs.

6

How can 9–10 Billion People be Fed Sustainably and Equitably by 2050?

H. Charles J. Godfray

There are currently about 7 billion people on Earth and by the middle of this century the number will most likely be between 9 and 10 billion. A greater proportion of these people will in real terms be wealthier than they are today and will demand a varied diet requiring greater resources in its production. Increasing demand for food will coincide with supply-side pressures: greater competition for water, land, and energy, and the accelerating effects of climate change. The need to produce food in ways that are more environmentally sustainable will become ever more pressing. And while global wealth will grow, not everyone will benefit, and the world will continue to be faced with the challenges of hunger and malnutrition, especially in the least developed countries. At the other end of the nutrition spectrum, we face a global epidemic of obesity.

Over recent decades the security of food supply at the global level has been some way down the political agenda. The food system, chiefly private sector and increasingly globalized, supplied food to consumers in the developed world at historically low prices so that the fraction of income spent on food in Europe and America has never been less. Indeed, many of the major policy issues in the rich world have involved problems of over-production and the maintenance of rural communities in the face of competition from developing countries with low wage advantages. The last 20 years have seen rapid growth in many developing countries and in particular within their agricultural sectors, increasing food supply and raising many food producers out of poverty. Even in the poorest countries the fraction of people suffering poverty and hunger was declining, and in the mid 2000s there was optimism that the first Millennium Development Goal—that no more than 8 per cent of people should go hungry in 2015—would be met.

Today, food security is a major policy priority for national governments and international organizations. The turnaround has occurred for several reasons. First, a number of prospective studies have concluded that there is a real danger that demand for food will rise more rapidly than the world's ability to supply it, leading to price rises of a magnitude that would risk economic and political instability. Second, there has been an increasing realization that environmental deterioration poses a real threat to food production. Factors such as insufficient access to water and the negative effects of climate change may severely affect yields. Finally, there has been the sharpest rise in global food prices since the oil crises of the 1970s, as well as episodes of high price volatility. Higher food prices have triggered civil unrest in a number of low-income countries and have contributed to changes in governments and regimes.

In the first section of this chapter I flesh out in a little more detail the argument that over the next few decades there is a high probability that the world will face a significant disjunction in the supply of and demand for food unless actions are taken today. An argument is then made that the threat of problems ahead is sufficiently high to justify action on all fronts—on increasing supply, moderating demand, reducing waste, and improving governance and efficiency. In the second section each of these are looked at in turn.

The Future of the Food System

The demand for food globally or in a particular area is a function of the number of people and their purchasing power. Wealthier people demand more food (calories) up to a limit and then diversify their diets. Diet is important, as different food types require different amounts of resources to produce. Thus a certain amount of grain can be used directly to feed humans or with less efficiency can be fed to livestock to produce meat for human consumption.

Current estimates for global population suggest numbers will rise until the mid-century, reaching a plateau of between 9 and 10 billion people (Figure 6.1). However, there is substantial uncertainty around this figure—with different assumptions giving figures of between 8 and 16 billion (UN 2013). If the world really had to face a population of 16 billion in the second half of this century the strains on the food system would be immense. Human populations voluntarily reduce fertility—the demographic transition—as they become more secure economically, and when they have access to education (particularly of girls) and contraception. There is increasing evidence that reducing population growth brings general economic benefits to developing

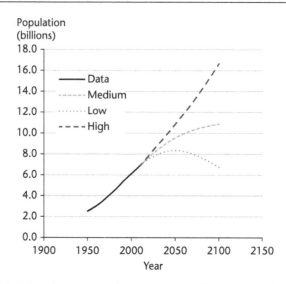

Figure 6.1. Global population growth with low, medium, and high fertility projections, 1950–2100

Note: based on data to 2010 and then projections.

Source: United Nations (2013).

countries.[1] In discussions on food policy, population is typically treated as exogenous, partly to make discussions more manageable, but also because of the sensitivities surrounding discussion of population policy. This is unfortunate, if understandable, as reducing population growth is critical to food security. Compared to the population debates of the 1970s, today we understand much better how population fertility can be reduced non-coercively and to the benefit of families and societies (Bongaarts 2009). These insights need to be put into operation today—there is a long gap between any changes in fertility resulting from policy intervention and reductions in population growth. And it is critical to stress that reducing the population growth rate—an issue chiefly in developing countries—is only part of the solution; equally important is reducing rates of per capita consumption in the rich world.

Economic growth provides the security that encourages people to have fewer children but allows them to go through the nutritional transition, a move from a diet dominated by starchy plant foods, through the major grains to a more protein-rich diet, often with meat a major component, as well as fruit and vegetables. Richer, more varied diets typically require more land, energy, and water to produce, though precisely how much can depend quite critically on the precise details of the diet. For example, the production

---

[1] See Dyson (2006) for a brief overview of the evidence and further references.

of grain-fed beef is highly demanding of land and water, while the production of 'white meat' (pig, poultry) requires fewer resources (Steinfeld et al. 2006). A pastoralist in Africa, grazing cattle on sustainable natural vegetation that requires no inputs and on land unsuitable for cultivation, has a very different footprint compared to an intensive beef producer. Predicting demand for food in the future involves making assumptions about how both people's incomes will alter and, contingent on this and myriad other factors, their behavioural-driven diet changes. A population of 10 billion people is about 40 per cent larger than today's which puts a lower bound on demand growth, but this figure assumes population growth will have decelerated, partly driven by economic growth that will also have led to a nutritional transition. An often-quoted figure for demand growth taking this into account is 70 per cent (FAO 2006), although if many parts of the world were to adopt an American/European diet the figure would become considerably higher, prob-ably in excess of 100 per cent.

There are further drivers that will affect demand growth as well as other aspects of the food system. The last 50 years have seen a marked growth in urbanization: over 50 per cent of the global population now lives in cities and the fastest-growing cities are in the developing world (Satterthwaite, McGranahan, and Tacoli 2010). Whereas 50 years ago the bulk of the world's poor were rural food producers, and disconnected from global markets, today an increasing fraction are urban food consumers whose economic access to food is affected to differing degrees (depending on how their government intervenes in the market) by world food prices. Large concentrations of food-insecure people quickly lead to civil disturbance. Urbanization also affects diets: economies of scale in cities allow processed foods rich in fats and sugar to be marketed to relatively poor people, with consequences for their health, as well as for the demand for the underlying foodstuffs. But some aspects of urbanization are positive for food security: cities offer economies of scale and allow greater efficiency in food processing and distribution, and if constructed appropriately food supply chains can lead to beneficial invest-ment in rural economies.

Food production requires land, water, energy, labour, and other inputs such as fertilizers. Land is clearly finite and existing pressure to convert land used for food to produce fibre and timber, or for urbanization, will almost certainly continue. Currently, significant tracts of land that can produce food are being used for biofuels, though, with the exception of sugar-cane bioethanol in Brazil, this is only cost-efficient (given current energy prices) if subsidized by govern-ment. Exactly how biofuel policy develops, as well as future energy prices, will have a major effect on land available for food production (Searchinger 2010).

Agriculture consumes approximately 70 per cent of the flows in fresh water available to mankind and in addition uses substantial non- (or very slowly) renewable water resources in underground aquifers (Strzepek and Boehlert 2010). Water flows in many rivers are now below designated 'environmental required flows' (ERFs) needed to maintain ecosystem services, a particular concern as ERFs' designation is often a political process leading to optimistic-ally low values. Major inland water bodies such as the Aral Sea and Lake Chad contain only a fraction of the water they did 50 years ago, while major fossil aquifers such as those in southern Australia, the south-central United States, and north-west and southern India will soon be functionally exhausted. Water shortage is already constraining and even reversing yield growth in many regions—for example, wheat production is being abandoned in much of the Arabian Peninsula as underground aquifers are depleted. Studies by defence research organizations of where future conflicts may arise highlight disagreements over water as a likely *casus belli*.

Food production and distribution requires energy for processing and trans-port while the production of nitrogen fertilizers by the Haber–Bosch process is particularly energy intensive. Increases in energy prices will directly increase the costs of food production, though they will also stimulate research on greater energy efficiency. The two other major mineral fertilizers—potash and phosphate—are mined, and there have been concerns about the size of reserves. Recent analyses suggest this is unlikely to be a near-term issue, but improved efficiency and research into alternative sources will become increas-ingly important (for example USGS 2013: 119).

The effects of climate change will increasingly become apparent as the century progresses. The frequency of extreme events will go up, and there will be secular changes in temperature and precipitation patterns. A major concern is shrinkage of montane snow fields and glaciers leading to lower and more variable river flows. The areas north and south of the Himalayas whose agriculture depends on rivers fed by glaciers are particularly likely to be affected. Further into the future, changes in sea level may affect low-lying agriculture regions. Integrated assessment models attempt to link crop and climate models to predict the effects of different climate scenarios on yields. These show that in some regions yields will increase, in particular along the northern margin of agriculture in America and Eurasia, but overall climate change will negatively affect yield, especially in the arid tropics (Parry et al. 2009).

The world thus faces a twin problem with the food system: increasing demand at a time of great pressure on the supply system. This is not the first time that this warning has been made. In the late 18th century Thomas Malthus argued the same point but his predictions of famine did not occur, largely because of the industrial revolution. More recently there was wide-spread pessimism in the 1960s and '70s but again innovation in the food system, the 'green revolution', allowed food production to keep pace with demand (problems of hunger being largely due to economic access to food rather than supply). Might the food system be able to respond to the present challenges without the need for policy intervention?

Several arguments suggest optimism should be tempered. First, there are actual physical limits to the capacity of the planet to support an ever-growing population; just because we haven't hit those limits in the past, it doesn't mean we are not up against them this time. The domination of virtually every biogeochemical cycle by anthropogenic effects suggests we may be in this region. Second, climate change is a type of systemic threat never before experienced by humans. Third, the world's politico-economic structures are now highly integrated and globalized; no longer can problems be geographically isolated. Finally, the argument that the food system will autonomously respond to the challenges of food security is not an argument to do nothing but instead suggests intervention should be made judiciously to address market failures and to work where possible with the grain of the natural economic response.

A dispassionate review of the evidence available strongly suggests that the threat of the demand for food outstripping supply is great enough, and the consequences of this happening severe enough, that radical action is needed throughout the food system (Nelson et al. 2009). In the second part of the chapter I explore how we might address the challenge of future food security, beginning with the supply side, going on to discuss demand, and finally exploring governance issues.

Meeting the Challenge

Producing more food

A few voices, concerned about agricultural expansion and its effects on the environment, have argued that we can meet future food demands purely by diet change and more equitable distribution (Soil Association 2010). However, most commentators think this approach would be highly risky by itself and argue that more food will need to be produced (Foresight 2011). It is important to distinguish between arguments about the need to increase production immediately and the importance of increasing production capacity. There are strong reasons to believe that moves to stimulate higher production in low-income countries would have multiple benefits: it would improve rural livelihoods, help disadvantaged parts of society (especially women) and lead to increased local food supply (FAO 2011). The explanations of why food production in poor countries is so low are typically lack of human and social capital (skills and institutions), lack of economic capital and access to market, and lack of infrastructure. In high-income countries production is already high and responsive to markets. The critical issue here is ensuring agriculture responds efficiently to market signals reflecting higher demand for food, and that the response is environmentally sustainable. A major policy issue in the rich world is how viable rural communities and economies can be sustained in high-income societies. Subsidies for food production are a discredited means of doing so and food security should not be used as an argument for their reinstatement.

If the argument is accepted that increasing food production capacity must be one plank of the response to the food security challenge then logically this could be achieved by intensifying production on current agricultural land or by bringing new land into agriculture. Humanity has already converted a large portion of the land potentially suitable for agriculture, but significant unexploited territory does exist, for example land currently forested in Amazonia, the Congo Basin, and South East Asia; some wetland areas such as those in South Sudan; and grassland savannah such as the Cerrado in Brazil and that in East Africa. In all cases the environmental cost of such conversion makes little sense, at least from a planetary perspective. Converting such areas releases very large amounts of greenhouse gases (Stern 2007), and devastates already threatened biodiversity, which is likely to have additional knock-on effects for agriculture, the impact of which may be spread unevenly.

Increased food production must thus come from our existing agricultural footprint—but this too has environmental consequences that both undermine our capacity to produce food in the future (soil degradation, for example) and that cause harm external to the food system (such as greenhouse gas emissions and nitrate pollution). This has led to calls for agricultural intensification rather than extensification but specifically for what has been called sustainable intensification—producing more with reduced environmental consequences (Royal Society 2009; Foresight 2011). Sustainable intensification has been taken up as a policy goal by both governments and international organizations, and embraced by the private sector and some NGOs.

Currently there is vigorous debate over exactly what sustainable intensification means. One camp, typically with an industry focus, sees sustainable intensification as a continuation of 'business as usual', increasing yields, and paying greater attention to input efficiency. An overlapping constituency interprets sustainability to mean economic rather than environmental sustainability. Voices, especially from the NGO community, see sustainable intensification as a Trojan horse to smuggle in a particular type of 'high-input Western' agriculture (including GM technologies) or to encourage a particular economic model of agriculture that favours large producers over small. The phrase sustainable intensification was coined by people who probably had arable crops in mind. Those concerned with animal welfare find the term particularly problematic, even an oxymoron, because in that community 'intensification' is synonymous with models of animal husbandry that lead to poor levels of welfare.

Attempts have been made to define and reclaim sustainable intensification in line with its original conception (Garnett and Godfray 2012). These efforts stress that sustainable intensification, or the same concept by a different name, follows logically from the need to produce more food sustainably from the same amount of land. They underline that in this context 'sustainable' refers to environmental sustainability, while fully acknowledging that there are other important food system agendas (of which more below) where issues of sustainability arise. Most critically they stress that sustainable intensification, if taken seriously, is genuinely radical—a call for a new type of food production and a new type of land management. It challenges the agricultural industry to make real progress on sustainability; not only by reducing local environmental harms through increased input efficiencies and other measures that frequently save the farmer money, but also by addressing more diffuse environmental damage—the externalities not captured in the economy of the food system. It also challenges NGOs concerned with environment and development to modify their campaigning positions to accept the need to produce more food, possibly substantially more food, in the coming decades. And finally, it poses huge challenges to policymakers to craft regulations and incentives to enable sustainable intensification to take place.

A more in-depth study would be needed to cover the great number of different techniques and technologies that can contribute to sustainable intensification (for reviews see Foresight 2011 and the detailed studies commissioned by the project[2]), and it is important to emphasize that there will be no silver bullet. No one strategy or set of strategies will be appropriate in all contexts—fit for a corn farm in Iowa and a cassava field in West Africa. Sustainable intensification identifies a goal but not the trajectory to get there.

One can conceptualize two stages in determining how to implement sustainable intensification, the first defining the set of possible strategies and the second picking the most appropriate. It is in defining the set of permissible strategies that sustainable intensification most explicitly overlaps with other food system agendas. For example, consider animal welfare: animal breeding targeted at specific traits such as muscle volume can increase meat yields though result in an animal that is congenitally unhealthy and will always be in a state of poor welfare (Dawkins 2011). Society may decide that such an option is unethical and should be forbidden. Now consider field crops. Though major yield increases can be achieved through conventional breeding

---

[2] These studies are available on the Foresight website, <http://www.bis.gov.uk/foresight/our-work/projects/published-projects/global-food-and-farming-futures/reports-and-publications>.

(especially if bolstered by marker-assisted methods) it is clear that some desirable traits can only be introduced into crops through genetic engineering. No one argues other than that GM technology should be strictly regulated but some countries, prompted largely by civil society pressure, adjudge the health and environmental risks of GM to be strong enough to ban the technology completely. Finally, there is an argument that to improve sustainable yields and food security in low-income countries, they should go through an accelerated form of the agricultural transition that has occurred in most of Europe; from farming dominated by high-employment smallholdings to large mechanized farms. One counterargument questions the premise that smallholder farming is unproductive, but another, and my point here, privileges employment and smallholder rights over productivity and would disallow a move to large farms as a possible means of sustainable intensification in low-income countries.[3]

There is an important role for research in helping resolve these issues; in setting the boundary conditions for sustainable intensification. Research can help us understand the conditions that promote good animal welfare, tell us whether GM carries health and environmental risks, and help us discover which development interventions actually help poor people. But these decisions all involve ethical and value judgements and finally decisions should be the province of elected politicians reflecting the will of civil society. Critically, these decisions cannot be made in a vacuum and their ramifications through the food system, and possible perverse outcomes, must be considered. For what it's worth, I shall give my view on these three issues. I think welfare considerations do constrain the possible pathways for the sustainable intensification of meat production, even if this results in higher meat prices (which, unfortunately but inevitably, affect mostly those on low incomes). GM technologies need to be strictly regulated and assessed, and such assessments should also consider the consequences of any excess concentration of power in a small number of corporate players. But to me there is nothing intrinsically wrong or different with these technologies that render them a priori unacceptable, and they can have positive environmental consequences if they allow farmers to reduce inputs.

Finally, the needs of the very poorest must be central to development and very many of the poorest are smallholders. But the evidence base concerning which agricultural interventions in which contexts work best is still very poorly developed. I worry about simplistic approaches to agricultural development, whether they are calls for Africa to transition rapidly to 'Western' forms of food production or for it uniformly to adopt a particular agro-ecological

---

[3] See also Conway (2012) for an excellent discussion of these issues.

form of agriculture. The growing emphasis on rigorous experimental evaluations of different interventions, realizing the importance of context, is to be welcomed (Banerjee and Duflo 2011).

Changing diets and food habits

The Western diet contains large amounts of meat, fruit, and other food types that require many more resources to produce compared to the more plant-based diets of other regions (and of our ancestors). Were a world of 9 to 10 billion people to converge on a Western diet then demand-side pressures would lead to a production response that would almost certainly have very major environmental costs (for example through greenhouse gas emissions from deforested land) and which most likely would be insufficient to keep food prices anywhere near their current levels (Nelson et al. 2009).

Of the 7 billion people alive today, 5 billion are either well nourished or over-nourished (obese or overweight). Of the remaining 2 billion, approximately half consume sufficient calories but have a poorly balanced diet and suffer some form of micronutrient deficiency; this group is often described as suffering from hidden hunger. The remaining billion—the bottom billion—suffer from calorie deficiencies and go to bed hungry, typically because they do not have the resources to purchase sufficient food (FAO 2012). The role of changing diets in food security will clearly mean different things to these three groups.

Significant pressure could be taken off the future food system if diets in high-income countries were to switch to less resource-intensive food types. The most often quoted example is the benefits that would accrue from high-income countries reducing meat consumption. However, care must be taken to distinguish the wide range of environmental impacts of different meat types and production methods. Feeding grain to animals is a poor way of turning sunlight into human food, though the conversion efficiencies vary considerably from grain-fed cattle (~10), to pigs (~3), to poultry (which may be as low as ~1.5).

Reducing meat consumption has triple benefits (Steinfeld et al. 2006). First, it reduces the demand for grain for animal feed and hence, other things being equal, keeps world grain prices lower, helping food security in poor countries. Second, there are environmental benefits from reduced demand for grain and soya, and some specific sources of greenhouse gas emissions associated with meat production (in particular methane from ruminant animals and nitrous oxides from manure) are lowered. Finally, for most people in high-income countries, eating less meat has positive health benefits. Moreover, there seems to be a positive correlation between harm to health and harm to the environment—reducing red meat (cattle, sheep, etc.) in favour of white meat (poultry) helps both (pork has a somewhat intermediate position).

It is much easier to persuade people to change their behaviour when it directly benefits the individual. That eating less meat improves personal health as well as having broader benefits would thus seem to be encouraging. The bad news is that it has proven to be extremely difficult to change diets by public health campaigns (Butland et al. 2007). Part of the problem may have been naivety in believing behaviour change would occur simply in response to improved public information, and there is some optimism that a more sophisticated use of ideas from psychology and behavioural economics may make more progress. But the human animal evolved to seek out sweet and fatty foods in an environment where these were seldom encountered in large quantities—diet change will always be a struggle.

Can consumers be persuaded to eat food that promotes different aspects of food security? There are a variety of schemes that attest to higher standards of food production: for example, in the United Kingdom products certified by the Soil Association (organic food), the Fairtrade Foundation, the Rainforest Alliance, or the Marine Stewardship Council. There is evidence that consumers will pay a premium for such food, though in the recession that followed the 2008 banking crisis sales of organic food plummeted. The benefits of the food types championed by these different organizations may also be contested. Consider, for example, organic food. The reduction in inputs in organic farming clearly reduces the environmental harm of farming but typically lower yields result. If the resulting yield loss is made up by increased production elsewhere, the consequent environmental harm might be much worse.

There are other ways to influence the composition of people's diets. One is to use fiscal instruments—to tax less-healthy food. There is currently much debate about soda taxes (targeted at high-sugar fizzy drinks) and fat taxes (targeted at fatty foods such as processed meat products). These measures have health objectives in mind, although they will also affect the demand for food and could in the future be designed specifically to address issues of food security. Different types of food production have different effects on the environment and hence varying costs, which are external to the food system and borne by local, national, and global society. Internalizing these costs would, at least in principle, incentivize the consumption of more sustainable types of food, though there are formidable technical hurdles to its implementation.

'Choice editing' is an ugly term to describe restricting consumers' access to particular food types. It can be done by retailers or by the government. An example of the former is the supermarkets that stock only fish from certified sustainable fisheries. Retailers may choice edit because of corporate social responsibility, or because they believe it will increase consumer trust in their brand. Governments also choice edit, for example through legislation forbidding the sale of meat that fails to meet animal welfare standards. At times of national emergencies such as wars governments have taken very active measures to influence diets.

Discussion of diet change is politically very sensitive. Large vested interests are involved as the food industry creates value by processing food—typically adding the salt, sugar, and fat that we crave but which harm our health, and which often also include food types that most damage the environment (Nestle 2007). Agricultural lobbies can be very powerful for historical reasons, often disproportionately so considering their contribution to GNP. Governments are concerned about threats that they are infringing civil liberties and creating a 'nanny state'. Fiscal measures on food are typically regressive, though it can be countered that the poor tend to suffer the most from bad diets (Gordon-Larsen, Guilkey, and Popkin 2011).

Governments have found it so difficult to act on diets that affect health that it is hard to be optimistic about concerted efforts to influence diets in response to food security threats that are not yet upon us. Politicians do not yet have a mandate from civil society to move decisively in this sphere. But this may change. We have known that tobacco kills us since the 1960s but it is only in the last two decades that governments have felt empowered to ban smoking in public places, drastically curb advertising, and fiscally punish smokers. A change in public attitude to the health consequences of smoking allowed politicians to act. As the consequences of food insecurity become more apparent, perhaps public opinion will react and allow governments to act. Hopefully it will not be too late.

Reducing waste

An oft-quoted statistic is that ~30 per cent of all food produced is never consumed, but is wasted (WRAP 2008). Some commentators have argued for higher figures, of up to 50 per cent. This has led to the view that reduction of waste is critical to addressing food security and might even be the magic bullet that allows the food system to continue otherwise unchanged. I argue here that reducing waste should indeed be a clear objective but council against over-optimism about how much can be achieved quickly.

The origin of waste in low-income and high-income countries is very different. In low-income countries waste occurs on the farm, in storage, and in the food supply chain. It is a consequence of poor investment; in harvesting techniques, the control of pests, and in infrastructure (refrigeration in the distribution network for example). Addressing waste in low-income countries has much in common with closing the yield gap. It requires substantial investment in human, social, physical, and economic capital, and the creation of a facilitating environment. Progress is under way, especially in the economies moving from low- to mid-income status, but it will inevitably be slow.

Agriculture and food supply chains in high-income countries tend to be much more efficient, and most waste occurs in the home, in the food service sector (restaurants, institutional food providers, etc.), or is associated with consumer preferences. For example, in high-income countries consumers have come to expect unblemished fruit and vegetables leading to much food being discarded before it reaches the shops (though typically it is used for other purposes). Food is historically cheap today and relatively well-off consumers accept food waste as a cost of having a conveniently well-stocked fridge or larder. The costs of food are also not high enough for the food service sector to reduce waste aggressively. Retail strategies such as 'buy one, get one free' may accidentally encourage waste. Many people lack the food knowledge to reduce waste and may be confused by 'best before' and 'use by' labelling (Foresight 2011).

Governments are actively trying to reduce waste—for example the 'Love food, hate waste' campaign in the United Kingdom—and there is some evidence for a reduction in the levels of discarded food. A combination of awareness raising, education, fiscal measures, and regulation are all likely to make some impact on food waste and be politically more acceptable to implement compared with measures designed to change diets. Were food prices to increase then this would incentivize waste reduction. It would be interesting to understand more about the elasticity of waste's relationship with price, and the degree to which this is affected by consumer food-processing skills. Nevertheless, food is still relatively very cheap for people in rich countries and, for non-cataclysmic food security scenarios, is likely to remain so. This suggests caution is called for in relying on the reduction of food waste as the major policy of addressing global food security.

Better governance

Improving food system governance is an enormous topic and will be critical in achieving food security. It has profound consequences on all aspects of the food system; from how individual shops provide food for villagers, to the macroeconomics of grain reserves. Space precludes a full discussion of the myriad aspects of food governance relevant to food security but a few topics are highlighted in the following paragraphs.

The 2008 banking crisis had many effects on the food system. One was a flow of investment funds from discredited sectors such as sub-prime mortgages into commodities such as food. Another was a profound distrust of complex financial instruments that extended to some of the derivative and index-based products developed to facilitate investment in food. Many people worried that one of the causes of the volatility of food prices after 2008 (possibly the major cause) was financial speculation.

The development of futures and forwards markets for agricultural products in the 19th and early 20th centuries did a huge amount to stimulate food production and address food insecurity. Part of the problem with low yields in developing countries today is the lack of appropriate financial infrastructure. Getting financial services right is critical for food security, and the evidence that speculation has been a major source of volatility since 2008 is not strong (Bayley 2012). Nevertheless, the recent performance of the financial service sector suggests great vigilance is needed to anticipate future problems. In particular, attention needs to be paid to transparency and accurate valuation of financial products, position limits, high-frequency automatic trading, and the general cost to the food system of the services provided by finance and banking. It is also critical that when governments intervene in the markets they do not open themselves up to speculative attack, a fate of many food reserve policies in the past.

The increased competition for land for biofuels has already been mentioned. Biofuels production creates an even stronger link between food prices and the notoriously volatile energy markets (Searchinger 2010). Much of biofuels policy is dominated by energy security considerations, and increasingly agricultural interests seeking to protect production and other subsidies. The argument that the possibility of biofuels production increases farmer options by allowing them to switch from food to fuel as the price differential alters is often negated by long-term contracts to supply biofuels that may act pro-cyclically and increase volatility. Biofuels policy urgently needs review, especially in the United States and Europe where it currently harms both food security and the environment.

In the last 40 years there has been major corporate consolidation in different sectors of the food system. There are four or five major agribusinesses involved in seeds and crop protection. Five or six international commodity companies mediate the bulk of trade in food. In most major countries a small number of supermarket chains dominate retail. This consolidation has been driven by economies of scale and brings significant benefits. Only very big firms can afford the research costs required to bring new crop varieties and agrichemicals to markets. Modern supermarkets provide consumers with an outstanding variety of cheap and safe food types.

The consolidation also raises important governance questions. While economic theory says two players are enough to have a functioning market, in reality small numbers of participants can lead markets to function less efficiently and reduce competition (Connor 2003; Sexton 2013). Many of the companies are very large and international, and may escape appropriate regulation which is often at the national or trade bloc level. These issues are of course not unique to the food sector, and present an ongoing challenge to successful globalization.

Finally, and another aspect of globalization, is the issue of to what extent nations should seek to be self-sufficient in food or rely on purchasing food on international markets. Because food is an essential non-substitutable commodity, its ready availability and accessibility is of enormous importance to governments. Governments have repeatedly pursued interventionist policies to stimulate agriculture or interfere with free trade; for example, reducing exports at times of scarcity and restricting imports at times of plenty. Though rich countries have moved away from direct production subsidies in recent decades, there are numerous other subsidies to food production in both the United States and Europe. Similarly, many developing countries restrict free trade in food.

Should the world move to free trade in food or, to quote a recent book title, should we heed the cry 'Food is different: Why we must get the WTO out of agriculture' (Rosset 2006)? It is perhaps helpful to think of three types of country. An exemplar of the first is Egypt, the world's largest importer of wheat. Countries like Egypt rely on a well-functioning global market in food, and, were this to fail to provide food at reasonable prices, the social and political consequences would be hugely disruptive. The growth of 'megacities', especially in the tropics, means more countries are entering this category and raising the risk of global political instability associated with the food system. Brazil and Ukraine are examples of the second type of country, which produces large agricultural surpluses; these countries would suffer in a seizing-up of global trade in food, but for the opposite reason (the United States is also in this category, though *sui generis*). Finally, there are many countries that could be food sufficient if they invested to different degrees in their own food production sector.

I would argue, to paraphrase the economist Joseph Stiglitz, that there is no going back from globalization and the challenge is to make globalization work in favour of food security and other planetary societal goods (Stiglitz 2002).[4] We have to use the comparative advantage of category-two countries to help feed those in category one. The political, social, and economic consequences of failing to do this would be dire, if not catastrophic. Arguments for self-sufficiency as a policy goal too often reflect agricultural exceptionalism and vested interests in the third category of countries. Crafting this efficient and equitable global food system will require rich countries finding a way to support their rural communities (surely a legitimate political goal) without

---

[4] See also Goldin and Mariathasan (forthcoming).

directly or indirectly distorting world food markets. It will also require high- and mid-income countries allowing low-income countries some temporary protection from full market forces until their agricultural sectors are mature enough to contribute to global food security.

References

Banerjee, A. H. and Duflo, E. (2011). *Poor Economics*. London: Penguin.

Bayley, B. (2012). *Speculation and the Recent Agricultural Price Spikes*. London: HM Treasury Briefing Note. Last accessed 29 June 2013. <http://www.staff.ncl.ac.uk/david.harvey/ACE2006/Principles/Bayley2012SpeculationBrief.pdf>.

Bongaarts, J. (2009). 'Human Population Growth and the Demographic Transition', *Philosophical Transactions of the Royal Society B-Biological Sciences*, 364: 2985–90.

Butland, B., Jebb S., Kopelman, P., McPherson, K., Thomas, S., Mardell, J., and Parry, V. (2007). *Tackling Obesities: Future Choices*, Foresight Report (2nd edn). London: Government Office of Science. Last accessed 21 April 2013. <http://www.bis.gov.uk/assets/foresight/docs/obesity/17.pdf>.

Connor, J. M. (2003). 'The Changing Structure of Global Food Markets: Dimensions, Effects, and Policy Implications', Presented at the OECD-sponsored conference on *Changing Dimensions of the Food Economy: Exploring the Policy Issues*, 6–7 February, The Hague, The Netherlands. Last accessed 7 August 2013. <http://ssrn.com/abstract=1711925>.

Conway, G. (2012). *One Billion Hungry: Can We Feed the World?* Ithaca, NY: Cornell University Press.

Dawkins, M. S. (2011). *Why Animals Matter*. Oxford: Oxford University Press.

Dyson, T. (2006). 'Population and Development' in D. A. Clark (ed.), *The Elgar Companion to Development Studies*. Cheltenham: Edward Elgar, pp. 436–41.

FAO (2012). *The State of Food Insecurity in the World [2012]. Economic Growth is Necessary but not Sufficient to Accelerate Reduction of Hunger and Malnutrition*. Rome: Food and Agricultural Organization. Last accessed 18 April 2013. <http://www.fao.org/docrep/016/i3027e/i3027e.pdf>.

FAO (2011). *Save and Grow: A Policymaker's Guide to the Sustainable Intensification of Smallholder Crop Production*. Rome: Food and Agricultural Organization. Last accessed 18 April 2013. <http://www.fao.org/docrep/014/i2215e/i2215e00.pdf>.

FAO (2006). *World Agriculture: Towards 2030/2050*, Interim Report. Rome: Food and Agricultural Organization. Last accessed 18 April 2013. <http://www.fao.org/fileadmin/user_upload/esag/docs/Interim_report_AT2050web.pdf>.

Foresight (2011). *The Future of Food and Farming: Challenges and Choices for Global Sustainability*, final project report. London: Government Office of Science. Last accessed 21 April 2103. <http://www.bis.gov.uk/assets/foresight/docs/food-and-farming/11-546-future-of-food-and-farming-report.pdf>.

Garnett, T. and Godfray, H. C. J. (2012). *Sustainable Intensification in Agriculture: Navigating a Course Through Competing Food System Priorities*. Oxford: Oxford Martin

Programme on the Future of Food and Food Climate Research Network. Last accessed 21 April 2013. <http://www.fcrn.org.uk/sites/default/files/SI_report_final.pdf>.

Goldin, I. and Mariathasan, M. (2014), *The Butterfly Defect: How Globalization Creates Systemic Risks, and What to Do About It*. Princeton, NJ: Princeton University Press.

Gordon-Larsen P., Guilkey D., and Popkin B. (2011). 'An Economic Analysis of Community-Level Fast Food Prices and Individual-Level Fast Food Intake: A Longitudinal Study', *Health Place*, 17(6): 1235–41.

Nelson, G. C., Rosegrant, M. W., Koo, J., Robertson, R., Sulser, T., Zhu, T., Ringler, C., Msangi, S., Palazzo, A., Batka, M., Magalhaes, M., Valmonte-Santos, R., Ewing, M., and Lee, D. (2009). *Climate Change: Impact on Agriculture and Costs of Adaptation*, Food Policy Report. Washington, DC: International Food Policy Research Institute. Last accessed 21 April 2013. <http://www.ifpri.org/sites/default/files/publications/pr21.pdf>.

Nestle, M. (2007). *Food Politics: How the Food Industry Influences Nutrition and Health* (revised edn). Berkeley, CA: University of California Press.

Parry, M., Evans, A., Rosegrant, M. W., and Wheeler, T. (2009). *Climate Change and Hunger: Responding to the Challenge*. Rome: World Food Programme.

Rosset, P. M. (2006). *Food is Diferent: Why We Must Get the WTO Out of Agriculture*. London: Zed Books.

Royal Society (2009). *Reaping the Benefits: Science and the Sustainable Intensification of Global Agriculture*, RS Policy Document 11/09. London: Royal Society.

Satterthwaite, D., McGranahan, G., and Tacoli, C. (2010). 'Urbanization and its Implications for Food and Farming', *Philosophical Transactions of the Royal Society B-Biological Sciences*, 365: 2809–20.

Searchinger, T. D. (2010). 'Biofuels and the Need for Additional Carbon', *Environmental Research Letters*, 5(2): 1–10.

Sexton, R. J. (2013). 'Market Power, Misconceptions, and Modern Agricultural Markets', *American Journal of Agricultural Economics*, 95(2): 209–19.

Soil Association (2010). *Telling Porkies: The Big Fat Lie About Doubling Food Production*. Bristol: Soil Association.

Steinfeld, H., Gerber, P., Wassenaar, T., Castel, V., Rosales, P., and de Haan, C. (2006). *Livestock's Long Shadow: Environmental Issues and Options*. Rome: Food and Agricultural Organization. Last accessed 18 April 2013. <ftp://ftp.fao.org/docrep/fao/010/A0701E/A0701E00.pdf>.

Stern, N. (2007). *The Economics of Climate Change*. Cambridge: Cambridge University Press.

Stiglitz, J. (2002). *Globalization and its Discontents*. London: Penguin.

Strzepek, K. and Boehlert, B. (2010). 'Competition for Water for the Food System', *Philosophical Transactions of the Royal Society B-Biological Sciences*, 365: 2927–40.

UN (2013). *World Population Prospects: the 2012 Revision*. New York: United Nations. Last accessed 29 June 2013. <http://esa.un.org/unpd/wpp/index.htm>.

USGS (2013). 'Phosphate Rock', *Mineral Commodities Summaries*, United States Geological Survey, January. Last accessed 21 April 2013. <http://minerals.usgs.gov/minerals/pubs/commodity/phosphate_rock/mcs-2013-phosp.pdf>.

WRAP (2008). *The Food We Waste*, Food Waste Report v.2, Waste and Resources Action Programme. Oxon: Banbury. Last accessed 21 April 2013. <https://www.ns.is/ns/upload/files/pdf-skrar/matarskyrsla1.pdf>.

7

Water Scarcity on a Blue Planet

Mark New

'The absence of a thing . . . this can be as deadly as the *presence*. The absence of air, eh? The absence of water? The absence of anything else we're addicted to.'

The Baron in Frank Herbert's popular novel, *Dune*.

(Herbert, 2005: 198–9, original emphasis).

It is a wellworn, but true cliché: water is essential for all life on earth, to a greater or lesser extent. At the most basic level it is required for a range of plant physiological processes that support the food web. Extreme water scarcity is the primary explanation for low diversity and biomass in hot and cold desert landscapes—in contrast, abundant water is an enabling factor in more humid environments (Hawkins et al. 2003; Lavers and Field 2006). For humans, water enables many of the features of our way of life and pleasures, from basic drinking and sanitation, to the food we eat, to the energy and products we consume, and for the amenity it provides directly for recreation and indirectly in supporting healthy ecosystems (Vörösmarty et al. 2010). As described below, the human 'footprint' on water has grown as population has increased, multiplied by growing per capita consumption of water, both directly, and indirectly through water embedded in goods and services. This chapter explores the implications of continued population growth for water scarcity at global and regional scales, by looking at both the demand and availability constraints, and the potentially confounding impacts of climate change, and considers possible demand-side and supply-side solutions. It is important to note that this chapter is focused on first-order water scarcity—that related to the physical limits to water availability. In many regions, second-order scarcity—related to lack of access to the water that is potentially available—is an equally pressing issue, but not related to absolute scarcity.

How Water Is and Has Been Used

Water use is often divided into three categories—blue, green, and grey—that relate to its source and destination. Blue water is defined as that held in surface and subsurface storage, rivers, lakes, wetlands, and groundwater, which can be physically abstracted, transported, and used. Green water is rainfall held in soils which is used for plant production; plants that are harvested or used for forage represent green water use. Grey water refers to return flows of blue water that is polluted to a greater or lesser extent; it is defined as the amount of fresh water that is required to dilute polluted return flows to tolerable levels of water quality (Hoekstra et al. 2011). The grey water requirement per unit volume of polluted water entering a water body increases with the severity of pollution.

The most common measure of water use by society relates to blue water. While estimates of water use are always uncertain, based as they are on extrapolation and estimation where measurements are unavailable, globally, about 4,400 km^3 of water was abstracted and used by society in 2010.[1] This abstraction supports three main uses of water: domestic/municipal consumption, industrial processes, and food production. Of these, the largest proportion was used for agricultural irrigation (64 per cent), followed by domestic use (22 per cent) and then industrial use (10 per cent).[2] These global figures hide huge variation across countries, depending on the balance between irrigated agriculture and economic sectors. For example, in Belgium the domestic–industrial–agriculture water use ratio is 13:85:1, while in South Africa it is 31:6:63 (Gleick et al. 2010).

A significant fraction of blue water that is abstracted returns to the terrestrial water cycle, for example as domestic and industrial waste. While consumptive water use is even more difficult to estimate than withdrawals, Shiklomanov and Rodda (2003) suggest that of the approximately 4,000 km^3 of blue water withdrawn each year, only about 2,600 km^3 is used consumptively. Thus withdrawal figures are in one sense misleading, in that only about 60 per cent of withdrawn water is consumed, although the 40 per cent that returns as grey water to the terrestrial water cycle is polluted to a lesser or greater extent, and therefore impacts on the availability of good quality water further downstream.

Figure 7.1 shows the growth in blue water use globally since 1900. Water use has increased sevenfold since 1900, and threefold since 1950, but the proportionate use between the three main sectors—agriculture, domestic, and industrial—has remained relatively constant. The strong link between water use and population is clear from Figure 7.1. As population has increased

---

[1] This figure is based on a projection derived from Morrison et al. (2009: 5, Figure 2).
[2] Author's calculation based on Morrison et al. (2009: 5, Figure 2).

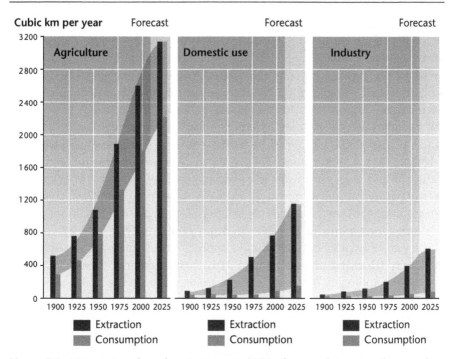

Figure 7.1. Historic trends and projections to 2025 of water abstraction from surface and ground waters

While every effort was made to contact the copyright holders of material in this book, there are instances where we have been unable to do so. If the copyright holders contact the author or publisher we will be pleased to rectify any omission at the earliest opportunity.

Source: UNDP (2008).

through the last century to the present, so water abstraction has increased to satisfy the increases in food production, manufactured goods, and domestic water goods demanded by this growing population.

Figure 7.1 implies that there have in fact been three phases of growth in global water abstraction. Up until about 1945 consumption increased roughly linearly with population growth, so that per capita consumption remained roughly constant. From 1945 through to 1980, however, per capita consumption increased considerably; here other factors come into play to amplify the effects of population growth. In the agricultural sector, the shift to irrigated, high-input agriculture to feed a growing, higher-consuming population resulted in larger water use per unit of food produced. Domestic water use increased, largely as a consequence of a growing urban population, coupled with much wider access to reticulated water supply. A growing middle class also consumed more goods and services, driving up manufacturing from an industry that generally was not required to use water efficiently.

From the mid 1980s, while total water abstraction has continued to increase, global per capita withdrawal has decreased. While there is great heterogeneity across regions, a number of factors are thought to be driving this recent trend. In some key regions, such as the United States and Europe, water supply limitations and recognition of the environmental impacts of over-abstraction have become important, and through regulation and/or pricing, efficiency of water use has become more of a factor. Similarly, while total irrigation abstraction has increased, the rate of increase is slowing, as the area available for irrigation has not grown as fast. Finally, the mid-century improvement in living standards and associated water use seen in the developed countries has not been replicated to the same extent in many developing countries; this does, however, suggests there is latent per capita growth in emerging economies and least-developed countries, especially in Africa, South America, and parts of Asia.

The water footprint is an alternative approach to estimating the water used by society (Hoekstra and Mekonnen 2012, and references therein). Using a bottom-up approach that first estimates water use in the production and consumption of goods and domestic water consumption, these authors estimate the global water footprint of humanity at ~9,100 km^3. Of this by far the largest proportion of consumed water is green, at ~6,700 km^3 per year (74 per cent), while blue and grey water consumption are estimated to be considerably lower at ~1,000 km^3 (11 per cent) and ~1,400 km^3 (15 per cent), respectively (Hoekstra and Mekonnen 2012: table 1).

How Much Water is Available?

These globally averaged consumptive water use figures can be expressed as a function of total physical water availability. The upper limit of accessible blue water resources is estimated at ~12 500–15 000 km^3 per year (Rockström et al. 2009), so in terms of planetary water availability, the blue and grey water use is a small fraction of the total (16–22 per cent, depending on estimates of consumption and availability). Even when blue water withdrawals are considered, this only amounts to 29–34 per cent of available blue water. Similarly, green water consumption is a small fraction of total available green water.

The figures for water availability above ignore the role of water in supporting ecosystem services, many of which are of a value to society over and above the service that water provides for consumption. Some of this is accounted for via dilution of grey water, but ecologically healthy blue water systems also act to assimilate and remove pollutants, support provisioning, and provide cultural and economic services for society (for example fishing, recreation, ecotourism). This ecological requirement, often termed the environmental flow or ecological reserve, constrains the proportion of available blue water that can be abstracted, stored, or consumed without causing severe ecological degradation (or loss of ecosystem services). The impact of water resource development on aquatic ecosystems is already significant, with 60 per cent of larger river systems affected by at least moderate flow regulation and fragmentation (Nilsson et al. 2005). The coupling between biodiversity impact and water use have been clearly elucidated by Vörösmarty et al. (2010) who show that in developed countries the reduction of threats to water security through water infrastructure investment has been at the expense of biodiversity. Further, in many developing country river basins biodiversity and water security threats are coincident, suggesting that interventions to ensure water security have the potential to negatively impact on biodiversity.

Considering these and other potential limits to the amount of available blue water has led to various proposals for water stress and water scarcity thresholds. A widely used index of water stress, initially used by Falkenmark and Widstrand (1992), and by others with various modifications, relates mean annual run-off to population; lower per capita run-off is taken to indicate higher first-order water stress. Under the Falkenmark index, 1,700 and 1,400 m^3 per year per person indicates states of water stress and water scarcity, respectively. At the planetary scale, Rockström et al. (2009) suggest that global consumptive withdrawals of blue water should be kept below 4,000–6,000 km^3 per year to avoid crossing continental-scale thresholds such as collapse of ecosystems, major shifts in moisture feedbacks into the planetary or regional hydrological cycle, or shifts in fresh-water inputs into oceans and consequent thermohaline impacts. Compared to these planetary boundaries, the Falkenmark stress and scarcity thresholds for the 2012 global population of 7 billion would correspond to an equivalent global water use of 11,900 to 9,800 km^3 per year respectively. These are more than double the threshold proposed by Rockström et al., at least partially explainable by Falkenmark and colleague's focus on total water availability rather than ecologically sustainable water use. However, regardless of the threshold chosen, current global blue water use is significantly below even the Rockström threshold.

These planetary figures clearly hide great geographic diversity in water stress and water scarcity. The Falkenmark index has been applied at river basin and national scales in several assessments, and shows great diversity of potential water scarcity or stress. More nuanced versions of this index, such as the ratio of actual withdrawals to available water resources (Alcamo et al. 2003; Vörösmarty et al. 2000) or the percentage of a river basin or country's territory affected by over-abstraction of water (YCLEP 2013), have also been developed; these are better representations of the actual situation.

Regardless of the index used, similar geographic patterns of water stress emerge, with 'hotspots' generally located in arid and semi-arid regions where water availability is low (Figure 7.2). However, a second class of water stress

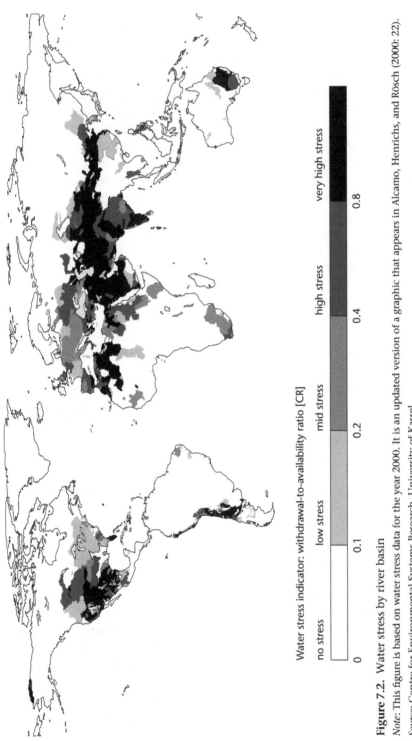

Water stress indicator: withdrawal-to-availability ratio [CR]

| no stress | low stress | mid stress | high stress | very high stress |

0   0.1   0.2   0.4   0.8

Figure 7.2. Water stress by river basin

Note: This figure is based on water stress data for the year 2000. It is an updated version of a graphic that appears in Alcamo, Henrichs, and Rösch (2000: 22).

Source: Centre for Environmental Systems Research, University of Kassel.

hotspots lies in regions of Europe and the northern United States where high population densities and high per capita water use are leading to stress in more humid environments.

Turton and Ohlsson (1999) describe the progression of water use in a political economy as one that moves from initial water abundance, where water use is not strongly institutionalized, through a series of transitions. This progression maps onto, and in some part explains, the trends described in this chapter. The first transition, into water scarcity (defined as a decrease in the volume of *available* water per capita over time), leads to the development of water institutions whose role is to redistribute water in space and time to the benefit of society. The focus of these institutions is invariably supply-side dominated. In the United States and Europe, this transition largely occurred in the 19th or early 20th centuries. In emerging economies, this transition has occurred more recently, or is occurring now. In both cases this transition enables the growth in water use seen in Figure 7.1, and the addition of new countries that undergo the transition feeds the continual growth in water withdrawal. The second transition, to water deficit, occurs when growth in demand cannot be met by supply-side measures, and leads to an era of demand-side adaptations, including efficiency, allocation, and competition between competing demands, and so on.

It is clear therefore that despite global water use currently being well below most commonly adopted scarcity and sustainability thresholds, some river and/or groundwater basins have 'filled up' to the extent that water abstraction is high relative to availability. The problem of course is that water is difficult and expensive to transport in bulk over large distances and so, unlike commodities such as food, oil, and minerals, global trade in bulk water has not developed. Indeed it has been cheaper to invest in expensive, unconventional water sources such as desalinization than to engage in bulk trade, or to exploit natural resources at levels that lead to significant environmental damage.

Water footprint calculations are useful for understanding the drivers of stress in different countries, by looking at the difference between the water footprint of production relative to consumption, and the flows of embedded or virtual water[3] between countries (Hoekstra and Mekonnen 2012). For example, the United States has between mid to very high withdrawal to availability in most of its major river basins (Figure 7.2), and this is reflected in a relatively high per capita blue and total water footprints of approximately 250 and 2800 m^3, respectively. Yet at the same time the United States is a net

---

[3] According to Hoekstra et al. (2011: 193) the virtual water content of a product is 'the volume of water consumed or polluted for producing the product, measured over its full production chain'; if such a product is exported, water is exported in virtual form. Therefore, virtual water content and the water footprint of a product are equivalent, although the water footprint is more sophisticated by differentiating between blue, green, and grey components of embedded water.

exporter of virtual water, by about 80 km^3 per year, which is equivalent to about another 10 per cent of its consumptive water footprint.[4] In contrast, the United Kingdom, which also has a number of severely over-abstracted catchments in the south-east, is a net importer of virtual water, offsetting its stress/scarcity via these imports which make up for about 60 per cent of the United Kingdom's total consumptive water footprint.

Future Water Use and Availability

From the preceding description of trends in water abstraction and consumption it is clear that an increasing and more economically developed, better fed, better serviced, and more consumerist population has caused the quadrupling of water abstraction over the last hundred years. At present, at the global scale, consumptive water use by humanity falls well below most proposed planetary limits of available water, even when an environmental or planetary 'reserve' is taken into account. However, these global figures are deceptive, hiding hotspots of water scarcity and high environmental damage from water use. These local scarcities can potentially be solved via virtual water trade, but for many poor countries the trade is difficult due to a lack of alternative sources of income with which to buy virtual water.

So, looking forward, there are two key factors that need to be considered in projecting the impacts of future populations on global and regional water resources. The first is of course population growth itself, and the geographical distribution of this future population. The second is climate change.

Population growth and per capita water use

Global population projections rest on numerous assumptions, but by all accounts a global population of 9 billion by 2050 is a reasonable expectation, driven mainly by growth in Asia and Africa (each roughly by 1 billion), while a population of 11.3 billion is possible.[5]

The question then arises as to what the implications of different possible populations are for global, regional, and national water use. To explore this, population numbers have to be combined with scenarios for water use. This has been attempted in a number of studies, mainly with respect to water requirements for food production (for example, Postel 1998) but also for total water withdrawals under various population and water use intensity scenarios (Alcamo, Henrichs, and Rösch 2000). With the new work on water

---

[4] See Hoeketra and Mekonnen (2012: 2). The units have been converted to km^3 for consistency.
[5] These figures refer to UN-DESA's (2011) medium and high population projections respectively.

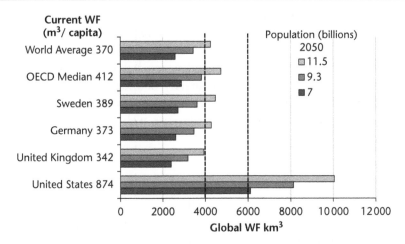

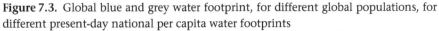

Figure 7.3. Global blue and grey water footprint, for different global populations, for different present-day national per capita water footprints

Note: Vertical lines show the planetary fresh water boundary (Röckstrom *et al.* 2009).

Source: author, based on water footprint data for each country from Mekonnen and Hoekstra (2011), appendix VIII.

footprints by the Water Footprint Network (Hoekstra and Mekonnen 2012)[6] one can use present-day water footprints from different countries to evaluate the implications of different water footprints for global and national water availability. Consider the present global average per capita blue and grey water footprint of 370 m[3] per year and contrast this with the water footprint of OECD countries such as the United States, Germany, and Sweden, with standards of living that the less-developed world might aspire to (Figure 7.3). Germany and Sweden have national consumptive water footprints below the OECD median of 412 m[3] per year, while the United States's water footprint is more than double this.

If today's global population of approximately 7 billion all had the standard of living of Germany, and its associated water footprint, the global water footprint would be ~2,600 km[3] per year—well below the planetary boundary proposed by Rockström et al. (2009). In contrast, a per capita water footprint equivalent to that of the United States would produce a global water footprint of ~6,100 km[3] per year, above even the upper range (6,000 km[3] per year) for the proposed planetary water boundary. These figures remain well below the Falkenmark global thresholds for water scarcity and stress, implying the water footprint can be satisfied, but only at the expense of environmental function, and may therefore not be sustainable in the long term.

---

[6] See also the Water Footprint Network's website, <http://www.waterfootprint.org>.

The alternative scenarios presented in Figure 7.3 indicate that global populations of 9.4 (and 11.3) billion would carry a global per capita water footprint of ~3,500 (~4,200) and ~8,130 (~10,050) km^3 for water footprints equivalent those of Germany and United States today, respectively. In the case of the former, the Rockström et al. (2009) planetary boundary will have just been breached by the larger population water footprint, while the United States water footprint would push global water use well beyond the planetary boundary.

Climate change, water availability, and water demand

Global warming has the potential to affect water availability on both the supply and demand sides. At the global scale, climate models suggest a warmer atmosphere will result in an intensified hydrological cycle; via enhanced evaporation from oceans and humid land areas, greater water holding capacity in the atmosphere, and as a consequence, more precipitation (Allen and Ingram 2002; Changing Watercycle Group 2014). However, these global-scale changes are unevenly distributed geographically, with the moist tropics and mid-latitudes projected to experience increased precipitation and the dry tropics, subtropics, and mid-latitudes projected to suffer reduced precipitation (Meehl et al. 2007; Zhang et al. 2007). The enhanced evaporative demand of a warmer climate is an important additional driver of reduced water availability, exacerbating the situation in areas with reduced or unchanged precipitation, and offsetting gains in areas with increased precipitation (Fung et al. 2011). In an assessment of the impacts of climate change on water stress, assuming greenhouse gas emissions continue to increase at the current high-end rates through to mid-century, New et al. (2011) estimated that over 50 per cent of major river basins worldwide would most likely experience an increase in water stress, of which 25 per cent would experience significant increases in stress (Table 7.1). Further, approximately half these basins were already experiencing water stress by the year 2000.

Annual average water stress figures hide a range of other potential impacts that may in specific circumstances be very important. For example, changes in seasonality, or reduced dry season flows, even with no reduction in mean annual run-off, can cause temporary stress, especially in areas where there is limited infrastructure to store water from the wet season (Taylor 2009). In semi-arid areas, drier conditions can lead to smaller water courses becoming ephemeral (de Wit and Stankiewicz 2006), adding to difficulties in water access for rural communities.

Climate change may also affect water demand. A range of studies (for example, Herrington 1996; New 2002) suggest increases in demand of between 3 and 10 per cent per degree of warming, although values vary widely

Table 7.1. Percentage of major river basins showing an increase in potential water stress due to climate change, under the RCP8.5 emissions scenario

Change in WSI[a]	Increase by > 0%			Increase by > 10%		
Percentile RCP8.5	5th	50th	95th	5th	50th	95th
Africa	23 (14)	68 (23)	64 (23)	9 (5)	32 (14)	32 (14)
Asia	7 (7)	23 (17)	20 (17)	0 (0)	0 (0)	0 (0)
Australasia	0 (0)	40 (20)	40 (20)	0 (0)	20 (20)	20 (20)
Europe	41 (22)	59 (41)	67 (48)	22 (11)	41 (22)	52 (33)
North America	42 (37)	58 (42)	68 (47)	32 (26)	32 (26)	37 (26)
South America	78 (11)	100 (11)	89 (11)	22 (11)	22 (11)	33 (11)
Global	29 (17)	54 (28)	54 (30)	14 (9)	24 (14)	29 (17)

[a] water stress index

Note: The table shows the percentage of major river basins showing an increase (>0%) or significant increase (>10%) in potential water stress due to climate change alone, under the 5th, 50th and 95th percentiles of the RCP8.5 emissions scenario 2060 global temperature change. The Figures in brackets show the percentage of basins with an increasing WSI and categorized as highly or moderately stressed in 2000 by Alcamo, Henrichs, and Rösch (2000).

Source: New et al. (2011: 11).

between and within water-use sectors. In the agricultural sector, there is considerable uncertainty about the effects of climate change on demand; in many instances increased irrigation efficiency could far outweigh any bio-physical increases in water requirements. Further, the (as yet poorly constrained) effects of carbon dioxide fertilization on plant water use efficiency may result in no net increase in plant water use requirements and perhaps an increase in run-off (Betts et al. 2007).

Overall, while the regional scale patterns of the *direction* of impact from climate change on water availability are becoming clear, there remains considerable uncertainty as to the magnitude of its impact, arising primarily from uncertainty in projections of climate models. Further, in the transition areas between humid and dry regions the direction of change in precipitation, and hence water availability, is also often uncertain.

Interaction of population and climate

A number of studies have examined the potential 'double whammy' of climate change and population growth on water scarcity (Arnell 2004; Arnell, Vuuren, and Isaac 2011; Fung, Lopez, and New 2011; New et al. 2011; Vörösmarty et al. 2000). In all, the general conclusion is that population and economically driven changes in demand for water will dominate changes in water stress in the future. For example, under a similar population scenario to the 9.4 billion in Figure 7.3 above, in the absence of climate change, approximately 60 per cent of the global population was projected to be living in moderately or highly stressed river basins in 2055 (Arnell 2004). When projected impacts of climate change on water resources in the 2050s is considered

Table 7.2. Percentage change in the number of people experiencing water stress with climate change, relative to without climate change, in 2055 under the A2 emissions and population scenario

Stress Level		Global Climate Model							
m³/cap/yr	class	HadCM3	ECHAM	CGCM	CSIRO	GFDL	CCSR	Mean	Std. Dev.
>1700	not stressed	−4.4	0.2	−2.1	−0.7	−9.7	7.4	−1.5	5.2
1000–1700	moderately stressed	9.8	46.7	−3.2	58.6	21.6	−14.1	19.9	25.8
500–1000	highly stressed	12.2	−23.4	8.9	−7.0	13.0	−1.8	0.3	12.9
<500	extremely stressed	−10.8	−12.9	−2.3	−34.5	−12.6	1.5	−12.0	11.5
<1700	—		2.3	−0.1	1.1	−0.2	5.0	−3.8	0.7	2.7

Note: Stress is defined in cubic metres per capita per annum. All figures rounded to one decimal place.
Source: author's calculation based on data from Arnell (2004), table 8, p. 41.

Table 7.3. Millions of people in catchments that shift into and out of water stress in different world regions, under the A2 population and emissions scenario

	Into Stress		Out of Stress		Into vs. Out of Stress	
	Mean	Std. Dev	Mean	Std. Dev	Difference	Ratio
Northern Africa	197	70	74	69	123	2.7
Western Africa	57	48	72	36	−14	0.8
Central Africa	18	24	20	20	−2	0.9
Eastern Africa	68	58	123	52	−55	0.6
Southern Africa	46	33	29	25	18	1.6
Mashriq	132	32	19	22	113	7
Arabian Peninsula	35	75	229	111	−193	0.2
Central Asia	56	57	54	50	2	1
South Asia	373	305	1794	318	−1421	0.2
South East Asia	4	4	2	2	2	2.6
Greater Mekong	41	32	6	7	34	6.5
North-west Pacific	404	329	477	336	−74	0.8
Australasia	0	0	0	0	—	—
Western Europe	142	61	13	25	129	10.8
Central Europe	125	25	0	0	125	—
Eastern Europe	21	5	1	1	20	21.3
Canada	7	2	0	0	7	—
United States	87	30	13	11	74	6.7
Caribbean	12	17	8	13	4	1.5
Meso-America	71	37	33	27	38	2.1
South America	31	22	21	15	10	1.5

Note: Stress is defined as catchment average runoff <1000 m³/cap/ann. The mean and standard deviation are derived from the six global climate model scenarios reported by Arnell.
Source: author's calculation based on data from Arnell (2004), table 12, p. 44.

in tandem with the population scenario (Table 7.2), the total number of people living in moderately to highly stressed catchments does not change significantly, although the distribution between stressed categories does vary, particularly between high and moderate stress (1000 m³ per capita per year).

Arnell (2004) also identified, on a regional basis, the balance between the numbers of people moving from zero or moderate water stress to a high or extreme stress situations (Table 7.3). While there is variation between results for different climate model projections, some regions can be identified as particularly vulnerable to a net switch to a high water stress situation: North and Southern Africa, Mashriq, South East Asia and Great Mekong, Europe, the United States, the Caribbean, and Meso-America. Thus, while climate change does not affect global levels of water stress, the global variations in its impacts on water availability are sure to modulate the geography of water stress in the future.

Regional Water Scarcity on a Blue Planet

A future where global use of fresh water exceeds total sustainable planetary availability is only really conceivable with a worst-case scenario of population growth coupled to a global per capita water footprint similar to that of the United States (Figure 7.3). Water footprints for other OECD countries which have excellent standards of living suggest that global water use below planetary boundaries is possible with existing methods of production and consumption. However, many river basins and countries are already experiencing first-order water shortages, and these are likely to increase in number and severity in future. Clearly, then, this global water budget excess hides a geography of water scarcity that warrants serious consideration from human well-being, economic, geopolitical, and environmental perspectives. How might stress in these hotspots be reduced?

Virtual water: an elegant but limited solution

The idea of virtual water trade as a solution to water scarcity has received considerable attention since it was first proposed in around 1994 (Allan 1998, 2003; World Water Council 2004). As described earlier, the amount of water consumed in the production of a product represents its 'virtual water' content (Allan 1998). Much of the virtual water trade is around food and fibre, and a significant proportion of this is not driven by water scarcity *per se*, but by other environmental conditions. For example, Canada is a large importer of virtual water in tropical fruit because it is climatically impossible to grow these fruit there. Increasingly, virtual water is also being traded in non-food and non-fibre products as well.

Virtual water trade as the solution to water scarcity is based on the proposition that in areas of water scarcity production of goods and services that have a high water footprint should be avoided, and that these goods should rather be imported from areas with water excess, reducing pressure on water resources in these water-stressed areas. To date only a few countries have made conscious efforts to reduce water scarcity via virtual water trade, with Israel and Jordan being most commonly highlighted (World Water Council 2004). However, many other countries engage subconsciously in virtual water trade to offset domestic shortfalls of food supply and to maintain social stability.

The fact that there has not been much evidence of deliberate policy choices to make water unavailable for water-intensive production suggests a number of political and economic barriers to virtual water trade (World Water Council 2004). These include: (1) financial costs, as not all countries have the alternative economic activities to generate the income needed for virtual water trade, leading to foreign reserve depletion and/or exorbitant food prices[7]; (2) fear of an increased dependency on main exporting countries; (3) damage to local agriculture (if unable to compete or adapt), due to importing food; and (4) interference in internal affairs by external trading partners.

Thus virtual water trade has potential as a deliberate policy for reducing water scarcity, but probably requires an international food, fibre, and goods trade system that guarantees stability of supply for national governments to countenance dependency on external foods. More likely is that the economics of food production in water scarce countries will lead to purchases of food and fibre from countries where food is cheaper to produce; some of these lower production costs may reflect water, but other factors are also of relevance, including land pressure, labour costs, and transport costs. There is evidence that this reorganization is to some extent already occurring; Dalin et al. (2012) showed that the number of global food trade connections has doubled in the last two decades, with major shifts in virtual water trade in food as Asia (and especially China) has grown its virtual water imports. This has resulted in a fourfold increase in the water saved by global imports of food in place of locally produced food to nearly 250 km^3 by 2007 (Dalin et al. 2012).

Water efficiency and water use reduction

Globally, it is estimated that nearly 50 per cent of water abstracted is returned to rivers after use or through lack of use (Table 7.4); for domestic and industrial use this figure is over 80 per cent, while for agriculture it is about 30 per cent. A proportion of abstracted water is lost even before it is used, due to leakage in

---

[7] This is particularly the case for developing countries where small-scale subsistence farming provides much of the local food and does not provide much in the way of extra income to purchase imported food.

Table 7.4. Global withdrawals, consumption, and return flow by sector in 2000

	Agriculture	Domestic	Industry	Total
Withdrawals (km^3)	2600	800	400	3800
Consumption (km^3)	1800	100	50	1950
Return flows (%)	31	88	88	49

Source: UNDP (2008) and author's calculation.

water distribution networks. Of the water that is used, much of the return flows is polluted or incompletely treated (grey water). Clearly then, there is scope for greater efficiency, in all three major domains of water use.

In water distribution systems, leakages are often extremely high—for example, 30 per cent in the United Kingdom prior to privatization, but now significantly reduced to an average of 20; currently 25 per cent in South Africa; and world average urban non-revenue water loss is around 37 per cent of withdrawals (see McKenzie, Siqalaba, and Wegelin 2012). Economically sustainable levels of leakage, defined as the leakage levels where further investment in leakage reduction is outweighed by the cost of supply from new sources of water, vary widely. The lowest reported levels of leakage are in Germany, at approximately 5 per cent (EEA 2003), where geology and soils are conducive to such low levels; other countries with low leakage levels include New Zealand and Australia, at around 10 per cent (McKenzie, Siqalaba, and Wegelin 2012: vii). Therefore, there is significant opportunity to meet at least some of future water demand via more efficient delivery, albeit at a cost.

Similarly, in irrigated agriculture, efficiency of field water application can vary from 50 per cent in open furrow systems, through 75 per cent in sprinkler systems, to 90 per cent in surface and subsurface drip (Brouwer, Prins, and Heibloem 1988). Switching to more efficient irrigation systems therefore can reduce agricultural water use, and has been occurring in many regions. However, these switches are invariably driven by water economics, only taking place where the cost of water or absolute lack of availability of new water drives this investment.

Opportunities for efficiency in industrial and domestic water use are also considerable. Many of these efficiencies are also economically beneficial, in that investment in efficiency produces a return over short to medium time scales. For example, in South Africa it has been estimated that 20 per cent of the projected 2030 shortfall of water availability in these sectors can be met by efficiency improvements that have at worst zero net cost (2030 Water Resources Group 2009).

Water reuse

Advances in water treatment make it possible to reuse virtually all waste water, but again at a cost. In Singapore, the NEWater water reuse initiative has resulted in 30 per cent of the public water supply being derived from treated and purified waste water, with a future target of 50 per cent by 2020 (Schnoor 2009).[8] While most of this treated water is allocated to industrial use, a proportion is mixed with natural water for public consumption, and the intention is to increase this proportion with time. Other examples of water reuse include the groundwater replenishment scheme in Orange County, California, where a combination of treated and untreated waste water provides 20 per cent of the recharge for the local aquifer; and Windhoek, Namibia, where 35 per cent of municipal water is derived from treated wastewater (Grant et al. 2012).

Water reuse therefore has considerable, demonstrated potential to improve the productive use of blue water that is abstracted. As with efficiency of distribution and use, its widespread adoption requires a number of economic, political, regulatory, and social acceptability barriers to be overcome (Grant et al. 2012). Water recycling at the utility level is only possible when it can be justified from a cost perspective, but this threshold has already been reached in many water-stressed areas; at this stage, political, regulatory, and even social acceptability issues tend to be surmountable.

Desalination

Desalination offers a supply-side solution to water scarcity, and is being widely implemented around the world. The most common plants make use of reverse osmosis, and it is estimated that there are over 15,000 desalination plants worldwide, with a combined capacity of some 32 km^3 per year (Poseiden Water 2013). This capacity is less than 1 per cent of global fresh water withdrawals, indicating that while desalination serves as an important additional source of water in water scarcity hotspots, its widespread application as an alternative to fresh water seems unlikely. The costs of desalination have also reduced substantially over the last few decades, but are starting to flatten out at just below US$1 per cubic metre, as more marginal efficiency gains have been offset by energy price rises. Nonetheless, desalination has become a viable alternative water supply option in areas where traditional fresh water supplies are scarce. One widely acknowledged externality of desalination is that the added energy inputs required, which can add to carbon emissions, are

---

[8] See also Singapore's national water agency website, <http://www.pub.gov.sg>.

powered by fossil fuel sources. However, an increasing number of desalination plants are being partly or wholly driven by renewable energy.

Conclusions

Historically, a growing population has inevitably caused rising demand for fresh water, and it is hard to envisage this changing over the next few decades. However, the rate of this growth in demand is critically dependent on the water footprint of individuals and nations. A global population with a water footprint of the average Western European citizen would result in global water use that is less than half that which would arise were the global footprint the same as the United States average. A world with a population of more than today's 7 billion and a footprint equivalent to that of the United States results in abstractions that exceed the recently proposed planetary boundary for safe utilization of global water. Keeping below these boundaries without compromising living standards is clearly possible; it depends on utilizing water in ways that *at a minimum* equal its productive use in Western Europe. Moreover, there are many opportunities to increase efficiency and enhance the productive use of water beyond the European norm, so that per capita and national water footprints are substantially reduced, creating a greater buffer between demand and availability.

However, assessment of fresh water budgets at the global scale masks a complex geography of water abundance and stress. Many countries in the dry subtropics experience absolute water scarcity, and many other countries in more humid areas have become water stressed, or are approaching water stress, as their national water footprints have increased. In these water stress hotspots, it is often the socio-economically vulnerable who are most affected—directly by lack of access to scarce water, and indirectly via local food insecurity, constraints on economic development, degraded aquatic ecosystems, and hydro-political tensions.

Ironically, climate change will be expected to increase the global fresh water budget, but exacerbate the existing broad patterns of water scarcity, with dry areas becoming drier and wet areas wetter. Although projections of changes in precipitation from climate models are uncertain over many regions, the best estimates suggests that the total number of people in 2050 who live in water stressed river basins will remain largely unchanged, in sharp contrast to the increases in stress projected as a function of population growth. These global impact metrics of course hide notable regional shifts, with many people moving out of stress in areas that become wetter and vice versa; of particular concern is a projected net 10 per cent increase in people experiencing extreme scarcity due to climate change.

A range of technical and behavioural solutions to local and global water scarcity already exist. These include: (1) demand-side options such as increased efficiency in reticulation, irrigation, industrial processes, and domestic use (both behavioural and technical); (2) supply-side options such as water reuse and desalination and large-scale water transfers; and (3) virtual water trade, enabling the flow of water embedded in food, fibre, and goods from where they are produced in water-abundant areas to where they are consumed in water-scarce locations. No single option is likely to be the answer in any location, but a portfolio approach that addresses both the demand and supply sides will be required. However, while solutions exist, and have been implemented in practice, there are significant barriers to widespread reduction in water footprints. These include: (1) economic barriers relating to the fact that the full economic costs of water are frequently not reflected in its price in many locations; (2) governance and political barriers; and (3) cultural preferences and lifestyle choices that result in high water footprints or reluctance to adopt new technologies such as water reuse.

Ultimately, the extent to which widespread water scarcity can be avoided is dependent on proactive water policies, via a mix of local, regional, and global solutions, that avoid as far as possible the Turton and Ohlsson (1999) transitions to water scarcity and water deficit. Without this, history suggests that severe water scarcity or deficit is inevitable before society responds at sufficient scale to solve the problem. The consequences of only responding to water scarcity crises rather than avoiding them are serious for both people, especially the most vulnerable, and the aquatic environment in water stressed regions.

References

Alcamo, J., Döll, P., Henrichs, T., Kaspar, F., Lehner, B., Rösch, T., and Siebert, S. (2003). 'Global Estimates of Water Withdrawals and Availability Under Current and Future "Business-As-Usual" Conditions', *Hydrological Sciences Journal*, 48(3): 339–48.

Alcamo, J., Henrichs, T., and Rösch, T. (2000). *World Water in 2025* (Kassel World Water Series Report No 2). Kassel: Centre for Envrionmental Systems Research, University of Kassel. Last accessed 11 June 2013. <http://www.usf.uni-kassel.de/usf/archiv/dokumente/kwws/kwws.2.pdf>.

Allan, J. A. (2003). 'Virtual Water—The Water, Food, and Trade Nexus: Useful Concept or Misleading Metaphor?' *Water International*, 28(1): 106–13.

Allan, J. A. (1998). 'Virtual Water: A Strategic Resource. Global Solutions to Regional Deficits', *Ground Water*, 36(4): 545–6.

Allen, M. R. and Ingram, W. J. (2002). 'Constraints On Future Changes in Climate and The Hydrologic Cycle', *Nature*, 419(6903), 224–32.

Arnell, N. W. (2004). 'Climate Change and Global Water Resources: SRES Emissions and Socio-Economic Ccenarios', *Global Environmental Change*, 14(1): 31–52.

Arnell, N. W., van Vuuren, D. P., and Isaac, M. (2011). 'The Implications of Climate Policy For The Impacts of Climate Change on Global Water Resources', *Global Environmental Change*, 21(2): 592–603.

Betts, R. A., Boucher, O., Collins, M., Cox, P. M., Falloon, P. D., Gedney, N., Hemming, D.L., Huntingford, C., Jones, C. D., Sexton, D. M., and Webb, M. J. (2007). 'Projected Increase in Continental Runoff Due to Plant Responses to Increasing Carbon Dioxide', *Nature*, 448(7157): 1037–41.

Brouwer, C., Prins, K., and Heibloem, M. (1988). *Irrigation Water Management: Irrigation Scheduling* (Training Manual No. 4). Rome: Food and Agricultural Organization. Last accessed 11 June 2013. <http://www.fao.org/docrep/T7202E/T7202E00.htm>.

Changing Watercycle Group (2014). 'Quantifying Changes in the Global Water Cycle', *Bulletin of the American Meteorological Society*, Under Review.

Dalin, C., Konar, M., Hanasaki, N., Rinaldo, A., and Rodriguez-Iturbe, I. (2012), 'Evolution of the Global Virtual Water Trade Network', *Proceedings of the National Academy of Sciences*, 109(16): 5989–94.

de Wit, M. and Stankiewicz, J. (2006). 'Changes in Surface Water Supply Across Africa with Predicted Climate Change', *Science*, 311(5769): 1917–21.

EEA (2003). '(WQ06) Water Use Efficiency (in Cities): Leakage', Indicator Fact Sheet (version 01.10.03). European Environment Agency. Last accessed 20 August 2013. <http://www.eea.europa.eu/data-and-maps/indicators/water-use-efficiency-in-cities-leakage/water-use-efficiency-in-cities-leakage>.

Falkenmark, M. and Widstrand, C. (1992). *Population and Water Resources: A Delicate Balance* (vol. 47, no. 3).Washington, DC: Population Bulletin.

Fung, F., Lopez, A., and New, M. (2011). 'Water Availability in + 2 Degrees C and + 4 Degrees C Worlds', *Philosophical Transactions of the Royal Society: A– Mathematical Physical and Engineering Sciences*, 369(1934): 99–116.

Gleick, P., Allen, L., Christian-Smith, J., Cohen, M. J., Cooley, H., Heberger, M., Morrison, J., Palaniappan, M., and Schulte, P. (2010). *The World's Water Volume 7: The Biennial Report on Freshwater Resources*. Washington, DC: Island Press.

Grant, S. B., Saphores, J-D., Feldman, D. L., Hamilton, A. J., Fletcher, T. D., Cook, P. L. M., Stewardson, M., Sanders, B. F., Levin, L. A., Ambrose, R. F., Deletic, A., Brown, R., Jiang, S. C., Rosso, D., Cooper, W. J., and Marusic, I. (2012). 'Taking the "Waste" Out of "Wastewater" for Human Water Security and Ecosystem Sustainability', *Science*, 337(6095): 681–6.

Hawkins, B. A., Field, R., Cornell, H. V., Currie, D. J., Guégan, J-F., Kaufman, D. M., Kerr, J. T., Mittelbach, G. G., Oberdorff, T., O'Brien, O. M., Porter, E. E., and Turner, J. R. G. (2003). 'Energy, Water, and Broad-Scale Geographic Patterns of Species Richness', *Ecology*, 84 (12): 3105–17.

Herbert, F. (2005). *The Great Dune Trilogy*. London: Gollancz.

Herrington, P. (1996). *Climate Change and The Demand for Water*. London: HMSO.

Hoekstra, A. Y., Chapagain, A. K., Aldaya, M. M., and Mekonnen, M. M. (2011). *The Water Footprint Assessment Manual: Setting the Global Standard*. London: Earthscan.

Hoekstra, A. Y. and Mekonnen, M. M. (2012). 'The Water Footprint of Humanity', *Proceedings of the National Academy of Sciences*, 109(9): 3232–7.

Lavers, C. and Field, R. (2006). 'A Resource-Based Conceptual Model of Plant Diversity That Reassesses Causality in the Productivity-Diversity Relationship', *Global Ecology and Biogeography*, 15(3): 213–24.

McKenzie, R., Siqalaba, Z., and Wegelin, W. (2012). *The State of Non-Revenue Water in South Africa* (WRC Report No. TT 512/12). South Africa: Water Research Commission.

Meehl, G. A., Stocker, T. F., Collins, W. D., Friedlingstein, P., Gaye, A. T., Gregory, J. M., Kitoh, A., Knutti, R., Murphy, J. M., Noda, A., Raper, S. C. B., Watterson, I. G., Weaver, A. J., and Zhao, Z-C. (2007). 'Global Climate Projections', in S. Solomon, D. Qin, M. Manning, Z. Chen, M. Marquis, K. B. Averyt, M. Tignor, and H. L. Miller (eds.), *Climate Change 2007: The Physical Science Basis.* (Contribution of Working Group I to the Fourth Assessment Report of the Intergovernmental Panel on Climate Change). Cambridge and New York: Cambridge University Press, pp. 747–846.

Mekonnen, M. M. and Hoekstra, A. Y. (2011). *National Water Footprint Accounts: the Green, Blue and Grey Water Footprint of Production and Consumption* (Value of Water Research Report Series No.50). Delft, The Netherlands: UNESCO-IHE Institute for Water Education. Last accessed 26 August 2013. <http://www.waterfootprint.org/?page=files/WaterStat-NationalWaterFootprints>.

Morrison, J., Morikawa, M., Murphy, M., and Schulte, P. (2009). *Water Scarcity and Climate Change: Growing Risks for Businesses and Investors*. Boston, MA: Pacific Institute for CERES. Last accesse 11 June 2013. <http://www.pacinst.org/reports/business_water_climate/full_report.pdf>.

New, M. (2002), 'Climate Change and Water Resources in the Southwest Cape, South Africa', *South African Journal of Science*, 98(7/8): 369–76.

New, M., Anderson, K., Bows, A., Fung, F., and Thornton, P. (2011). *SR8: The Possible Impacts of High Levels of Climate Change in 2060 and Implications for Migration.* (Review for UK Government's Foresight Project, Migration and Global Environmental Change). London: Foresight. Last accessed 11 June 2013. <http://www.bis.gov.uk/assets/foresight/docs/migration/science-reviews/11-1126-sr8-impact-high-levels-climate-change-2060-for-migration.pdf>.

Nilsson, C., Reidy, C. A., Dynesius, M., and Revenga, C. (2005). 'Fragmentation and Flow Regulation of the World's Large River Systems', *Science*, 308(5720): 405–8.

Poseiden Water (2013). 'Overview [Desalination]'. Last accessed 21 May 2013. <http://poseidonwater.com/desalination/overview>.

Postel, S. L. (1998). 'Water For Food Production: Will there be Enough in 2025?', *Bioscience*, 48(8): 629–37.

Rockström, J., Steffen, W., Noone, K., Persson, Å., Chapin, F. S. III, Lambin, E., Lenton, T. M., Scheffer, M., Folke, C., Schellnhuber, H., Nykvist, B., De Wit, C. A., Hughes, T., van der Leeuw, S., Rodhe, H., Sörlin, S., Snyder, P. K., Costanza, R., Svedin, U., Falkenmark, M., Karlberg, L., Corell, R. W., Fabry, V. J., Hansen, J., Walker, B., Liverman, D., Richardson, K., Crutzen, P., and Foley, J. (2009). 'Planetary Boundaries: Exploring the Safe Operating Space for Humanity', *Ecology and Society*, 14(2): <http://www.ecologyandsociety.org/vol14/iss2/art32/>.

Schnoor, J. L. (2009). 'NEWater Future?' *Environmental Science and Technology*, 43(17): 6441–2.

Shiklomanov, I. A. and Rodda, J. C. (2003). *World Water Resources at the Beginning of the 21st Century*. Cambridge: Cambridge University Press.

Taylor, R. (2009). 'Rethinking Water Scarcity: the Role of Storage', *Transactions of the American Geophysical Union*, 90(28): 237–8.

Turton, A. R. and Ohlsson, L. (1999). 'Water Scarity and Social Stability: Towards a Deeper Understanding of the Key Concepts Needed to Manage Water Scarcity in Developing Countries', *Occasional Papers 17*. London: SOAS-KCL Water Issues Group, School of Oriental and African Studies. Last accessed 21 January 2013. <http://www.soas.ac.uk/water/publications/papers/file38360.pdf>.

UNDP (2008). 'Trends in Global Water Use By Sector' in *Vital Water Graphics: An Overview of the State of the World's Fresh and Marine Waters—2nd Edition*. United Nations Development Programme. Last accessed 21 May 2013. <http://www.unep.org/dewa/vitalwater/index.html>.

UN-DESA (2011). *World Population Prospects: The 2010 Revision*. New York: United Nations, Department of Economic and Social Affairs, Population Division.

Vörösmarty, C. J., Green, P., Salisbury, J., and Lammers, R. B. (2000). 'Global Water Resources: Vulnerability from Climate Change Acid Population Growth', *Science*, 289 (5477): 284–8.

Vörösmarty C. J., McIntyre P. B., Gessner M. O., Dudgeon, D., Prusevich, A., Green, P., Glidden, S., Bunn, S. E., Sullivan, C. A., Liermann, C. R., and Davies, P. M. (2010). 'Global Threats to Human Water Security and River Biodiversity', *Nature*, 467(7315): 555–61.

Water Resource Group (2009). *Charting Our Water Future: Economic Frameworks to Inform Decision-Making*. Washington, DC: The 2030 Water Resource Group. Last accessed 11 June 2013. <http://www.2030wrg.org/wp-content/uploads/2012/06/Charting_Our_Water_Future_Final.pdf>.

World Water Council (ed.) (2004). *E-Conference Synthesis: Virtual Water Trade—Conscious Choices*. The Hague, The Netherlands: WWC Publications.

YCLEP (2013). 'Environmental Performance Index', Yale Centre for Environmental Law and Policy. Last accessed 11 June 2013. <http://epi.yale.edu/>.

Zhang, X. B., Zwiers, F. W., Hegerl, G. C., Lambert, F. H., Gillett, N. P., Solomon, S., Stott, P. A., and Nozawa, T. (2007). 'Detection of Human Influence on Twentieth-Century Precipitation Trends', *Nature*, 448 (7152), 461–5.

8

The Metabolism of a
Human-Dominated Planet

Yadvinder Malhi

This Age of Humans, this Anthropocene, is ecologically like no other in the long history of the Earth's biosphere. In all natural ecosystems, energy and work flow from the 'bottom up'. Plants and phytoplankton dominate the ecological metabolism of natural ecosystems, capturing energy from the sun and converting it into chemical energy usable for the work of functioning, growing, and reproducing. Much of this captured energy is used by the plants themselves, a fraction percolates up into consumers (especially fungi, bacteria, and soil fauna), and an even smaller fraction filters up into larger creatures.

In the past 10,000 years, the blink of an eye in the 4.6 billion-year history of Earth, this upwards flow of energy in the biosphere has been fundamentally perturbed. *Homo sapiens*, a single, highly social species of large primate with an unusual ability to share complex ideas and innovations through verbal language, began to actively colonize natural ecosystems and direct their energetic production to maximize its own consumption, through the innovation of agriculture. Previously this species, a component of the biosphere like any other species, probably had less influence on Earth's life-support systems than, say, elephants or mammoths, but these innovations gradually expanded human influence on ecosystem function in many regions. Later, less than 300 years ago, this species began to exploit on a large scale a source of energy previously not significantly utilized by other denizens of the biosphere (whether plants, animals, fungi, or microbes): the fossil, energy-rich remains of ancient inhabitants of the biosphere buried hundreds of millions of years previously (ancient plants in the form of coal, and ancient plankton in the forms of oil and gas). This rapid expansion in available energy enabled humans to expand rapidly in numbers, activity, and interconnectedness, to colonize previously forbidding ecosystems such as tropical forests and polar latitudes, and to maximize rates of harvest of other species; to efficiently exploit previously inaccessible material resources, and to generate waste products in such quantities that they threaten to shift the entire Earth system into fundamentally different biophysical states. Uniquely in the history of Earth, this new energy supply is concentrated not at the bottom trophic level (that is, plants) but at a higher trophic level (a large primate and associated domesticates such as cattle).

Hence, when considering the question 'is the planet full?' from an environmental perspective, it is helpful to tackle this question in terms of resource flow, and compare the resource flow appropriated by humans to that which would have existed in the absence of humans. Here, I tackle this question in terms of arguably the most fundamental of resources: *energy*. Energy is an interesting biological metric because, in the broadest sense, it represents the capacity of an organism (whether plant, bacterium, or human) or species to do 'work'; to exploit and modify its surroundings to advantage its survival prospects and those of its descendants. The more energy a species or organism has access to, the more able and likely it is to exploit and modify its environment. Energy is also a particularly useful metric because it enables the direct comparison of biological processes (photosynthesis, growth, metabolism) with socio-economic processes (food production, industrial energy production) in a common energetic currency.

This chapter takes a metabolic view of the planet, and examines how the *extended metabolism* of the human species compares in magnitude to the metabolism of the entire biosphere. Describing human activity on Earth as an integral component of biosphere activity can provide a useful perspective for analysing human–biosphere relations. I demonstrate that the energetic metabolism of our species has grown in size to be comparable in magnitude to the natural metabolic cycles of the terrestrial biosphere. This feature underlies almost all environmental challenges we face in the 21st century, ranging through resource depletion; overharvesting of other species; excessive waste products entering into land, oceans and atmosphere; climate change, and habitat and biodiversity loss.

My basic thesis is that when we consider humanity and the biosphere from a metabolic perspective, it is very clear that that the Earth is 'full', in the sense that the natural metabolism (here defined as the metabolism of the planet as it would have been in the absence of humans, or roughly that preceding human influence) is becoming dominated by the extended metabolism of one component species, and in particular one species that sits at a high trophic level where energy flows were previously small. What this means for the long-term functioning of the biosphere, and future for ourselves and fellow denizens of the biosphere, is far from clear, but it is certain that the biosphere will continue to be modified in multiple ways by this abundance of human extended metabolism.

My aim is not to suggest that metabolism explains everything, in some form of universal theory of metabolic determinism. It is rather to argue that a metabolic perspective on humanity and the biosphere can give new perspectives and insights into the influence of humanity on the planet.

Definitions

Metabolism is defined as a biological process, and can be defined as the rate at which energy is exchanged between an organism and its environment; transformed within an organism; and allocated to maintenance, growth, and reproduction (Brown et al. 2004). The purely biological context can be extended to encompass human societies through the concept of 'sociometabolism' (Fischer-Kowalski and Haberl 1998; Krausmann et al. 2008), which is the rate at which energy is exchanged between a human society and its environment, and transformed within a society. Hence biological metabolism is fuelled almost solely by light capture by plants, and then by consumption by other organisms of the chemical free energy embodied in plant biomass. Sociometabolism, in contrast, incorporates biomass resource consumption for food or fuel, but also energy generation and consumption from other sources, including fossil fuels, and nuclear, solar, and wind power.

All biological metabolism and a significant part of sociometabolism is fuelled by the consumption of biological material (plants or animals) and is therefore strongly coupled to the flow of elements essential to biological function (in particular carbon and major nutrients such as nitrogen and phosphorus). Hence energetic metabolism is strongly linked to the mass flow of key resources such as nitrogen and phosphorus.

The Biological Metabolism of Earth

Before quantifying the relative magnitude of human energy use relative to that of the biosphere, it is informative to first estimate the metabolic energy flowing through the biosphere prior to major human influence.

Almost all of the energy that powers the biosphere ultimately originates from solar energy (a tiny fraction comes from geothermal processes). 174 PW (1 PW $= 1$ petawatt $= 10^{15}$ W) of solar energy bathes the planet's upper atmosphere, of which 30 per cent is reflected back to space. Components of the terrestrial biosphere (in particular plants and cyanobacteria) have evolved to capture a fraction of this energy in concert with capturing carbon and water, lock the energy into carbon-based chemical bonds through the process of photosynthesis, and then utilize this energy in a controlled manner to power metabolisms that enable growth, resource exploitation, defence, and reproduction.

Because all abundant forms of biosphere energy capture require carbon (C) atoms as the basis of the carbon-bond-based energy storage, such capture is conventionally expressed in terms of carbon units, and is termed gross primary productivity (GPP). The GPP of the biosphere is about 210 Pg C year^{-1} (1 Pg C=1 petagram of carbon=1 thousand million tonnes of carbon= 10^{15} g C) of which 120 Pg C is on land and 90 Pg C is in the oceans (Field et al. 1998). The biosphere probably approached these levels of energy consumption in the Carboniferous period (359–299 million years ago) when plants became extensive on the land surface, and in particular during the late Cretaceous period (140–100 million years ago), when densely veined angiosperm plants with high photosynthetic capacity became the dominant form of plant life (Brodribb and Feild 2010).

For our purposes (and in a common currency of metabolic energy), it is useful to express the rates of global photosynthesis in units of energy conversion. The standard free energy for the reduction of one mole of carbon dioxide (CO_2) to the level of glucose is + 478 kJ mol^{-1}, or 39.83 kJ g C^{-1}. Using this conversion factor, the total global (terrestrial and marine) photosynthetic metabolism of the biosphere is 265 TW (1 TW=1 terawatt=10^{12} W), of which 150 TW (60 per cent) is through the land biosphere, and 115 TW (40 per cent) through the marine biosphere. This total biosphere metabolism represents 0.2 per cent of total surface solar energy.

This is the total photosynthetic flux. About 50–70 per cent of this captured energy is used by the plants and phytoplankton themselves to power their own metabolisms (termed autotrophic respiration) and about 30–50 per cent is used to produce plant/phytoplankton biomass (termed net primary production, or NPP), which is eventually consumed and metabolized by herbivores, detritivores, bacteria, and fungi (in what is termed heterotrophic respiration) (Malhi, Baldocchi and Jarvis 1999). Expressing NPP in energy units and using the values of terrestrial NPP and conversion factors outlined above, the total biomass energy made available by plants to other organisms is therefore about 75 TW on land, and 57 TW in the oceans.

The Metabolism of the Human Organism

The average active adult human metabolizes sugars to produce energy at a rate of 120 W (Burnside et al. 2012; equivalent to two typical old-fashioned tungsten light bulbs, or the amount of sunlight falling on an A3 sheet of paper when the sun is overhead in the tropics). A basal resting human metabolism is 60–80 W (Brown et al. 2004). This roughly corresponds to what would be expected for a mammal of our size, though our energy use is disproportionately allocated to maintenance of our unusually large and resource-demanding brains (which consume 20–25 per cent of our basal metabolic energy, around 15–20 W). As a result, less energy is allocated to other aspects such as growth, and humans have an unusually slow growth rate for a mammal our size. Despite our high mammal metabolism, we grow at the rate of an equivalent mass reptile (for example, a boa constrictor), an order of magnitude times slower than would be expected for a mammal our size (Burnside et al. 2012: 196).

The History of Human Sociometabolism

Next I explore how human energy use (human sociometabolism) compares to the natural energy use of the biosphere. This term includes the direct consumption of resources for our biological metabolism, but also indirect consumption through appropriation of ecosystems (agriculture) and animal domestication, and the use of biomass, fossil fuel, or other energy supplied for societal activity.

First we examine the human use of energy and materials during three stages of human societal development: preagricultural, agricultural, and industrial. This section draws on the concept of sociometabolic regimes and transitions introduced by Haberl (2006). Quantifying the sociometabolism of humanity requires accounting for both energy flows (which are relatively easily garnered for modern societies from energy statistics) and material flows (the flow of biomass used for human or livestock nutrition). The material flows are an important component of the metabolism of pre-industrial societies, and can still be a significant component of modern societies.

The hunter-gatherer sociometabolism

Prior to the Neolithic revolution in agriculture, the estimated global human population was low. Modern *Homo sapiens* had expanded out of Africa 50,000–100,000 years ago, and managed to displace pre-existing *Homo* populations such as Neanderthals in Europe, *Homo erectus* in Asia, and most likely other recently discovered but poorly described human species such as Denisovans and the enigmatic Red Deer Cave People (Krause et al. 2010; Curnoe et al. 2012). Quite what gave *Homo sapiens* such a competitive advantage is the subject of intense debate, but a very plausible hypothesis is the development of complex language that enabled transmission of complex knowledge, rapid cultural evolution, and the emergence of increasingly social and intercon-nected human societies. By 40,000 years ago *Homo sapiens* had reached hom-inid-free Australia; by 10,000 years ago it had crossed the Bering Straits and rapidly colonized the hominid-free Americas.[1]

Despite this global spread, human societies remained hunter-gatherer, as they had been during the millions of years of preceding evolution, albeit becoming increasingly effective hunters through the development of improved technologies such as spears, arrows, and fish hooks. Hunter-gatherer lifestyles did not have an entirely benign effect on ecosystems. The use and spread of fire altered many ecosystems, for example in Australia (Rule et al. 2012). There is abundant evidence of extensive extinction of large animals in many continents coinciding with the arrival of human hunters (Barnosky et al. 2004). The impact of preagricultural humans on ecosystems is often underappreciated. Prior to human arrival, much of North and South America and Australia would have appeared as African game parks appear today, abundant in large herbivores and carnivores, some familiar (lions, cheetahs, elephants) and some exotic (giant marsupial lions and wombats, sabretooth tigers, giant ground sloths, armadillo-like glyptodonts). Around the time of human arrival, 33 species of large animal (typically only animals of body mass equivalent or larger than human mass) became extinct in North America, 50 species in South America, and 21 species in Australia (Barnosky 2008). The only regions with low extinction rates were Africa, and to a lesser extent South Asia, where the megafauna had co-evolved with *Homo sapiens*, and perhaps had learned to be wary of this puny, strange-sounding, ground-dwelling primate. The extinction of the large fauna had knock-on consequences for ecosystem structure and nutrient cycling, with the encroachment of forests into previously browsed grasslands in ecosystems ranging from Siberia to the tropics, and reduction of movement of nutrients through animal dung (Doughty, Wolf, and Malhi 2013). The expansion of dark boreal forests into mammoth-maintained grasslands at high latitudes in the wake of mammoth extinction may indeed have induced an early, moderate global warming (Doughty, Wolf, and Field 2010). In high latitudes the light absorption effect of trees (especially in snow cover conditions) outweighs any carbon dioxide-associated cooling effect from carbon storage (Bala et al. 2007).

Examination of modern-day hunter-gatherer societies can give some indi-cation of energy use by preagricultural societies. Table 8.1 summarizes an estimate of sociometabolism of hunter-gather societies, derived from Kraus-mann et al. (2008). The energy use per capita of a hunter-gatherer is about

---

[1] See Goldin, Cameron, and Balarajan (2011, ch. 1) for a brief account of human migration from prehistory to Columbus.

Table 8.1. Aspects of the sociometabolism of hunter-gatherer, pre-industrial agricultural, and industrial societies

Metric	Units	Socio-metabolic mode		
		Hunter-gatherer	Agricultural	Industrial
Population density	Humans km^{-2}	0.02–0.10	40	400
Agricultural population	%	0	>80	<10
Extended metabolism	W per capita	300	2000	8000
Total energy use per unit area	W km^{-2}	6–30	82 × 10^3	3.3 × 10^6
Proportion of biome metabolism	%	<2 × 10^{-4}	3–6	210
Biomass share of energy use	%	> 99	> 95	10–30
NPP appropriation	Mg C km^{-2} year^{-1}	0.005–0.024	62	515
Proportion of local NPP	%	6–30 × 10^{-4}	8	69

Source: derived from Krausmann et al. (2008 table 1).

300 W, and this is almost entirely in the process of acquiring food for consumption, and to a much lesser extent other materials and the use of fire. This sociometabolism is greater than the 80–120 W required for human physiological metabolism, because of the inefficiencies in both acquiring foodstuffs, and in human conversion of food into metabolic energy, and also in the use of biomass energy sources for fuel.

The hunter-gatherer lifestyle can only appropriate a small fraction of the energy in the ecosystem landscape (fruit, tubers, other foodstuffs, animals, wood fuel), and can therefore only support low human population densities (typically 0.02–0.10 humans km^{-2}; Table 8.1). The overall impact is low (albeit heavy on the animals hunted), with low appropriation of ecosystem productivity typically of a magnitude of 5–24 kg C km^{-2} year^{-1}, equivalent to 6–30 W km^{-2}. This compares to a baseline ecosystem metabolism of 3.2 MW km^{-2} (GPP 2500 Mg C km^{-2} year^{-1}; NPP 1250 Mg C m^{-2} year^{-1}) for a tropical savannah environment (Roy and Saugier 2001). Hence human sociometabolism was six orders of magnitude smaller than the biological metabolism of the surrounding African savannah landscape in which we first appeared.

Homo sapiens and its antecedent *Homo* species have existed in a hunter-gatherer lifestyle for over a million years, with slow improvement in resource gathering efficiency as brains expanded and technologies improved, and notable waves of global expansion out of Africa. From a metabolic perspective however, total human metabolic activity was low and had modest impact on the planet; probably less impact than elephants and mammoths. This pattern was punctuated by a major transition that began about ten thousand years ago: the Neolithic revolution and the advent of farming.

The Agricultural Sociometabolism

Farming originated almost simultaneously (on human prehistory timescales) at several locations in the early Holocene (5,000–10,000 years ago), including in Mesopotamia and Anatolia, the Yangtze valley, New Guinea, West Africa, Meso-America, and the Andes (Diamond 2002). This suggests that this transition was somewhat inevitable given the stage of human language ability and cultural connectedness, and once the climate had moistened and stabilized sufficiently after the latest ice age. Following the development of farming, Neolithic cultures carried agricultural and pastoralist knowledge and approaches across the terrestrial surface, to the extent that hunter-gatherer cultures now form a tiny minority of humankind. The Neolithic transition did not necessarily lead to an improvement in individual human well-being, as health and life expectancy declined in congested, disease-ridden communities, and nutrition declined with monotonous agricultural diets (Larsen 1995). Through their efficient colonization and exploitation of ecosystem metabolism, however, the agricultural societies were able to support much greater populations of humans, and hence outcompete hunter-gatherer societies. The languages of the expanding Neolithic or Iron Age farmers and pastoralists dominate the global language maps of modern humanity, whether Indo-European across Eurasia (Bouckaert et al. 2012), Chinese in East Asia, or Bantu in sub-Saharan Africa. The transition from hunter-gatherer to farmer/pastoralist is largely complete for most of the human population. A very small fraction of humanity still retains a hunter-gatherer lifestyle.

Colonization of ecosystems

From a metabolic viewpoint, the key advance of the Neolithic revolution was the 'colonization' of the ecosystem landscape, with many ecosystem processes ending up being regulated or controlled by humans. Instead of harvesting or slightly modifying whatever foodstuffs the natural ecosystem was able to provide, the vegetation landscape was effectively 'colonized' (Fischer-Kowalski and Haberl 1998) and altered to produce a higher density and abundance of foodstuffs well suited for human consumption, especially cereals such as wheat (Middle East), rice (Asia) and maize (Americas). The domestication of key animals also greatly increased our colonization of natural ecosystems, with increased grazing by cattle, pigs, and goats (among others) converting large areas of human-inedible foodstuffs into small amounts of nutrient-rich meat. Biomass (either directly for fuel or as food for animals) is still the dominant energy source of agricultural societies, despite occasional use of wind or hydropower.

Pre-industrial agricultural societies often reduced the natural NPP of the regions they inhabited, as the natural ecosystem was replaced by a less optimized agricultural system (Haberl et al. 2007). A notable exception was semi-arid river valleys such as the Indus and Nile, where irrigation and controlled water flow greatly increased the previous productivity of the landscape. On a regional level, a large fraction of NPP can be appropriated and utilized by agricultural societies.

The intensity and efficiency of agricultural production increased over time. Table 8.1 presents data on sociometabolism from an advanced pre-industrial agricultural society (in this example an Austrian agrarian society in the mid-18th century, just prior to the industrial revolution). Compared to the hunter-gatherer sociometabolic regime, by the 18th century human sociometabolism per capita had increased by one to two orders of magnitude. Such a society supports a population density of up to 40 people km^{-2}, with a sociometabolism of around 2,000 W per capita. This is equivalent to a per unit area energy consumption of 82 kW km^{-2} (or 65 Mg C km^{-2} $year^{-1}$), three to four orders of magnitude greater than that of a hunter-gatherer society. This is still only 3–6 per cent[2] of the natural metabolism of the ecosystem that has been colonized (the temperate ecosystems most extensively colonized have about half the metabolism of tropical savannahs). Unlike the case of the hunter-gatherer, the ecosystem has been substantially altered to provide for this sociometabolism, and such alteration now represents a significant modification of local biological metabolism.

Locally, non-industrial agricultural societies can appropriate up to 80 per cent of NPP (Haberl et al. 2007), especially in densely populated, highly productive agricultural regions such as the Ganges plain, East China, and Java. By the time of the onset of the industrial revolution, humans had appropriated approximately 4 per cent of global terrestrial NPP. In suitable regions with high natural fertility the degree of agricultural appropriation of ecosystem metabolism was high, but there remained vast regions of the biosphere, most notably much of the tropical and boreal forest realm, where humanity did not have the metabolic resources to effectively colonize the biosphere.

A key feature of agricultural sociometabolism is its strong dependency on land area. The sociometabolism of a pre-industrial agricultural society was largely a function of the amount of ecosystem land area it was able to colonize. Agriculture made permanent settlement both possible (there was no need to roam a large area as per area energy density increased) and also necessary (it was necessary to nurture, manage, and protect crops). Hence the size of

---

[2] The figures have been calculated from the information in table 8.1.

metabolism per capita was broadly limited by the area per capita appropriated, notwithstanding gradual improvements in agricultural efficiency over the millennia. Eventually, many agrarian societies faced a Malthusian trap where population density increased in response to greater sociometabolic energy (and was needed as labour to exploit that sociometabolic energy), but the total amount of energy available was constrained by land area. Such an agricultural landscape is 'full' in the sense that the population exists at near the metabolic carrying capacity of the landscape, and is vulnerable to shocks; droughts and political instability can tip the sociometabolism into decline and lead to famine and depopulation.

The Industrial Sociometabolism

Pre-industrial agricultural humanity derived almost all of its energy, whether food or fuel, from natural ecosystems, and thus its sociometabolism ultimately was constrained by land area. Agricultural efficiency could be improved, but there were basic challenges to how much energy could be extracted from a specific land area of ecosystem, and therefore how dense a human population could be supported.

The next major sociometabolic transition was the industrial revolution, which, while having technological precedents, began to fundamentally shift societies in the mid-18th century in north-west Europe. The key characteristic of the industrial revolution was large-scale access to new dense sources of fossil energy not directly dependent on contemporary ecosystems, and hence not directly area dependent as hunter-gatherer or agricultural sociometabolism was. Hence humanity introduced a deep time dimension to its energy supply; rather than only being able exploit embodied solar energy captured by the biosphere in the preceding few years, it started exploiting fossil energy— embodied solar energy that was captured by the biosphere many millions of years ago and slowly accumulated and concentrated in the lithosphere.

From its initiation in north-west Europe, the industrial transition intensi- fied and spread across Europe and North America in the 19th century, and in the second half of the 20th century underwent further rapid expansion in much of Asia and parts of Africa and South America. The transition is still underway, and a substantial fraction of humanity still lives a predominantly agricultural lifestyle. This fraction is decreasing rapidly in the 21st century, most notably in and around the expanding cities and megacities of Asia, Latin America, and Africa.

It might be expected that abundant fossil energy might ease and displace pressure on the biosphere, by reducing pressure on fuelwood extraction, for example. In fact, the extra energy availability through industrialization also enables higher NPP extraction and material flows from the biosphere. For example, there is more metabolic energy available to do the work of extracting nitrogen from the air or phosphorus from rocks to make and transport fertilizer, to chop down forests to make new available land, or to build transportation networks linking remote regions of biosphere—such as the American West in the late 19th century or the Amazon frontier in the late 20th century—to centres of industrial metabolism. The availability of abundant fossil energy has generally led to increased exploitation of the biosphere (Ellis et al. 2010). There are interesting local exceptions; in mature industrial societies woodlands are no longer viewed as fuel or food reserves and have been much less intensively exploited or managed for fuel, and on marginal agricultural areas (such as the Eastern United States), agricultural lands have been abandoned to encroaching forests.

Two key features of industrial sociometabolism are (1) that biomass energy (whether for food or fuel) is only a small contributor to total sociometabolism compared to fossil fuels and other high-density energy sources, and (2) that there is sufficient surplus energy to build and maintain efficient transportation networks, meaning that population centres do not need to be co-located with food and energy production centres. Hence human sociometabolism and population density are decoupled from land area, enabling populations to both grow rapidly and be concentrated in towns, cities, and megacities, where human cultural and information exchange and partition of labour is much more efficient. As part of this transition humanity is moving from being an overwhelmingly rural creature to a predominantly urban one.

Table 8.1 shows the sociometabolism of a typical modern industrial society; England (not the whole United Kingdom) around 2010. Per capita energy consumption is here calculated as the sum of human biological metabolism (daily calorific intake) plus the energy obtained from all other sources (including fossil fuels and renewable energy sources). England has a sociometabolism of about 8,000 W per capita and a population density of 407 people km^{-2}. Hence its mean sociometabolism is 3.3 MW km^{-2}, approximately double that of the temperate forest ecosystem it has colonized and displaced (shown in Table 8.2). Biomass consumption makes up 10–30 per cent of this metabolism, or about 300–900 kW km^{-2} (Table 8.1).

Table 8.2 compares England with another advanced industrial society, the conterminous United States, which has higher per capita sociometabolism (about 12,000 W) but much lower population density (38 people km^{-2}). For this society its area-mean sociometabolism is 0.5 MW km^{-2}, about 15 per cent of the ecosystem metabolism (Table 8.2). However, this includes the thinly populated central regions; in areas such as California or the East Coast the sociometabolism exceeds the natural biological metabolism, as it does in England.

Table 8.2. The modern sociometabolism of high-density and low-density industrial societies (England and the conterminous USA) compared to natural biome metabolism

Region	Per capita sociometabolism[a]	Population density[b]	Per area metabolism	Total sociometabolism	Biometabolism[c]
England	8000 W	407 km^{-2}	3.3 MW km^{-2}	0.4 TW	0.2 TW
Conterminous USA	12000 W	38 km^{-2}	0.5 MW km^{-2}	4 TW	9 TW

Notes
[a] derived from Krausmann et al. (2008, table 1).
[b] ONS (2013: 2) and derived from USCB (2013).
[c] extracted from the dataset for specific countries in Field et al. (1998).
Source: author's calculation unless otherwise stated.

Globally, the mean per capita metabolism of humanity today is 2,200 W, reflecting the fact that much of humanity still lives a low-income, agricultural lifestyle.

A World of Resource-Consuming Giant Apes

Other animals have very limited sociometabolism beyond their basic bio-logical metabolism; their total energy appropriation is very close to their metabolic need, and they tend to forage from ecosystems rather than colonize and modify ecosystems through agriculture. How does our extraordinarily enhanced sociometabolism compare to the *biological metabolism* of other animals?

To answer this question we can draw on insights from the metabolic scaling theory of ecology (Brown et al. 2004), and in particular Kleiber's Law, the observation that animal metabolism, B, scaled with body mass, M, approximates as a three-quarter power law:

$$B = k.M^{3/4} \text{ or } B/M = k.M^{-1/4}$$

This implies that larger animals have slower metabolisms per unit of mass. An elephant uses much less energy per unit of mass than a mouse. The metabolic theory of ecology proposes that this decline in metabolic rate is associated with the constraints of the transport network (blood circulation, artery and vein architecture) in larger organisms, which limits maximum metabolic rates. The exact mechanism and value of the power coefficient (here three-quarters) is the subject of some debate (Price et al. 2012), but the broad observation remains valid, that metabolism scales with body mass as a power law that approximates to $M^{3/4}$.

Figure 8.1 plots physiological metabolism against body size for a number of representative animals, including humans. Elephants have larger biological

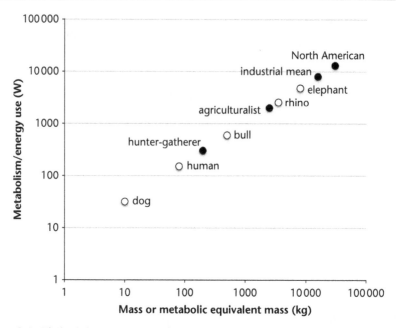

Figure 8.1. Kleiber's law re-examined

Note: Open circles plot biological metabolism against mass for a variety of animals. The solid circles plotting sociometabolism for humans represent various stages of history: hunter-gatherer, pre-industrial agrarian, and modern industrial (with a separate plot for North American).
Method: The values of animal biological metabolism are calculated by the application of Kleiber's Law to the average mass of adult animals (sourced from Wikipedia). The equivalent for human sociometabolism calculated from the values in Table 8.1 and the inverse application of Kleiber's Law.

Source: author.

metabolisms than humans, but per unit mass their metabolism is slower, and associated correlates of metabolic rate (such as heart rate) are smaller and timescales (gestation time, gut residence time, natural lifetime) are longer.

Next let us explore sociometabolism for various stages of human lifestyle, plotted on the same diagram (based on Table 8.1). In this case the position on the horizontal axis represents the metabolic equivalent mass: how large the human would have to be to have a biological metabolism of the same size as their sociometabolism. The average hunter-gatherer has a sociometabolism of 300 W, roughly three times their physiological metabolism. This includes direct extraction of food, and also use of materials for fuel. The pre-industrial agrarian human (18th-century agrarian Austria) has a sociometabolism of 2000 W, almost all derived from the colonization of the biosphere through agriculture. This is equivalent to the physiological metabolism of a 2.5-tonne rhino. A modern industrial human has a sociometabolism of 8000 W (or 12,000 W if a North American). This is equivalent to the physiological metabolism of a 10-tonne mammal (or a 15-tonne mammal in North America), about 1.4 to 2 times the mass of a large African elephant, the largest extant land mammal. A 10–15-tonne primate, such as King Kong, has existed only in literature (Moses 2005). For an alternative perspective on human impacts on the natural environment, imagine the United Kingdom as a landscape with 63 million 10-tonne apes roaming the countryside, or the United States as a landscape with 310 million 15-tonne King Kongs!

Our access to (primarily) fossil energy has enabled us to sustain exceptional levels of resource consumption and exceptional population densities. We are something new in the metabolic history of this planet; a hypersocial mega-faunal mammal, half-ape and half-ant. It is inevitable that such an organism has major impacts on the functions and metabolism of the wider planet.

A Timeline of Global Sociometabolism

We can multiple the per capita consumption rates of different types of human society by global population estimates to estimate the global socio-metabolism of humanity (Haberl 2006; Haberl et al. 2011). Prior to the Neo-lithic revolution, the total metabolism of humanity was about 300–3000 MW (0.0003–0.003 TW). This compares with global terrestrial GPP of 150 TW, or NPP of 75 TW, and was thus five to six orders of magnitude smaller than terrestrial ecosystem metabolism (Table 8.3).

Following the Neolithic revolution and the colonization of ecosystems, human sociometabolism gradually grew from about 0.3 TW in the early Neolithic (10,000 years ago), to about 3 TW just prior to the industrial revo-lution; an increase of between three and four orders of magnitude over pre-agricultural metabolism, but still only 2 per cent of global terrestrial GPP (Table 8.3). (Regionally, this fraction could be much larger.)

The industrial transition, which is far from complete for two-thirds of humanity, has thus far increased human sociometabolism to about 25 TW (Haberl 2006), about 17 per cent of potential terrestrial GPP or 34 per cent of NPP[3] (Table 8.3). Of this total metabolism, around 50 per cent is still powered by the biosphere by material flows of biomass food and energy. The remaining 50 per cent is powered by other sources, and overwhelming by fossil fuels (Haberl 2006). Hence currently it is the ability of humanity to exploit the energy that was locked up in the deep past by the biosphere (a fourth, temporal dimension of energy exploitation) that has powered the current

---

[3] Brown et al. (2011) estimated a smaller number for global total human sociometabolism of 17 TW. However, for material flows they only considered human biological metabolism, not including other material flows such as the metabolism of domesticated animals or biomass appropriation for fuel. Hence a higher number such as 25 TW is more plausible. These higher estimates modified from Brown et al. are the basis of the calculations in this section and the section entitled 'The Metabolism of the 21st Century'.

Table 8.3. Global human sociometabolism in comparison to the metabolism of the land biosphere, in various sociometabolic stages and under alternative scenarios for 2050

Period	Global metabolism	Percent of land biosphere metabolism	Human population	Biomass-derived metabolism
Pre-agricultural	0.0003–0.003 TW	2–20 × 10–4%		0.0003–0.003 TW
Pre-industrial	3 TW	2%		3 TW
Modern	25 TW	17%	7 billion	13 TW
2050 (WEC/UNDP)	48 TW	32%	9.3 billion	20 TW
2050 'Global US'	180 TW	120%	9.3 billion	
2050 'Global China'	60 TW	40%	9.3 billion	

Note: The derivation of the final three rows is explained in the main text.
Source: first three rows derived from Haberl (2006) and Haberl et al. (2011).

rapid expansion of human sociometabolism. The 13 TW of metabolism that come directly from biomass are equal to 22 per cent of terrestrial biomass production. The remainder of the sociometabolism is overwhelming powered by fossil fuels.

The total sociometabolism of the conterminous United States is about 4 TW (about 19 per cent of which is biomass material flow). The total natural metabolism (GPP) of the same area is about 9 TW (Table 8.2). For England, the total sociometabolism is around 0.4 TW, and the total natural metabolism is around 0.2 TW—hence in England sociometabolism already dominates over natural metabolism.

The Metabolism of the 21st Century

Now let us examine the 21st-century world. How does contemporary socio-metabolism compare with the current metabolism of the terrestrial biosphere? I focus on the land biosphere, as human appropriation of energy from the biosphere is still overwhelmingly from land, despite intensive harvesting of ocean fisheries. As we have seen, the total photosynthetic energy use of the land biosphere (GPP) is about 150 TW, and the total rate of energy fixation in plant biomass (NPP) is about 75 TW. Hence current human sociometabolism is equivalent to 11 per cent of terrestrial photosynthesis, or 22 per cent of NPP. For comparison, the Amazon rainforest, which amounts to about half of the world's rainforests, accounts for approximately 17 per cent of global photosynthesis (Malhi 2012), or 25 TW of metabolic energy. Human socio-metabolism is approaching that of the entire Amazon rainforest biome, the most biologically productive region of the land biosphere.

The figure of human metabolism accounting for 11 per cent of global terrestrial metabolism may appear reassuringly small, but in fact it is astonishing that a single vertebrate species has a total metabolism that approaches that of global vegetation. In natural ecosystems (with the exception of heavily grazed grasslands) all vertebrates have typically accounted for much less than 1 per cent of metabolic activity. As calculated above, in densely populated and industrialized regions such as Western Europe or Eastern China, human sociometabolism already greatly exceeds pre-existing or remnant natural metabolism.

Moreover, there is every indication that, if possible, human sociometabolic activity will increase rapidly this century if energy and resource supply limitations can be met. Using a medium World Energy Council energy use scenario, and a medium United Nations Population Division scenario of 9.3 billion people, human sociometabolism is on course to reach 48 TW by 2050 (Haberl 2006: 94), 32 per cent of terrestrial GPP and 64 per cent of NPP (Table 8.3). The biomass-derived component of metabolism is expected to rise to around 20 TW, or 28 per cent of terrestrial NPP (Table 8.3). The human superorganism would be consuming one third of the biological production of the land surface.

There are strong correlates between energy use and standard of living, and it is hard to conceive of increasing the standards of living of the world's population without a commensurate increase in energy use. To raise the global population of 6.6 billion[4] to the standard of living of the United States would require an increase of global energy consumption from 25 to 113 TW (as in Brown et al. 2011, but modified to the higher estimate of contemporary sociometabolism calculated here), equal to 1.5 times all of terrestrial NPP or 75 per cent of terrestrial photosynthesis. For a projected global population of 9.5 billion in 2050, maintaining a lifestyle equivalent to the current United States lifestyle would require 180 TW, seven times current global energy use, and 1.2 times the total metabolism of the terrestrial biosphere. Even a global population at the current mean Chinese standards of living would require 60 TW, 2.5 times current global energy consumption and 40 per cent of total terrestrial metabolism.

Urban metabolism

It is insightful to explore the current human socio-economic metabolism in the context of urban areas. Just as the Neolithic revolution heralded the transformation of our species from a nomadic species to a predominantly small settlement (village) species, the industrial revolution heralded the

---

[4] The projection cited here is based on 2006 data. World population reached 6.7 billion in mid 2007, and continues to expand well beyond the 7 billion mark.

transformation to a predominantly large settlement (urban) species. The facts that our energy supply is no longer tied to immediately accessible land area, and that our abundance of energy has enabled development of efficient transportation and distribution networks have made it possible for *Homo sapiens* to live in high density urban areas.

In the early 21st century we are in the full fury of this transition: over 50 per cent of the human population is now urban and this proportion is expected to approach 70 per cent by 2050 (UN-DESA 2012). For most continents, urban dwellers already exceed 70 per cent of the total population, and in the two less urban continents (Asia and Africa) the urban proportions are around 39 to 45 per cent and are increasing at 2 to 4 per cent per decade (UN-DESA 2012). This trend is not just in the high-profile megacities, but in numerous smaller towns and cities. We are increasingly a hypersocial species living in colonies of hundreds of thousands to millions of individuals, akin to social insects (Wilson 2012). How does the metabolism of our cities compare to that of the social insects, say in a termite colony?

First, let us consider social insect colonies. Rather surprisingly, social insect colonies seem to follow Kleiber's Law, in an extrapolation of the metabolism of individual insects (Hou et al. 2010). In terms of metabolic physiology, a termite colony behaves much like a single gigantic termite of equivalent size. This means that the metabolism per unit mass of termite (or per individual termite) is slower in a large colony than in a small one. Quite why this happens remains a puzzle, but may be associated with the decreased amount of foraging required per individual in a large termite colony.

Now let us turn to social *Homo sapiens* colonies, in the form of cities. Do towns or cities also 'slow down' (per individual human) as they get larger? As anyone from the hinterland who spends a day in London, New York, São Paulo, Lagos, Mumbai, or Tokyo can testify, they most certainly do not. Bettencourt et al. (2007) compiled data of various measures of activity in cities worldwide. They found that many metrics scaled superlinearly with city size (beta > 1). This included (most amusingly) the rate at which people walk, but also other metrics such as wages, income, gross domestic product, bank deposits, and rates of invention. All of these are approximate metrics of sociometabolism.

A number of metrics associated directly with population scaled isometrically with city size (beta ~1), including the number of jobs, number of houses, and consumption of water. These are metrics that broadly track individual human needs, and hence track human population. Other metrics associated with infrastructure networks (for example, number of fuel stations, length of electrical cables, total road surface) scale sublinearly (beta < 1). These metrics show economies of scale in energy transport, similar to individual organisms and termite colonies.

So, unlike social insects, social humans become more active the bigger their colony gets, because of the intensified opportunities of knowledge exchange, innovation, and efficient partition of labour. Rather than functioning like termite colonies, human cities are more akin to stars, which burn more fiercely the larger they get (Bettencourt 2013). Cities are immense social reactors for humanity, burning more fiercely with activity and innovation the larger their human mix.

Growth driven by linear scaling is exponential (Bettencourt et al. 2007). Hence insect megacolonies show sub-exponential growth in metabolism over time; human megacolonies show superexponential growth. Superexponential growth has its challenges, though—under fixed background conditions it is impossible to sustain because ultimately the resources needed to sustain the city's sociometabolim become limited (that is, the city reaches environmental carrying capacity—its environment becomes 'full'), leading to possible metabolic collapse.

How have cities circumvented this? Bettencourt et al. (2007) suggest that innovation is the key. Innovation in the generation, extraction, transportation, and use of socio-metabolic energy and other resources avoids resource collapse. Cities are founts of local innovation, and also now increasingly connected to exchange innovation at a global scale. Each innovation staves off resource collapse, but also points to the next resource limitation. Bettencourt et al. (2007) illustrate this by examining time series data of New York City's rate of population growth, and show periods of increased and decreased growth that match this model. The innovation can be technical, but can also come in the form of governance, such as well-organized public transport systems.

Summary and Conclusions: An Anthropocene Perspective

In this chapter I have argued that a socio-metabolic perspective can provide valuable insights into the question 'is our planet full?'. In the sense that our species' metabolism is coming to dominate and overwhelm the natural background metabolism of the planet, the answer to that question is an undeniable 'yes'. This does not mean that it cannot or will not be filled even more, but that such fullness is having inevitable consequences on all aspects of planetary and biosphere function.

Most of the current range of environmental challenges can be traced back to the size of our sociometabolism relative to that of the local ecosystem or the planet as a whole, from resource overconsumption (overfishing, habitat loss, biodiversity loss, depletion in phosphorus) to excessive metabolic waste production (atmospheric pollution and climate change, excess nitrogen, waste-disposal capacity). Hence many of the current challenges of sustainability can be viewed through the lens of energetic metabolism. How do we reduce carbon dioxide waste by-products while maintaining the work done by our global metabolism? How do we maintain the biomass supply our metabolism requires without other species losing habitat and living space? Even with a potential future cheap and non-polluting energy supply (cheap solar, or nuclear fusion) can we continue to increase our sociometabolism indefinitely, or will limits to other material sources (food biomass, or phosphorus) constrain it? And what are the consequences for the other denizens of the biosphere?

Humanity, this hyperactive, hypersocial, megafaunal ape, has a heavy impact on the planet, fundamentally powered by a fossil fuel sociometabolism that provides us with abundant energy to transform the planet. Even if our sociometabolism shifts from fossil fuels to some form of energy with less problematic waste products, the other consequences of our active ability to consume and transform the planet remain.

The preceding examination of urban areas is a good analogy for our human predicament as a whole (not least because humanity has become more and more urban, and will become overwhelmingly urban over the course of the 21st century). Modern human history is a constant race between resource overconsumption and innovation. As humans aggregate in the social reactors that are cities and communicate with ever-greater intensity through planet-spanning telecommunications, and as greater numbers of human minds become embedded in this planet-spanning communications network, the pace of innovation has managed to keep pace with the pace of resource consumption, leading to ever-increasing global sociometabolism that in many regions greatly exceeds the metabolism of the natural biosphere. As global sociometabolism approaches the total biological metabolism of the land surface biosphere, will innovation be able to keep winning the race against resource overconsumption? And can this state of continuous dynamic instability be sustained indefinitely, or will a new stable state of resource use be attained? If the latter is even possible, what would it look like?

The innovations that our urbanized and interconnected species can bring to bear on these challenges are not only technological; they can also be innovations in governance and administration, as we continually seek new ways to self organize our local, regional, and global polity to effectively utilize our shared and limited resources, to limit our impacts on fellow species, and to meet the challenge of collectively managing our global resources. A great challenge of our time is that the size and global reach of our sociometabolism has led to resource-limitation and waste-production challenges at a global scale—a scale at which our existing governance structures struggle to act effectively. One obvious example is the slow pace of progress to a global agreement for action on climate change, despite the rapid rise of greenhouse gases in the atmosphere that is apparent to (almost) all.

Is there a limit to the size of global human sociometabolism? Can we determine some sort of planetary boundary for sociometabolism that to some extent integrates several existing proposed planetary boundaries? The answer is not clear. One aspect that is likely to be limited is the fraction of metabolism (currently 50 per cent of our total sociometabolism) linked to material resource flow, as it is difficult to change the ability of the biosphere to increase its supply of such resources while at the same time providing some resources and space for its other inhabitants and maintaining overall function and stability. The portion of sociometabolism not directly linked to biosphere material resource flow (most of industrial energy) is not so strongly constrained by the ability of the biosphere to supply, and any planetary boundary in sociometabolism needs to be considered in terms of its impacts on the biosphere, atmosphere, and hydrosphere, whether through waste products (especially in the case of fossil fuels) or simply through the effects of the sheer number and activity of high-energy industrial humans in altering the planet's surface and biospheric function.

As a major 'force of Nature' humanity has come to define the Anthropocene. The human expansion and domination of the Earth system over the past 10,000 years, albeit fleetingly recent in the 4.6 billion year context of Earth history, represents a major transition in the nature of life on Earth, comparable energetically to the colonization of land by plants. A major challenge of our time is to innovate and develop the global governance structures to minimize the overexploitation and degradation of the global commons, and to avoid critical and dangerous thresholds in the biosphere and atmosphere, while at the same time maintaining the creativity and ability of humanity to innovate in both the social and technological spheres. The innovations can be technological, but they can also be innovations in governance, as we continually seek new ways to self organize our global polity to effectively govern our shared and limited resources, to limit our impacts on fellow species, and to meet the challenge of collectively managing the Anthropocene.

References

Bala, G., Caldeira, K., Wickett, M., Phillips, T. J., Lobell, D. B., Delire, C., and Mirin, A. (2007). 'Combined Climate and Carbon-Cycle Effects of Large-Scale Deforestation', *Proceedings of the National Academy of Sciences*, 104(16): 6550–5.

Barnosky, A. D. (2008). 'Megafauna Biomass Tradeoff as a Driver of Quaternary and Future Extinctions', *Proceedings of the National Academy of Sciences*, 105: 11543–8.

Barnosky, A. D., Koch, P. L., Feranec, R. S., Wing, S. L., and Shabel, A. B. (2004). 'Assessing the Causes of Late Pleistocene Extinctions on the Continents', *Science*, 306: 70–5.

Bettencourt, L. M. A. (2013). 'The Origin of Scaling in Cities', *Science*, 240, 1438–41.

Bettencourt, L. M. A., Lobo, J., Helbing, D., Kuhnert, C., and West, G. B. (2007). 'Growth, Innovation, Scaling, and the Pace of Life in Cities', *Proceedings of the National Academy of Sciences*, 104: 7301–6.

Bouckaert, R., Lemey, P., Dunn, M., Greenhill, S. J., Alekseyenko, A. V., Drummond, A. J., Gray, R. D., Suchard, M. A., and Atkinson, Q. D. (2012). 'Mapping the Origins and Expansion of the Indo-European Language Family', *Science*, 337: 957–60.

Brodribb, T. J. and Feild, T. S. (2010). 'Leaf Hydraulic Evolution Led a Surge in Leaf Photosynthetic Capacity During Early Angiosperm Diversification', *Ecology Letters*, 13: 175–83.

Brown, J. H., Burnside, W. R., Davidson, A. D., DeLong, J. P., Dunn, W. C., Hamilton, M., Mercado-Silva, N., Nekola, J. C., Okie, J. G., Woodruff, W. H., and Zuo, W. Y. (2011). 'Energetic Limits to Economic Growth', *Bioscience*, 61: 19–26.

Brown, J. H., Gillooly, J. F., Allen, A. P., Savage, V. M., and West, G. B. (2004). 'Toward a Metabolic Theory of Ecology', *Ecology*, 85: 1771–89.

Burnside, W. R., Brown, J. H., Burger, O., Hamilton, M. J., Moses, M., and Bettencourt, L. M. A. (2012). 'Human Macroecology: Linking Pattern and Process in Big-Picture Human Ecology', *Biological Reviews*, 87: 194–208.

Curnoe, D., Xueping, J., Herries, A. I. R., Kanning, B., Taçon, P. S. C., Zhende, B., Fink, D., Yunsheng, Z., Hellstrom, J., Yun, L., Cassis, G., Bing, S., Wroe, S., Shi, H., Parr, W. C. H., Shengmin, H., and Rogers, N. (2012). 'Human Remains from the Pleistocene-Holocene Transition of Southwest China Suggest a Complex Evolutionary History for East Asians', *PLoS ONE*, 7(3): e31918.

Diamond, J. (2002). 'Evolution, Consequences and Future of Plant and Animal Domestication', *Nature*, 418: 700–7.

Doughty, C. E., Wolf, A., and Field, C. B. (2010). 'Biophysical Feedbacks Between the Pleistocene Megafauna Extinction and Climate: The first Human-Induced Global Warming?' *Geophysical Research Letters*, 37(15): L15703.

Doughty, C. E., Wolf, A., and Malhi, Y. (2013). 'The Legacy of Pleistocene Megafaunal Extinctions on Nutrient Distribution in Amazonia', *Nature Geoscience*, 6: 761–4.

Ellis, E. C., Goldewijk, K. K., Siebert, S., Lightman, D., and Ramankutty, N. (2010). 'Anthropogenic Transformation of the Biomes, 1700 to 2000', *Global Ecology and Biogeography*, 19: 589–606.

Field, C. B., Behrenfeld, M. J., Randerson, J. T., and Falkowski, P. (1998). 'Primary Production of the Biosphere: Integrating Terrestrial and Oceanic Components', *Science*, 281: 237–40.

Fischer-Kowalski, M. and Haberl, H. (1998). 'Sustainable Development: Socio-Economic Metabolism and Colonization of Nature', *International Social Science Journal*, 50(158): 573–87.

Goldin, I., Cameron, G., and Balarajan, M. (2011). *Exceptional People: How Migration Shaped Our World and Will Define Our Future.* Princeton, NJ: Princeton University Press.

Haberl, H. (2006). 'The Global Socioeconomic Energetic Metabolism as a Sustainability Problem', *Energy*, 31: 87–99.

Haberl, H., Erb, K. H., Krausmann, F., Gaube, V., Bondeau, A., Plutzar, C., Gingrich, S., Lucht, W., and Fischer-Kowalski, M. (2007). 'Quantifying and Mapping the Human Appropriation of Net Primary Production in Earth's Terrestrial Ecosystems', *Proceedings of the National Academy of Sciences*, 104, 12942–5.

Haberl, H., Fischer-Kowalski, M., Krausmann, F., Martinez-Alier, J., and Winiwarter, V. (2011). 'A Socio-Metabolic Transition Towards Sustainability? Challenges for Another Great Transformation', *Sustainable Development*, 19: 1–14.

Hou, C., Kaspari, M., Zanden, H. B. V., and Gillooly, J. F. (2010). 'Energetic Basis of Colonial Living in Social Insects', *Proceedings of the National Academy of Sciences*, 107: 3634–8.

Krause, J., Fu, Q., Good, J. M., Viola, B., Shunkov, M. V., Derevianko, A. P., and Pääbo, S. (2010), 'The Complete Mitochondrial DNA Genome of an Unknown Hominin from Southern Siberia', *Nature*, 464(7290): 894–7.

Krausmann, F., Fischer-Kowalski, M., Schandl, H., and Eisenmenger, N. (2008). 'The Global Sociometabolic Transition', *Journal of Industrial Ecology*, 12(5–6): 637–56.

Larsen, C. S. (1995). 'Biological Changes in Human Populations with Agriculture', *Annual Review of Anthropology*, 24: 185–213.

Malhi, Y. (2012). 'The Productivity, Metabolism and Carbon Cycle of Tropical Forest Vegetation', *Journal of Ecology*, 100(1): 65–75.

Malhi, Y., Baldocchi, D. D., and Jarvis, P. G. (1999). 'The Carbon Balance of Tropical, Temperate and Boreal Forests', *Plant Cell and Environment*, 22: 715–40.

Moses, M. E. (2005). *Metabolic Scaling from Individuals to Societies*. Ph.D. Thesis, University of New Mexico.

ONS (2013). 'Population and Household Estimates for the United Kingdom, March 2011', Statistical Bulletin, 21 March. Newport: Office for National Statistics. Last accessed 31 August 2013. <http://www.ons.gov.uk/ons/dcp171778_304116.pdf>.

Price, C. A., Weitz, J. S., Savage, V. M., Stegen, J., Clarke, A., Coomes, D. A., Dodds, P. S., Etienne, R. S., Kerkhoff, A. J., McCulloh, K., Niklas, K. J., Olff, H., and Swenson, N. G. (2012). 'Testing the Metabolic Theory of Ecology', *Ecology Letters*, 15, 1465–74.

Roy, J. and Saugier, B. (2001). 'Terrestrial Primary Productivity: Definitions and Milestones' in J. Roy, M. A. Mooney, and B. Saugier (eds), *Terrestrial Global Productivity*. San Diego, USA: Academic Press, pp. 1–6.

Rule, S., Brook, B. W., Haberle, S. G., Turney, C. S. M., Kershaw, A. P., and Johnson, C. N. (2012). 'The Aftermath of Megafaunal Extinction: Ecosystem Transformation in Pleistocene Australia', *Science*, 335: 1483–6.

UN-DESA (2012). *World Population Prospects: The 2011 Revision*. New York: United Nations, Department of Economic and Social Affairs, Population Division.

USCB (2013). *United States Census, 2010*. Washington, DC: United States Census Bureau. Last accessed 29 August 2013. <http://www.census.gov/>.

Wilson, E. O. (2012). *The Social Conquest of Earth*. New York: Liveright Publishing Corporation.

9

Safe, Effective, and Affordable Health Care for a Bulging Population

Robyn Norton

Currently, most people in the world do not have access to safe, effective, and affordable health care. However, the provision of such care is not only an aspiration, but an expectation of increasing numbers of the world's population, especially for the growing middle class in both low- and middle-income countries. If these expectations are to be met, and indeed if safe, effective, and affordable health care is to be extended to the poorest, then significant changes will be required in the way in which health care is currently organized.

With further population growth and continued increasing expectations of quality health care, if these changes are not made, governments will be challenged in their ability to meet these demands, and potentially access to health care or lack of access may well pose a security risk. Additionally, if these changes are not made, then fewer people are likely to have access to quality health care, life expectancy may well decrease in some countries and for some populations, the numbers living with disability may increase, and overall quality of life may deteriorate.

In the first part of this chapter, the rationale for suggesting that current health-care systems are unable to meet current and future demands is outlined. Evidence is provided to show how changing lifestyles and behaviours have and will continue to contribute to significant changes in the global patterns of disease and disability. Data are also provided on the utilization and costs of current health care and the potentially catastrophic cost implications of further-increased demand for services.[1]

---

[1] The focus of this chapter is on the increasing importance of non-communicable disease in rich and poor countries alike. The impact of infectious diseases such as malaria, tuberculosis, and HIV/AIDS—and their implications for health-care systems—has been discussed elsewhere (for example, WHO 1999).

In the second half of the chapter, a positive way forward is outlined. New models of health-care delivery, such that a health-care crisis can be averted and the provision of universal health care can be facilitated, are proposed. Examples of the development and evaluation of these new models within low-income and middle-income settings are provided. The challenges and potential solutions to implementing these models within high-income settings are also discussed. In closing, the rationale and necessity to agree on a bold vision and commitment to making substantial changes to existing health-care systems, as opposed to incremental changes, is championed.

The Changing Health-care Landscape: an Overview, with Evidence

Changes in economic growth, urbanization, and ageing

Put simply, more people means more people wanting to access health care. However, population growth alone has not been the driver of increased health-care demand. Population growth has been accompanied by changes in economic growth, urbanization, and ageing, each of which, both separately and collectively, is likely to have contributed to this increasing demand.

While global population growth has been significant in the past century, such growth is eclipsed by the profound size and increase in economic growth, and while the level of growth has been uneven across different countries and regions of the world, GDP per capita has increased in all countries (IMF 2000). With increased wealth and purchasing power, not only is there an expectation from individuals that they can access and pay for better health care, but their greater purchasing power means they can, for example, buy and eat more food and purchase a range of consumer goods that make their lives more comfortable, such as motor vehicles, refrigerators, and televisions.

Accompanying economic growth has been a significant increase in levels of urbanization across the world, no doubt fuelled in large part by the desire of rural residents to also participate in the health, education, and wealth being generated by those living in cities. As a consequence, more than 50 per cent of the world's population now lives in urban environments (WHO and UN-HABITAT 2010). In Asia, for example, growth in GDP per capita has increased twofold over the past 50 years and during this period the proportion of the population living in urban environments has increased from less than 5 per cent in 1960 to almost 40 per cent in 2005 (UN-HABITAT 2010). While urbanization is associated with many positive changes, including increased access to health services, it is also associated with increased access to 'fast foods', decreased access to environments that facilitate physical activity, and increasing levels of motorization (numbers of vehicles per head of population) (WHO and UN-HABITAT 2010).

Equally, profound changes have occurred in the past century in the numbers in the population living to older age. Since 1970, life expectancy has increased globally from 56.4 years to 67.5 years for males and from 61.2 years to 73.3 years for females (Wang et al. 2012). Continuing increases are predicted over the next 40 years and particularly notable are the huge predicted increases in the numbers of individuals over the age of 80 years, with the estimates for China suggesting an increase from about 10 million older individuals in 2000 to over 100 million in 2050 (Perls 2009). It is perhaps not surprising, then, that this demographic change alone has led to increased demand for health services, given the greater health-care needs of older people, in combination with the greater availability of treatment options to manage their health-care conditions.

While there is debate about the causal relationship between economic growth, urbanization, and ageing, and the specific contributions of each, collectively these factors have had and are likely to continue to have a major impact on population health behaviours and conditions, on patterns of death and disability, and also on expectations of access to health care and the costs of such health care. The experiences of high-income countries, who have led these changes in the last century, provide some insights into what might occur in the near future in the large emerging market populations, including China and India. However, the rapid pace of transition in these countries, combined with their very large populations, suggests that the future impact of these changes may be even more dramatic than observed previously.

Changes in health behaviours and conditions

Of particular relevance to the increased demand for health-care services globally is the increasingly significant impact of major changes in health behaviours and conditions related to the growth in non-communicable diseases. In the following section, some example behaviours and conditions illustrate the profound changes that have been occurring and are likely to drive health-care demand in the coming years.

TOBACCO CONSUMPTION

One of the most significant contributors to the global disease burden is the use of tobacco products (Lim et al. 2012). Currently the burden of disease and the consumption of tobacco are greatest in high-income countries (accounting for 18 per cent of total deaths), followed by middle-income countries (11 per cent of deaths) and low-income countries (4 per cent of deaths) (WHO 2009). However, rates of tobacco use have declined significantly in high-income countries in recent years as the impact of various tobacco-control strategies take effect. By comparison, tobacco use is increasing dramatically in middle-income and low-income countries, such that the WHO is predicting that tobacco use could cause up to a billion premature deaths in the 21st century (WHO 2011).

Recent findings from the Global Adult Tobacco Survey identify several factors which in combination suggest that in the coming years, without urgent action, these predictions will become a reality. Of the estimated 852 million smokers worldwide, already 301 million (35 per cent) are in China and 225 million (26 per cent) are in India (Giovino et al. 2012). While globally smoking rates are lower in men than women, women are increasingly starting to smoke at equivalent ages to men, and while smoking cessation is increasing in high-income countries, in most low- and middle-income countries cessation rates are very low.

DIETARY INTAKE

Over the past few decades there has been a dramatic global 'nutrition transition' in terms of the amount and types of foods that are consumed, and while until recently this was perceived predominantly as a 'Western' phenomenon, increasing evidence shows that the same changes are occurring in low- and middle-income countries (Popkin, Adair, and Ng 2012). In essence this transition includes increases in the consumption of refined carbohydrates, added sugars (especially in beverages), fats, and animal-source foods, in combination with decreases in the consumption of fruit and vegetables, nuts, seeds, and grains.

Evidence that this transition is occurring in low- and middle-income settings is exemplified by recent research examining temporal trends in the food consumption of children and adolescents in China between 1991 and 2009, as identified through the China Health and Nutrition Surveys. Over this period, daily fat intake has increased substantially, such that the proportion of children and adolescents consuming a diet with more than 30 per cent of energy from fat has increased from 20 per cent to 49 per cent (Cui and Dibley 2012). Notably, the largest changes were observed in low-income urban households and high-income rural households, suggesting that these trends are moving in a very similar direction to that observed in high-income countries.

PHYSICAL ACTIVITY

Worldwide, almost a third of the adult population is defined as being physically inactive, with higher levels of physical inactivity being observed in high-income countries compared with low- and middle-income countries (Hallal et al. 2012). Physical activity is defined as the composite of leisure-time physical activity (such as engagement in sports), work-related physical activity, physical activity associated with housework, and transport-related activity (such as walking to and from work). While levels of leisure-time activity are higher in high-income countries, adults in high-income countries have lower levels of occupational, household, and transport related activity (Hallal et al. 2012). Decreases in physical activity in high-income countries over the past few decades are purported to be associated with increasing urbanization, mechanization, and motorization—and in particular the introduction of technological developments aimed at decreasing the amount of physical labour required to accomplish tasks (Hallal et al. 2012).

While currently greater levels of physical inactivity are observed in high-income compared with low-income countries, there is growing concern that within a very short period this situation might be reversed. The potential impact of urbanization on physical activity levels in low-income countries is illustrated by findings from the *Indian Migration Study*, which examined the relationship between rural-to-urban migration and physical activity. In this study with a population of more than 6,000 individuals, levels of physical activity were low across all population groups, suggesting that already they were leading 'sedentary/lightly active lifestyles', with women being less active than men (Sullivan et al. 2011). Physical activity levels were highest in rural residents, whereas migrant and urban residents had similarly lower levels of activity. Conversely, levels of sedentary behaviour and television viewing were higher and comparable in migrant and urban residents, and significantly higher than in rural populations. With projected rises in the proportion of Indians living in urban settings, from 26 per cent in 1991 to 40 per cent in 2030 (Sankhe et al. 2010), these findings suggest that overall levels of physical activity in the Indian population are likely to decrease dramatically over a very short period of time.

OVERWEIGHT AND OBESITY
Since the 1970s the global prevalence of overweight and obesity has increased substantially, driven by the combination of changes in dietary intake and reduced physical activity. By 2008, an estimated 1.46 billion adults worldwide were defined as being overweight (with a body mass index or BMI $> 25 \text{kg/m}^2$) and 502 million were defined as being obese (BMI $> 30 \text{kg/m}^2$) (Finucane et al. 2011). Additionally, 170 million children and adolescents (< 18 years) were defined as being overweight or obese, with up to 25 per cent of children in some countries falling into these categories (Swinburn et al. 2011).

While the increased prevalence of overweight and obesity was initially led by high-income countries, rapid increases in the prevalence of overweight and obesity have now been documented in many low-income and middle-income countries (Popkin, Adair, and Ng 2012). In high-income countries, the highest levels of overweight and obesity are observed in poorer communities and households, whereas in low-income and middle-income countries, rates are highest among the urban affluent (Swinburn et al. 2011). However, more and more reports are emerging showing that rates are increasing among children and adolescents as well as in rural communities. For example, a meta-analysis from China, which examined trends in overweight and obese children and adolescents between 1981 and 2010, showed increases from 1.8 per cent and 0.4 per cent respectively in 1981–1985 to 13.1 per cent and 7.5 per cent in 2006–2010 (Yu et al. 2012). The prevalence of overweight and obesity was higher in boys than girls and higher in urban compared with rural areas. Alarmingly, the highest rates of increase were seen among toddlers.

Changes in patterns of death and disability

The dramatic global changes observed in the past century—and particularly in the last fifty years—in economic growth and urbanization have, overall, had a major positive impact on human health, as evidenced by the fact that the majority of the world's population are living longer and arguably more healthy lives. However, these changes have also been accompanied by significant transformations in health behaviours and conditions, as illustrated by the examples above, which have not surprisingly contributed to major shifts in the global patterns of death and disability.

In the early 20th century, infectious diseases, nutritional deficiencies, and maternal and perinatal conditions were the predominant causes of death and disability. By the beginning of the 21st century, while such conditions still accounted for about 50 per cent of deaths in low-income countries, they accounted for less than 20 per cent of deaths in middle-income countries and less than 10 per cent of deaths in high-income countries (Mathers and Loncar 2006). The most recent findings from the Global Burden of Disease (GBD) study show a continuing decline in the significance of such conditions, from 34 per cent of total global mortality in 1990 to 25 per cent in 2010 (Lozano et al. 2012).

More specifically, deaths from these causes have been overtaken by deaths from non-communicable diseases, and in 2010 non-communicable diseases accounted for two of every three deaths in the world (Lozano et al. 2012). In particular, ischaemic heart disease and stroke accounted for 25 per cent of deaths (the same number of deaths as from all infectious diseases, nutritional deficiencies, and maternal and perinatal conditions), and cancer accounted for 15 per cent. Non-communicable diseases accounted for five of the leading ten causes of diseases, and while overall communicable diseases decreased in the rankings, non-communicable diseases increased (Table 9.1).

While in part the predominance of non-communicable diseases reflects the growing numbers of older people dying from these conditions, calculations of

169

Table 9.1. The ten leading causes of death in 1990 and 2010

Cause of death	Classification of cause of death[a]	1990 ranking	2010 ranking	Direction of change
Ischaemic heart disease	II	1	1	–
Stroke	II	2	2	–
Chronic obstructive pulmonary disease	II	4	3	↑
Lower respiratory infections	I	3	4	↓
Lung cancer	II	8	5	↑
HIV/AIDS	I	35	6	↑
Diarrhoea	I	5	7	↓
Road injuries	III	10	8	↑
Diabetes	II	15	9	↑
Tuberculosis	I	6	10	↓

[a] Group I = communicable, maternal, perinatal, and nutritional conditions; Group II = non-communicable diseases; and Group III = injuries.

Source: adapted from Lozano et al. (2012: 2113).

the amount of life lost due to premature mortality (years of life lost or YLLs), also show the predominance and increasing significance of non-communicable diseases. The proportion of YLLs from non-communicable diseases increased from 33 per cent in 1990 to 43 per cent in 2010, and in 2010 ischaemic heart disease was the leading cause of YLLs (whereas in 1990, lower respiratory infections were the leading cause of YLLs) (Lozano et al. 2012). Several additional cause-specific non-communicable diseases increased in importance over this period, including stroke, lung cancer, liver cirrhosis, diabetes, liver cancer, and chronic kidney disease.

Until the publication of the GBD study few data were available on the global burden of disability, and as a consequence limited information was available on the burden of ill health associated with conditions that primarily cause ill health but not death—conditions which nevertheless have a potentially significant impact on health-care utilization and costs. With the launch of the first GBD study in 1990, and subsequent analyses of data for 2000 and 2010, recent trends in disability—measured in terms of years lived with disability (YLD)—can be determined. Over the past 20 years, the number of YLDs has increased by 33 per cent, largely driven by increases in population growth and to a lesser degree by increases in population ageing (Vos et al. 2012). Non-communicable diseases account for the largest proportion of YLDs, increasing from 75 per cent in 1990 to 79 per cent in 2010, with 21 of the 25 leading causes being non-communicable diseases (up from 19 of 25 in 1990). The main cause-specific contributors to global YLDs were mental and behavioural

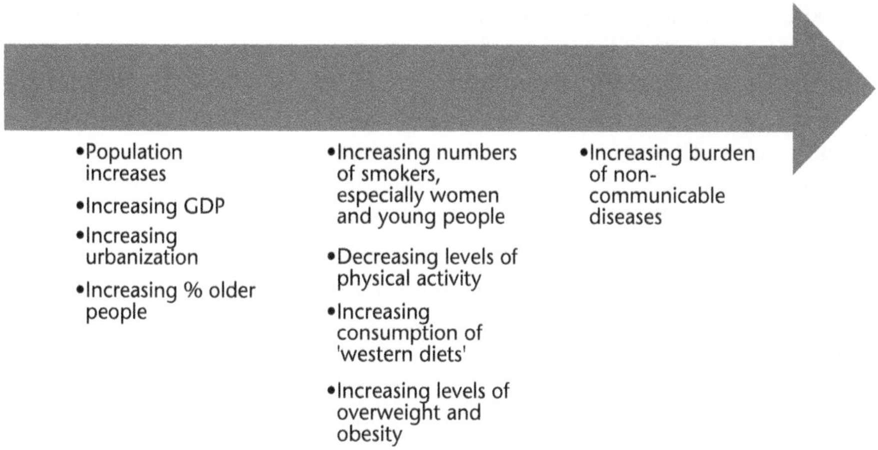

- •Population increases
- •Increasing GDP
- •Increasing urbanization
- •Increasing % older people

- •Increasing numbers of smokers, especially women and young people
- •Decreasing levels of physical activity
- •Increasing consumption of 'western diets'
- •Increasing levels of overweight and obesity

- •Increasing burden of non-communicable diseases

Figure 9.1. Key drivers in the emerging economies of projected further increases in non-communicable diseases

Source: author.

disorders, musculoskeletal disorders (low back pain was the leading cause of YLDs), and diabetes.

Projections about the future burden of death and disability, based on the *Global Burden of Disease 2010* study (IHME 2013), are not yet available. However, estimates from the WHO, based on 2002 data, projected that deaths from non-communicable diseases would likely increase and account for 69 per cent of the global burden of deaths in 2030 (Mathers and Loncar 2006). This proportion has almost been surpassed already, with deaths from non-communicable diseases accounting for 65.5 per cent of the global burden of disease in 2010 (Lozano et al. 2012). Given the recent and projected changes in health behaviours and conditions outlined in the previous section, especially those affecting the large emerging markets of China and India, projections of an even greater impact of such conditions on the global health burden in future years would seem entirely realistic (Figure 9.1).

Changes in health-care utilization and costs

As a result of population growth combined with increasing proportions of older people, increases in the utilization of health-care services and increases in total health-care costs would be expected. However, with the disease burden transitioning from a predominance of communicable to non-communicable diseases and with growing numbers of the population living with disability, health-service provision has also changed from predominantly providing acute

171

episodic care to the provision of ongoing chronic care. As a consequence, the utilization and costs of health care have risen dramatically.

In the United Kingdom, over the 25 years from 1985 to 2010, health-care costs rose more than sixfold, with projections of continuing increases in coming years (Chantrill 2013a). These increases almost exclusively reflect the increased costs of providing clinical treatment services, with little change in the costs associated with the provision of preventive or public health services. These cost increases are substantially more than the observed increases in GDP, such that whereas the latter has doubled over the 15 years from 1995 to 2010, clinical service costs have more than tripled (Chantrill 2013b).

In large part these increasing costs are being driven by the staff costs. In 2012/13 the budget of the UK National Health Service (NHS) was GBP 109 billion, with staff accounting for the largest proportion of these costs (60 per cent), a further 20 per cent being the costs of drugs, and the remaining 20 per cent being the costs of other aspects of health-care service (NHS Choices 2013). In the last two decades, there have been substantial increases in staff numbers and staff remuneration as well as pharmaceutical costs. In 2012/13, there were 1.7 million staff employed in the NHS, of which just under half were clinical staff (NHS Choices 2013). Between 2002 and 2012, clinical staff numbers grew by 17 per cent, with the numbers of doctors increasing by 40 per cent.[2]

The United Kingdom experience is not unique, and is arguably less dramatic than that observed in some other high-income countries, such as the United States. In most high-income countries, health-care costs as a proportion of GDP have doubled over the forty years since 1970 (Kaiser Family Foundation 2011). In the United Kingdom, for example, the proportion of expenditure on health-care costs has doubled from about 4 per cent of GDP in 1970 to about 8 per cent in 2008. In the United States, over the same period, costs have risen from 7 per cent to 16 per cent. The most recent figures available from the United States suggest that almost 18 per cent of the GDP is now spent on health care—the highest proportion of any country in the world (Blumenthal and Dixon 2012).

Such increases are not only being observed in high-income countries where the burden of non-communicable diseases is greatest, but they can already be observed in an increasing number of low-income and middle-income countries. In China, in the ten years between 2000 and 2009, health-care expenditure increased almost fourfold, a much faster increase than the rate of economic growth (Tang, Tao, and Bekedam 2012: 4). In 2009 the government

---

[2] Author's calculation based on NHS Confederation (2013) figures.

further committed to doubling the average annual governmental expenditure on health care, over the following three years, as the first phase towards achieving comprehensive universal health coverage by 2020 (Zhu 2009). However, while such budgetary increases potentially provide an opportunity to improve the health of the whole population, there is increasing concern that the growing burden of non-communicable diseases in China threatens to significantly undermine these equity initiatives, and that resources will need to focus instead on providing care for those with these conditions (Alcorn and Ouyang 2012).

A Positive Way Forward—an Outline Proposal with Supportive Data

For most high-income countries, then, more of the same in terms of the provision of health-care services is not viable. With continued population growth, population ageing, and the burden of non-communicable diseases maintaining its predominance, health-care costs will continue to rise if there is not significant change.

Burgeoning health-care costs, combined with increasing concerns about the large numbers of the poor who are unable to afford access to care, is not just an economic but a political issue in both rich and poor countries, as observed in the 2012 United States presidential elections (Oberlander 2012). Equally, health-care reform is on the United Kingdom political agenda, and for both countries the key issue is how to provide comparable or ideally better health outcomes while reducing costs to sustainable levels that are close to or ideally no higher than growth in GDP (Blumenthal and Dixon 2012).

For middle-income and low-income countries, health-care systems modelled on those of countries such as the United States and the United Kingdom are not going to provide the solutions for managing the forthcoming tsunami of non-communicable diseases. Certainly the current model of doctor-centric care that is practiced in high-income countries is not going to be affordable. If India, for example, wanted to achieve the same ratio of doctors per 10,000 population as the NHS, then they would need to scale up from their current level of roughly 757,000 doctors to 3,193,000 doctors.[3] The costs of such an undertaking would be vast, let alone the logistics of training so many physicians, and the benefits in terms of improvements in health care would take many years to make the required impact.

[3] WHO (2012, table 6) and author's estimate.

Consequently, in order to meet the challenges of providing safe, effective, and affordable health care for the growing numbers of individuals with non-communicable diseases in low- and middle-income countries, very different—and arguably revolutionary—approaches to health care will be required. While a range of strategies might be employed, key components will need to include the greater utilization of lower-cost health-care workers—often referred to as task-shifting—with a greater focus on the provision of health care (including preventive care) in the community and in ambulatory settings rather than in tertiary environments (Fulton et al. 2011), greater utilization of low-cost health technologies (Howitt et al. 2012), and greater access to essential medicines (Hogerzeil et al. 2013).

New models for health-care delivery in resource-poor settings

In the following section, examples of each of the above approaches are outlined. The first two examples focus on the utilization of lower-cost health-care workers, supported by low-cost health technologies, working in primary care settings in rural areas of India and China. The third example illustrates the potential of a low-cost polypill to improve access to cardiovascular medication.

UTILIZATION OF LOWER-COST HEALTH-CARE WORKERS

The transition from malnutrition to over-nutrition and from a burden of disease profile that is predominantly focused on communicable diseases and maternal and child ill health to one which is dominated by non-communicable diseases is especially evident in the urban affluent middle-classes in India. However, such diseases are now the most common causes of adult death in rural villages in Andhra Pradesh, a state on India's East Coast (Joshi et al. 2006). More than half of all deaths are due to such conditions, and a significant proportion of these deaths occur in those of working age.

As in most Indian states, there are too few doctors to provide essential medical care, many people have little understanding of the benefits that medical care can provide, and for many the cost of care for conditions such as heart disease is unaffordable. As a consequence, those who develop serious heart disease receive no or minimal regular medical care. For example, only 16 per cent of individuals with a history of heart attack in rural Andhra Pradesh were found to be receiving aspirin and only 9 per cent of individuals with a history of stroke—a treatment that arguably is affordable for all (Joshi et al. 2009: 1952). While it might be expected that such individuals might not be able to access more expensive treatments, the fact that over 80 per cent of these individuals weren't even receiving the cheapest, evidence-based care suggests there are problems with the current health-care delivery system.

Each village in Andhra Pradesh has an Accredited Social Health Activist or ASHA, usually a woman with modest education, who visits homes, mainly to provide antenatal care to women and to check up on their children after birth. The wages of these workers are about 70 per cent less than those of physicians. These women, with suitable training and support might well be able to fill the current gaps in identifying and managing those with non-communicable diseases. To determine whether in fact they can provide such care, ASHAs in more than 50 villages have now been trained to use simple, standardized algorithms to screen and identify individuals with heart disease or at high risk of its occurrence and to make appropriate recommendations (again with the assistance of standardized algorithms) about the sorts of treatment these individuals should be taking. They are also trained to refer high-risk individuals to local doctors for further care (Joshi et al. 2012).

This approach has led to significant increases in the referral of high-risk patients to local doctors and has shown that ASHAs are able to identify similar or better percentages of high-risk individuals than are the local doctors (Joshi et al. 2012). Importantly also, there is almost unanimous agreement between ASHAs and physicians regarding the best strategies to treat patients with coronary heart disease.

In rural China, a similar approach is being used to improve the management of health care, especially for individuals at high risk of stroke—a condition that is particularly prevalent in much of China as a consequence, in part, of the very high levels of salt intake. The China Rural Health Initiative (Life-Seeds), supported by the Chinese Ministry of Health, is being undertaken in five rural provinces, in about 120 villages, involving about one million people (George Institute, 2013). Village health-care workers (barefoot doctors), who have modest levels of education, have been trained using simple, standardized algorithms, to screen, manage, and refer high-risk individuals. Evaluation of the impact of this initiative is in progress.

UTILIZATION OF LOW-COST TECHNOLOGIES

As a result of the successes with the utilization of lower-cost health-care workers in Andhra Pradesh, the approach is now being extended to more than 150 villages and one million people, but will incorporate new technologies designed to provide ASHAs with patient-specific information to guide appraisal, referral, and treatment (George Institute, 2012).The impact of this programme on the proportion of people receiving appropriate care will be evaluated, together with the impact of such care on the risks of serious medical problems such as heart attack.

This initiative—SMART (Systematic Medical Appraisal, Referral, and Treatment) Health India—has seized on the potential for smartphone technology given that mobile phone networks reach approximately 80 per cent of the population, combined with increasing evidence that electronic decision support systems improve patient care (Kawamoto et al. 2005). Each ASHA will have access to a smartphone programmed with custom-designed software, enabling her to input information about her patients and receive personalized, evidence-based recommendations about patient management. Simultaneously, the phone automatically transmits the patient information to a secure sever for storage in an electronic medical record accessible to local doctors and hospitals. The system also allows patients, using their own phones (which need not be smartphones) to access health-care information, receive reminders to take medication, or arrange appointments with the ASHA or doctor. Importantly, this process ensures that there is quality control over the information provided, allowing for regular assessment of performance management and continuous improvement—all at a cost that is arguably affordable.

As in India, the second phase of the LifeSeeds initiative in China is being planned, involving smartphone technology to allow the assessment, diagnosis, treatment, follow-up, and referral of patients, while monitoring the quality of care. The initial focus is on the primary and secondary prevention of stroke, heart disease, and kidney disease. However, the application of this approach to the management of blood pressure, lipids, glucose, antiplatelet therapy, and tobacco cessation, involving patient-focussed strategies is being developed. The latter builds on research that has shown the positive impact of behavioural change support, information, and reminders sent by mobile phone SMS text messaging, in increasing tobacco abstinence (Free et al. 2011).

Further initiatives that are likely to enhance the usefulness of lower cost health workers in managing the burden of non-communicable diseases include the development of remote electronic sensors for mobile phones (Howitt et al. 2012). Such sensors will enable for example, the measurement of blood pressure, heart rate, ECGs, and heart sounds, which when transmitted directly to local doctors and hospitals, will enhance diagnosis, management and follow-up.

ACCESS TO ESSENTIAL MEDICINES

As illustrated in the findings from the rural villages in Andhra Pradesh, access to essential cardiovascular medications in low- and middle-income countries is woefully low. While in the United Kingdom the cost of medicines to the health service is less than 20 per cent, in many low- and middle-income countries, medicines account for 20–60 per cent of health spending, most being purchased through out-of-pocket payments, and for many people their costs are unaffordable (Cameron et al. 2009). Access to medications to manage non-communicable diseases is significantly lower than access to drugs for acute conditions, both in the public and private sectors (Cameron et al. 2009) and there are substantial differentials in access to cardiovascular medication in low-income countries compared with middle-income and higher-income countries (Yusuf et al. 2011).

A range of detailed strategies has been proposed to better improve access to essential medicines for non-communicable diseases, learning in large part from the experiences and policies developed in relation to both communicable diseases and especially HIV treatment (Hogerzeil et al. 2013). One approach that is showing promise is the development of fixed-dose, one-a-day combination polypills. Such formulations take advantage of the strong evidence base available for many treatments, the availability of off-patent medications, and the desire to maximize compliance through the use of one rather than several pills. Indeed, fixed-dose combination pills for HIV, tuberculosis, and malaria have been shown to minimize prescribing error and missed doses while reducing costs by up to 50 per cent (Panchagnula et al. 2004). Additionally, the use of fixed-dose combinations can be more easily and safely prescribed by lower-cost health-care workers and additionally simplify patient education and counselling.

The combination of aspirin plus agents to lower blood pressure and cholesterol, in one pill taken daily, is the subject of a range of trials being undertaken in both high- and low-income countries. Initial findings suggest that these combinations have the potential to halve predicted heart disease and stroke risk in individuals with raised cardiovascular risk (PILL Collaborative Group et al. 2011). More recent findings in patients with established cardiovascular disease and diabetes, randomized in India and in Europe to receive a fixed-dose combination therapy versus usual care, showed that at 15 months adherence was significantly greater in those using the fixed-dose combination (86 per cent) compared with those receiving usual care (65 per cent). As a consequence, both systolic blood pressure and LDL-cholesterol levels were improved in the fixed dose-combination group (O'Riordan 2012).

New models for health-care delivery in high-income settings

This last example provides promising evidence that innovative low-cost solutions to reducing health-care costs and improving access to health-care services are applicable not only in low-income countries but also have relevance in high-income countries. Equally, strategies that utilize lower-cost health-care workers in non-tertiary settings supported by appropriate technology could be part of the solution to providing safe, effective, and affordable health care in high-income countries. The principles that underlie the development of SMART Health India are clearly applicable. Namely, conditions that are amenable to treatment by algorithms should be managed by non-physician health-care workers, whereas those that are not amenable should be managed by doctors.

Much of the increasingly positive evidence put forward about the value of task shifting has emerged from low-income settings (McPake and Mensah 2008). As such, both the concept of transferring knowledge from low-income countries to high-income countries and the proposal that tasks undertaken by physicians might be undertaken by lower-cost health-care workers are likely to be considered controversial. Such a radically different approach is likely to be resisted by many in the medical profession, citing safety as an overwhelming concern. Likewise, there is likely to be resistance from patients who have expectations that they will receive care from physicians. Overcoming concerns from doctors and patients alike will thus require evidence of efficacy, safety, and cost-effectiveness through the conduct of large-scale, randomized controlled trials. Arguably, in the current climate of major health reform, prioritizing the conduct of such research should be high on the agenda.

Health care in high-income countries is already heavily dependent on technologies, so recognizing and utilizing technology as part of a strategic approach to providing more accessible health care in high-income countries should be relatively easy. However, as with most new drug developments, new technologies often involve higher- rather than lower-priced technologies. Consequently, encouraging and rewarding the development of frugal (and disruptive) technologies to improve health care in high-income countries, as well as low-income countries, will be a crucial component of strategies to reduce health-care costs (Howitt et al. 2012).

Conclusions

Is health care or the potential lack of safe, effective, and affordable health care a constraint for future population growth and the future quality of life? Arguably yes, if we continue to pursue the models of health care that are currently operating in most high-income countries. For populations in high-income countries, continued growth in per capita health-care expenditure is not feasible. Limiting or reducing health-care expenditure without changes to the current health-care models will likely mean that fewer people have access to safe, effective, and affordable health care. For populations in low-income countries, in which demand for health care is increasing, developing health-care systems that copy the models of care in high-income countries will likely be both impractical (within the short timeframes required) and unaffordable (Figure 9.2).

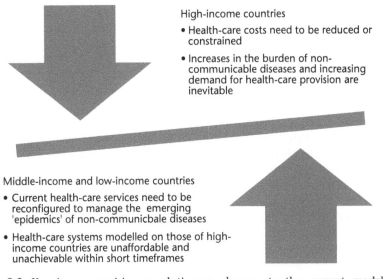

High-income countries
- Health-care costs need to be reduced or constrained
- Increases in the burden of non-communicable diseases and increasing demand for health-care provision are inevitable

Middle-income and low-income countries
- Current health-care services need to be reconfigured to manage the emerging 'epidemics' of non-communicbale diseases
- Health-care systems modelled on those of high-income countries are unaffordable and unachievable within short timeframes

Figure 9.2. Key issues requiring revolutionary changes to the current models of health-care delivery

Source: author.

In both scenarios, the consequence of not taking a radically different approach to the provision of health care has the potential to lead to fewer, not more, people leading long and healthy lives. However, this is an unnecessary scenario, given increasing evidence that lower-cost options can be at least as safe and effective as high-cost options. While much of the evidence is being generated in low-income settings, this should not be a barrier to uptake in high-income countries. What will be required is a bold vision, a willingness to embrace frugal and disruptive approaches, and a commitment to ensuring that new approaches are rigorously evaluated. The implementation of new models of health-care delivery, in tandem with the development and utilization of new technologies and drugs, offers a positive way forward, suggesting we can avert a crisis in health care and fulfil the promise and expectations of long, healthy, and disability-free lives.

References

Alcorn, T. and Ouyang, Y. (2012). 'Diabetes Saps Health and Wealth from China's Rise', *Lancet*, 379(9833): 2227–8.

Blumenthal, D. and Dixon, J. (2012). 'Health-Care Reforms in the USA and England: Areas for Useful Learning', *Lancet*, 380(9850): 1352–7.

Cameron, A., Ewen, M., Ross-Degnan, D., Ball, D., and Laing, D. (2009). 'Medicine Prices, Availability, and Affordability in 36 Developing and Middle-Income Countries: A Secondary Analysis', *Lancet*, 373(9659): 240–9.

Chantrill, C. (2013a). 'Health Care: United Kingdom from FY 1980 to FY 2015', UK Public Spending Website. Last accessed 20 May 2013. <http://www.ukpublicspending.co.uk/spending_chart_1980_2015UKb_12c1li111mcn_10t>.

Chantrill, C. (2013b). 'Medical Services: United Kingdom from FY 1980 to FY 2015', UK Public Spending Website. Last accessed 20 May 2013. <http://www.ukpublicspending.co.uk/spending_chart_1980_2015UKb_12c1li111mcn_13t>.

Cui, Z. and Dibley, M. (2012). 'Trends in Dietary Energy, Fat, Carbohydrate and Protein Intake in Chinese Children and Adolescents from 1991 to 2009', *British Journal of Nutrition*, 108(7): 1292–9.

Finucane, M. M., Stevens, G. A., Cowan, M. J., Danaei, G., Lin, J. K., and Pacoirek, C. J. (2011). 'National, Regional, and Global Trends in Body-Mass Index Since 1980: Systematic Analysis of Health Examination Surveys and Epidemiological Studies with 960 Country-Years and 9.1 Million Participants', *Lancet*, 377(9765): 557–67.

Free, C., Knight, R., Robertson, S., Whittaker, R., Edwards P., Zhou W., Rodgers, A., Cairns, J., Kenward, M. G., and Roberts, I. (2011). 'Smoking Cessation Support Delivered via Mobile Phone Text Messaging (txt2stop): A Single-Blind, Randomized Trial', *Lancet*, 378(9785): 49–55.

Fulton, B. D., Scheffler, R. M., Sparkes, S. P., Auh, E. Y., Vujicec, M., and Soucat, A. (2011). 'Health Workforce Skill Mix and Task Shifting in Low Income Countries: A Review of Recent Evidence', *Human Resources for Health*, 9 (1). Last accessed 20 May 2013. <http://www.human-resources-health.com/content/pdf/1478-4491-9-1.pdf>.

George Institute (2013) 'LifeSeeds—The China Rural Health Initiative', The George Institute for Global Health, China. Last accessed 20 May 2013. <http://www.georgeinstitute.org.cn/projects/lifeseeds-the-rurual-health-initiative>.

George Institute (2012), 'How Health Tracker India Works', YouTube Video, 9 December. Last accessed 20 May 2013. <http://www.youtube.com/watch?v=olhk_SRdqmk>.

Giovino, G. A., Mirza, S. A., Samet J. M., Gupta, P. C., Jarvis, M. J., Bhala, N., Peto R., Zatonski, W., Hsia, J., Morton, J., Palipudi, K. M., Asma, S., and GATS Collaborative Group. (2012). 'Tobacco Use in 3 Billion Individuals From 16 Countries: An Analysis of Nationally Representative Cross-Sectional Household Surveys', *Lancet*, 380(9842): 668–79.

Hallal, P. C., Anderson, L. B., Bull, F. C., Guthold, R., Haskell, W., and Ekelund, U. (2012). 'Global Physical Activity Levels: Surveillance, Progress, Pitfalls, and Prospects', *Lancet*, 380 (9838): 247–57.

Hogerzeil, H. V., Liberman, J., Wirtz, V. J., Kishore, S. P., Selvaraj, S., Kiddell-Monroe, R., Mwangi-Powell, F. N., and von Schoen-Angerer, T. (2013). 'Promotion of Access to Essential Medicines for Non-Communicable Diseases: Practical Implications of the UN Political Declaration', *Lancet*, 381 (9867): 680–9.

Howitt, P., Darzi, A., Yang, G. Z., Ashrafian, H., Atun, R., Barlow, J. Blakemore, A., Bull, A. M. J., Car, J., Conteh, L., Cooke, G. S., Ford, N., Gregson, S. A. J., Kerr, K., King, D., Kulendran, M., Malkin, R. A., Majeed, A., Matlin, S., Merrifield, R., Penfold, H. A.,

Reid, S. D., Smith, P. C., Stevens, M. M., Templeton, M. R., Vincent, C., and Wilson, E. (2012), 'Technologies for Global Health', *Lancet*, 380(9840): 507–35.

IHME (2013). *Global Burdon of Disease 2010: Generating Evidence, Guiding Policy*. Seattle, Washington: Institute for Health Metrics and Evaluation.

IMF. (2000). 'The World Economy in the Twentieth Century: Striking Developments and Policy Lessons', chapter 5 in *IMF World Economic Outlook May 2000: Asset Prices and the Business Cycle*. Washington, DC: International Monetary Fund, pp. 149–80. Last accessed 9 April 2013. <http://www.imf.org/external/pubs/ft/weo/2000/01/pdf/chapter5.pdf>.

Joshi, R., Cardona, M., Iyengar, S., Sukumar, A., Raju, C. R., Raju, K. R., Raju, K., Reddy, K. S., Lopez, A., and Neal, B. (2006). 'Chronic Diseases Now A Leading Cause of Death in Rural India—Mortality Data from the Andhra Pradesh Rural Health Initiative', *International Journal Epidemiology*, 35(6): 1522–9.

Joshi, R., Chow, C. K., Raju, P. K., Gottumukkala, A. K., Reddy, K. S., MacMahon, S., Heritier, S., Li, Q., Dandona, R., and Neal, B. (2012). 'The Rural Andhra Pradesh Cardiovascular Prevention Study (RADCAPS): A Cluster Randomized Trial', *Journal of the American College of Cardiology*, 59(13): 1188–96.

Joshi, R., Chow, C. K., Raju, P. K., Raju, R., Reddy, K. S., MacMahon, S., Lopez, A. D., and Neal, B. (2009). 'Fatal and Nonfatal Cardiovascular Disease and the Use of Therapies for Secondary Prevention in a Rural Region of India', *Circulation*, 119(14): 1950–5.

Kaiser Family Foundation (2011). 'Health Care Spending in the United States and Selected OECD Countries', The Henry J. Kaiser Family Foundation, 12 April. Last accessed 9 April 2013. <http://www.kff.org/insurance/snapshot/OECD042111.cfm>.

Kawamoto, K, Houlihan, C. A., Balas, E. A., and Lobach, D. F. (2005). 'Improving Clinical Practice Using Clinical Decision Support Systems: a Systematic Review of Trials to Identify Features Critical to Success', *British Medical Journal*, 330(765): online. <http://dx.doi.org/10.1136/bmj.38398.500764.8F>.

Lim, S. S., Vos, T., Flaxman, A. D., Danaei, G., Shibuya, K., Adair-Rohani, H., et al. (2012). 'A Comparative Risk Assessment of Burden of Disease and Injury Attributable to 67 Risk Factors and Risk Factor Clusters in 21 Regions, 1990–2010: A Systematic Analysis for the Global Burden of Disease Study', *Lancet*, 380(9859): 2224–60.

Lozano, R., Naghavi M., Foreman, K., Lim, S., Shibuya, K., Aboyans, V. et al. (2012). 'Global and Regional Mortality from 235 Causes of Death for 20 Age Groups in 1990 and 2010: A Systematic Analysis for the Global Burden of Disease Study', *Lancet*, 380 (9859): 2095–128.

Mathers, C. D. and Loncar, D. (2006). 'Projections of Global Mortality and Burden of Disease from 2002 to 2030', *PLoS Med*, 3 (11): 2011–30.

McPake, B. and Mensah, K. (2008). 'Task Shifting in Healthcare in Resource Poor Countries', *Lancet*, 372(9642): 870–1.

NHS Choices (2013). 'About the National Health Service (NHS)', (28 January last reviewed). Last accessed 20 May 2013. <http://www.nhs.uk/NHSEngland/thenhs/about/Pages/overview.aspx>.

NHS Confederation (2013). 'Key Statistics on the NHS', last updated May. Last accessed 20 May 2013. <http://www.nhsconfed.org/priorities/political-engagement/Pages/NHS-statistics.aspx>.

O'Riordan, M. (2012). 'UMPIRE's Ruling: Fixed-Dose Combo Improves Adherence, Lowers Cholesterol and BP', *Heartwire*, 5 November. Last accessed 20 May 2013. <http://www.theheart.org/article/1469635.do>.

Oberlander, J. (2012). 'Unfinished Journey—A Century of Healthcare Reform in the Unites States', *New England Journal of Medicine*, 367(7): 585–90.

Panchagnula, R., Agrawal, S., Ashokraj, Y., Varma, M., Sateesh, K., Bhardwaj, V., Bedi, S., Gulati, I., Parmar, J., Kaul, C. L., Blomberg, B., Fourie, B., Roscigno, G., Wire, R., Laing, R., Evans, P., and Moore, T. (2004). 'Fixed Dose Combinations for Tuberculosis: Lessons Learned from Clinical, Formulation and Regulatory Perspective', *Methods and Findings in Experiential Clinical Pharmacology*, 20(9): 703–21.

Perls, T. (2009). 'Health and Disease in People Over 85', *British Medical Journal*, 339: b4715.

PILL Collaborative Group, Rodgers, A., Patel, A., Berwanger, O., Bots, M., Grimm, R., Grobbee, D. E., Jackson, R., Neal, B., Neaton, J., Poulter, N., Rafter, N., Raju, P. K., Reddy, S., Thom, S., Vander Hoorn, S., and Webster, R. (2011). 'An International Randomized Placebo-Controlled Trial of a Four-Component Combination Pill ("polypill") in People with Raised Cardiovascular Risk', *PLoS One*, 6(5): e19857.

Popkin, B. M., Adair L. S., and Ng, S. W. (2012). 'The Global Nutrition Transition: The Pandemic of Obesity in Developing Countries', *Nutrition Reviews*, 70(1): 3–21.

Sankhe, S., Vittal, I., Dobbs, R., Mohan, A., Gulati, A., Ablett, J., Gupta, S., Kim, A., Paul, S., Sanghvi, A., and Sethy, G. (2010). *India's Urban Awakening: Building Inclusive Cities, Sustaining Economic Growth*. New Delhi: McKinsey Global Institute. Last accessed, 5 April 2013. <http://www.mckinsey.com/insights/urbanization/urban_awakening_in_india>.

Sullivan, R., Kinra, S., Ekelund, U., Bharathi, A.V., Vaz, M., Kurpad, A., Collier, T., Reddy, K. S., Prabhakaran, D., Ben-Shlomo, Y., Smith, G. D., Ebrahim, S., and Kuper, H. (2011). 'Socio-Demographic Patterning of Physical Activity Across Migrant Groups in India: Results from the Indian Migration Study', *PLoS One*, 6(10): e24898.

Swinburn, B., Sacks, G., Hall, K. D., McPherson, K., Finegood, D. T., Moodie, M. L., and Gortmaker, S. (2011). 'The Global Obesity Pandemic: Shaped by Global Drivers and Local Environments', *Lancet*, 378(9793): 804–14.

Tang, S., Tao, J., and Bekedam, H. (2012). 'Controlling Cost Escalation of Healthcare: Making Universal Health Coverage Sustainable in China', *BMC Public Health*, 12(Suppl 1): S8.

UN-HABITAT (2010). *State of the World's Cities 2010/2011—Cities for All: Bridging the Urban Divide*. London: United Nations Human Settlements Programme (UN-HABITAT). Last accessed 15 March 2013. <http://www.unhabitat.org/pmss/listItemDetails.aspx?publicationID=2917>.

Vos, T., Flaxman, A. D., Naghavi, M., Lozano, R., Michaud, C., Ezzati, M. et al. (2012). 'Years Lived with Disability (YLDs) for 1160 Sequelae of 289 Diseases and Injuries 1990–2010: A Systematic Analysis for the Global Burden of Disease Study', *Lancet*, 380(9859): 2163–96.

Wang, H., Dwyer-Lindgren, L., Lofgren, K. T., Knoll Rajaratnam, J., Marcus, J. R., Levin-Rector, A., Levitz, C. E., Lopez, A. D., and Murray, C. J. L. (2012), 'Age-specific and Sex-specific Mortality in 187 Countries, 1970–2010: A Systematic Analysis for the Global Burden of Disease Study 2010', *Lancet*, 380(9859): 2071–94.

WHO (2012). *WHO World Health Statistics 2012*. Geneva: World Health Organization. Last accessed 22 May 2013. <http://apps.who.int/iris/bitstream/10665/44844/1/9789241564441_eng.pdf>.

WHO (2011). *WHO Report on the Global Tobacco Epidemic: 2011*. Geneva: World Health Organization. Last accessed 22 May 2012. <http://whqlibdoc.who.int/publications/2011/9789240687813_eng.pdf>.

WHO (2009). *Global Health Risks: Mortality and Burden of Disease Attributable to Selected Major Risks*. Geneva: World Health Organization. Last accessed 15 March 2013. <http://www.who.int/healthinfo/global_burden_disease/GlobalHealthRisks_report_full.pdf>.

WHO (1999). *Removing Obstacles to Healthy Development*. Geneva, Switzerland: World Health Organization.

WHO and UN-HABITAT (2010). *Hidden Cities: Unmasking and Overcoming Health Inequities in Urban Settings*. Kobe: World Health Organization Centre for Health Development; and Nairobi: United Nations Settlements Programme. Last accessed 22 May 2013. <http://www.unhabitat.org/pmss/getElectronicVersion.aspx?nr=3049&alt=1>.

Yu, Z., Han, S., Chu, J., Xu, J., Zhu, C., and Guo, X. (2012). 'Trends in Overweight and Obesity among Children and Adolescents in China from 1981 to 2010: A Meta-Analysis', *PLoS One*, 7(12): 1–14.

Yusuf, S., Islam, S., Chow, C. K., Rangarajan, S., Dagenais, G., Diaz, R., Gupta, R., Kelishadi, R., Iqbal, R., Avezum, A., Kruger, A., Kutty, R., Lanas, F., Lisheng, L., Wei, L., Lopez-Jaramillo, P., Oguz, A., Rahman, O., Swidan, H., Yusoff, K., Zatonski, W., Rosengren, A., Teo, K. K., and PURE Study Investigators (2011). 'Use of Secondary Prevention Drugs for Cardiovascular Disease in the Community in High-income, Middle-income, and Low-income Countries (the PURE Study): A Prospective Epidemiological Survey', *Lancet*, 378(9798): 1231–43.

Zhu, C. (2009). 'Launch of the Health-care Reform Plan in China', *Lancet*, 373(9672): 1322–4.

10

Sourcing Mineral Resources—Problems and Solutions

Anthony Hartwell

The development of human societies has been based on the ability to exploit the Earth's mineral resources, and this has been linked with the harnessing of suitable energy supplies. Since modern industrial societies are dependent on the utilization of large volumes of mineral resources, it is important to consider if concerns about future availability suggest that the planet is full.

Another way of stating the question that forms the title of this book would be, 'Does the demand for mineral resources by the human population exceed the capacity of the Earth to supply them?' In the 19th century, Mark Twain (Samuel Langhorne Clemens) is said to have made the following recommendation: 'Buy land, they're not making it anymore.' Now that most parts of the Earth's 'hospitable' land surface is inhabited, and global population continues to rise, the average area of land available to provide the resources required is becoming smaller but the global demand for resources is increasing. The question could be put in another way: 'Can advances in technology continue to deliver effective improvements in land productivity—what are the limits?'

The Earth's resources are finite. The current trends for growth in the global population and demand for resources imply that there will come a time when terrestrial supplies would not be sufficient to meet demand. This Malthusian view, developed by Meadows, Randers and Meadows (2004) for the Club of Rome (CoR 2013), has recently been revived because of concerns about the availability of special metals that are required for several high-technology applications—for example the use of some rare earth elements (REEs) in automotive, wind turbine, and aerospace applications (Kooroshy, Korteweg, and de Ridder 2010).

To date the concerns of 'Malthusians' have not fully materialized because significant technical developments have been made (allowing for increased agriculture yields, and enabling the discovery and exploitation of lower-grade mineral and energy resources, thereby supporting growing populations). Some suggest that this justifies a 'laissez-faire' approach to the future based on the assumption that technological developments will continue to address whatever resource issues arise. This line of argument implies that investing now to address any issue that may occur in the future—even ones that could have an adverse impact on the long-term future of human society, such as climate change—would be inefficient because someone will come up with a better solution in the future. Jean Monnet (1978: 109) suggested that 'People only accept change when they are faced with necessity and only recognise necessity when a crisis is upon them'. However, even if the human track record has not been auspicious (Diamond 2005) perhaps it would be wiser to investigate the potential for future problems and seek to avoid them. The approach adopted in this chapter is to examine trends in mineral resource supply and demand, in order to identify actions that could minimize the degradation of the Earth's capacity to support future generations. It is assumed that as the developing economies expand, the demand for minerals will increase.

The focus of this chapter is on future availability of mineral resources, although it recognizes that the broader ecological context must also be taken into account. It will be suggested that, for the foreseeable future, it is not the absolute availability of these materials that will be a constraint. However, based on current trends it is important to consider how these resources are utilized because the impact of converting them into the forms required, and volumes demanded, by human societies will have significant implications for important global systems such as the atmosphere, oceans, and ecosystems. The focus will be on one important segment of mineral resources—metals—because these are products of energy-intensive industries and perform essential functions in the systems used by modern high-technology industries. Details on the determination of the overall Ecological Footprints of organizations and nations can be obtained from the Global Footprint Network (GFN 2013).

The current trends of increasing global population and growing demand for resources per capita (global average), indicate that there will be a continued increase in the demand for resources (SERI 2009). Although the focus of this chapter is on the availability of metals, the links with energy and environmental issues will be demonstrated. The supply of food is not examined here—although of course this is also interrelated with energy and some other resources such as water and fertilizers. The future of energy supplies is not addressed in detail here because there are many detailed studies on this

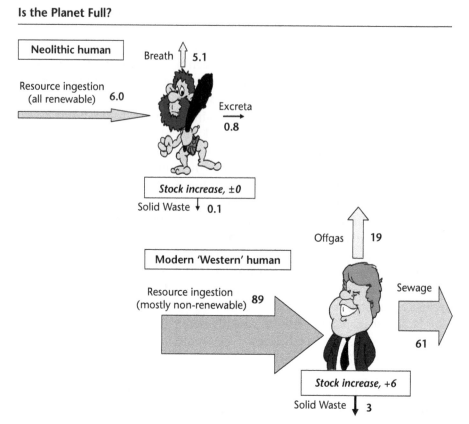

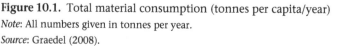

Figure 10.1. Total material consumption (tonnes per capita/year)

Note: All numbers given in tonnes per year.

Source: Graedel (2008).

subject (see, for example, IEA 2013). However, some aspects of the energy utilization are examined because it is important to recognize the link between the production, and use, of mineral resources and energy consumption.

Demand for Mineral Resources

Throughout history, human societies have strived to obtain the resources that meet the needs of their culture (Figure 10.1). Where hunter-gatherers have managed to adapt their lifestyle to live off the available natural resources they have been able to live within the boundaries of their ecosystem. As local populations grew and demand exceeded the local supply of resources, all or part of the group could migrate to new areas. Recent developments in archaeology and genetics have illustrated how rapidly modern humans migrated from their original African home across the globe over a relatively short period of time (National Geographic 2013). Human ingenuity has enabled habitation to spread across the entire globe, whether this was driven by local pressures on population and resources or by the spirit of adventure and exploration. In some regions the transition from hunter-gathering communities to societies based on agriculture increased the need to develop systems for managing the environment (land clearance and tillage, water supply, food storage) and eventually the means to defend their territorial base from invasion by external groups. The development of new materials and technologies facilitated this transition from a nomadic or semi-nomadic lifestyle to permanent settlements. Studies that analyse the flow of resources suggest that as societies become more affluent, in terms of Gross Domestic Product per capita, the demand for energy and materials increases (SERI 2009).

One of the ways of differentiating between modern humans (*Homo sapiens*) and earlier ancestors is their toolmaking skills. Early humans made use of materials that were readily available, such as wood and stones, but archaeological evidence indicates that over time *Homo sapiens* developed techniques for converting a range of natural resources into more and more sophisticated tools. The transition from a hunter-gatherer lifestyle into fixed farming and urban communities provided both the need and opportunity for an increase in the resources utilized by human communities (Diamond 2005).

It is interesting to note that several stages in the development of human societies have been defined in terms of the materials utilized for tools and weapons. Archaeologists have defined cultures according to their use of materials (Stone Age, Bronze Age, Iron Age) and some authors have suggested extensions to this series (Sass 2011). Late Stone Age technologies required the identification of suitable raw materials for making tools and when high quality materials were found there is evidence, for example at the Grimes Graves site in the United Kingdom, to show that underground mining techniques were used to extract them (NTO 2007). Quite sophisticated techniques were developed to produce a range of elaborate tools and weapons through manual labour.

Until the industrial revolution, the growth in human population may have been constrained by a range of interconnected factors such as disease, natural disasters (including variations in climate), wars, and the availability of food, water, and other resources (Diamond 2005). However, advances in a range of sciences and technologies enabled the development of methods for processing and utilizing mineral resources and fossil fuels. These technological advances began to overcome these constraints and the global human population has continued to grow.

Early human societies in different parts of the world operated in economies that had relatively few external links and were predominantly self-sufficient. Trade grew with the development of towns and cities, and the development of transport and communication systems since the Industrial Revolution has resulted in the globalization of the economic systems. However, it is not only in the business arena that globalization has become an important factor. In the past environmental issues were often considered to be local or regional but there is now recognition that these can influence global systems (for example, Chlorinated Fluorocarbons (CFCs) and ozone depletion; greenhouse gases and climate change; carbon dioxide and ocean acidification). This has highlighted the need to consider the Earth's systems from a holistic view—examining the wider implications of the demand for resources at the local, regional, and global scale.

Estimates of the future demand for resources are usually based on projections from current demand and estimates of the requirements for new applications. Although the consideration of future energy supplies is not the subject of this chapter it is important to recognize the important links between the demand for materials and energy. One very important difference between the use of metals and fossil fuels is considered below.

Sources of Raw Materials

In the past few years concerns have been raised about the availability of resources, with particular concern about oil. Parallels have been drawn between the concept of 'peak oil' and other minerals (Giurco et al. 2010). Projections of the future supplies of metals have suggested potential shortages (Cohen 2007: 34–41; Ragnarsdóttir 2008). These estimates are usually based on two factors. The first is a prediction for the future consumption rate of the material, which can be based on projections from past data. A value based on extrapolation from recent trends in demand is normally used but, as the stock market analysts are obliged to point out: past performance is not necessarily a guide to the future. The second factor is the available volume of the resource—this is not based on an estimate of an absolute value calculated from the composition of the Earth's crust but is usually derived from information on estimates of the resources that can be recovered in a viable process. As the term 'viable process' suggests this is not a fixed value. It will depend on the grade and quality of the ore, the location, energy costs, environmental factors, social considerations, and last but not least on the price of the mineral.

Figure 10.2 illustrates the way in which mineral deposits are classified by the United States Geological Survey (USGS 1980). There are regulations that mining companies registered on stock exchanges must comply with. The volume of the resources that they declare must be verified according to specific regulations; for example, in Canada, the National Instrument 43–101F1 (CIM 2013). To identify material as reserves mining companies must conduct the exploration necessary to demonstrate that these exist. There are significant

Cumulative production	Identified resources			Undiscovered resources	
	Demonstrated		Inferred	Probability range	
	Measured	Indicated		Hypothetical	Speculative
Economic	RESERVES		Inferred reserves		
Marginally economic	Marginal reserves		Inferred marginal reserves		
Sub-economic	Demonstrated sub-economic resources		Inferred sub-economic resources		
Other occurrences	*Includes nonconventional and low-grade materials*				

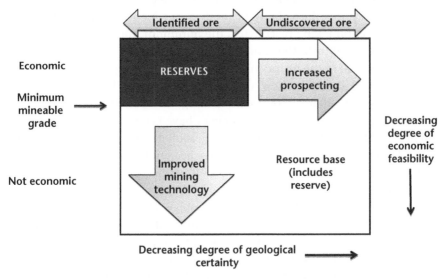

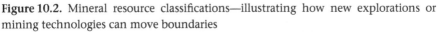

Figure 10.2. Mineral resource classifications—illustrating how new explorations or mining technologies can move boundaries

Source: USGS (1980: 5), top; and Ashby and Jones (2009: 22), bottom.

costs associated with proving reserves (drilling and analyses) so companies will only incur the costs required to ensure that they prove sufficient reserves to support the planning requirements for the future viability of their operations. Therefore any calculation on future supplies based on estimates of reserves at a given time will only have limited value. This is because additional exploration and development work, potential developments in mining and mineral processing technologies, and/or significant changes in prices would alter the boundary positions in Figure 10.2 and thus the volume of material

189

defined as reserves. The upper part of the diagram outlines how different types of resources and reserves can be defined at a specific point in time. Reserves are defined according to economic considerations and geological data. Exploration data is used to determine the vertical lines delineating the boundaries between measured, indicated, and inferred reserves. The lower diagram shows how these borders can be moved to the right (increasing the volume of reserves) by additional prospecting—if these identify additional resources of sufficient quality.

A number of factors influence the horizontal lines differentiating between reserves, marginal reserves, and sub-economic reserves. On the one hand, if the cost of extraction increases and the sale price of the mineral is static or falling then the volume of economic reserves would fall. On the other hand, the development of new processes or technologies can reduce the cost of extraction making more material economic to recover. During a period of rising mineral prices the volume of reserves can increase without any additional exploration taking place. Thus the minimum mineable grade (cut-off grade) is influenced by both economic and technological factors.

An examination of the history of copper production illustrates these points. Radetzki (2009) describes how copper resources have been exploited by humans for more than 7,000 years. During this period there have been many changes in the way copper resources have been identified, developed, and processed. Initially surface outcrops of visibly recognizable minerals, with relatively high copper contents, would have been utilized and then the layers, or veins, of minerals would have been followed underground (as was the case for the flint resources at Grimes Graves). This would have increased the amount of labour required to recover the resource. The value placed on copper and tin was high enough in ancient times to justify the use of long-distance trading routes, such as those from the Mediterranean to Northern Portugal, Spain, Britain, and Ireland (Comendador-Rey et al. 2008). Both of these metals are required to produce bronze alloys which have better properties for weapons and tools than unalloyed copper. The extensive underground workings for copper at Great Orme, in North Wales, were developed, and effectively exhausted, prior to the Roman invasion of Britain. The production of copper and other metals in the United Kingdom was limited until the knowledge of how to harness the energy contained in coal was developed.

The beginning of the Industrial Revolution may initially have been stimulated by the development of large-scale copper production facilities in the Swansea area where coal was available to smelt the copper ores that were then being mined in Cornwall and Anglesey. Until the development of low-cost transportation systems, the sources of ores and energy (coal) were the main factors determining the location of metal-production facilities. Since the Welsh Process for copper production required more coal than ore it made

Table 10.1. World mine production of copper

Year	Thousand tonnes	Cumulative growth, %/year	Main producing countries (global share, %)
1750	10		China 70, Europe 30
1800	15	0.8	Europe 53, China 47
1850	53	2.6	United Kingdom 23
1900	490	4.5	United States 56, Spain 11
1910	890	6.1	United States 56, Mexico 6
1920	960	0.8	United States 58, Chile 10
1930	1,540	4.8	United States 42, Chile 14, Canada 9
1940	2,360	4.4	United States 34, Chile 16, Canada 13
1950	2,490	0.5	United States 33, Chile 15, Zambia 11
1960	4,420	5.9	United States 22, Zambia 13, Chile 12
1970	6,340	3.7	United States 25, USSR 15, Chile 11
1980	7,740	2	United States 15, Chile 14, USSR 13
1990	8,990	1.5	Chile 18, USA 18, USSR 10
2000	13,230	3.9	Chile 35, USA 8, Peru 7
2007	15,520	2.3	Chile 36, Peru 8, USA 8
2010	16,134	1.1	Chile 34, Peru 8, China 7, USA 7

Note: The annual production figures for metals can vary somewhat depending on the source. When comparing figures it is important to ensure that data refers to the same product. For example, the values for mine output, smelter output, and refined output will be different.

Source: Radetzki (2009: 179); final row from COCHILCO (2013).

sense to locate the smelters near Swansea which became a world centre for copper production—earning the nickname 'Copperopolis' (Sullivan 2012). The growth of copper production after the Industrial Revolution can be seen from Table 10.1 which also indicates the share of the output from the leading copper producing nations (see also Radetzki 2009). Between 1910 and 2010 the global output from copper mines increased from less than one million to more than sixteen million tonnes per year. This was achieved whilst the average ore grades declined—with several high-grade mines becoming exhausted and new, low-grade, deposits being developed.

Despite the fact that this decline in the average ore grade has meant that much higher tonnages of ore have to be processed to produce one tonne of copper, advances in technologies and process efficiencies have meant that the long-term trend since 1850, has been for the index-adjusted price of copper to fall—until the recent commodity boom (see Figure 10.3).

Despite the continued growth in copper production, estimates of reserves available for future production have tended to increase rather than decline—see Figure 10.4. This data for copper illustrates the reasons why any projections for the lifespan of metal supplies based on current estimates of future consumption rates and current estimates of reserves (for example Cohen 2007) may be misleading.

Crowson (2011: 5) highlights this issue:

The global mine production of copper from the early 1930s onwards greatly exceeded the estimated reserves at the start of the period, but estimates of reserves

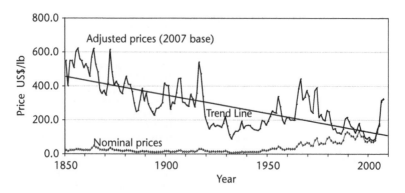

Figure 10.3. Price of copper—nominal and adjusted to 2007 base
Source: Radetzki (2009: 184).

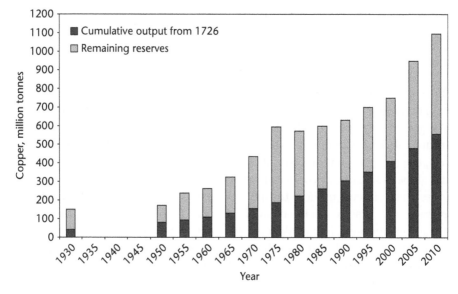

Figure 10.4. Cumulative copper output and identified reserves, 1930–2010
Source: Crowson (2011: 4).

rose more rapidly than cumulative production. In 2010, the US Geological Survey assessed global reserves of copper at 540 Mt...and in January 2011 its estimate had increased to 630 Mt...

The techniques used and investments required for the development of low- and high-grade deposits are very different. Large deposits of low-grade material near the surface can be developed by relatively low-cost open-pit mining methods (see Figure 10.5 (a)). These can benefit from the installation of large processing plants that can deliver economies of scale. High-grade ores often

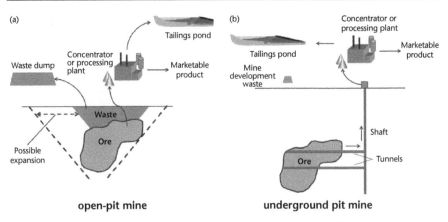

Figure 10.5. Schematic diagrams of an open and an underground pit mine

Source: adapted from Dunbar (2012a: 4 and 31).

Note: The author is grateful to W. Scott Dunbar for revising and supplying these figures for the present volume.

occur in narrow zones and many of the deposits visible at or near to the surface have been exhausted. Geological exploration can identify these high-grade resources below the surface but these require the use of underground mining methods which require significant investments and time to establish (see Figure 10.5 (b)).

The processing of mineral deposits targets one or more of the metals contained. If these are present in low concentrations then a significant volume of residues or by-products will be generated. The main conventional mining methods are illustrated in Figure 10.5 (see also Dunbar 2012a). The grade of material recovered from underground mines is usually higher than from open-pit mines. During the mining process other material will need to be removed to allow the ore to be recovered. In open-pit mining, see Figure 10.5 (a), this is called overburden. In underground mining, see Figure 10.5 (b), the rock removed during construction and development of the mine may be referred to as development waste—this material can be used to backfill worked-out areas of the mine. Once an underground mine is in production the aim will be to minimize the amount of barren material brought to the surface. Mining groups are now developing systems to enhance the safety of mining activities and minimize the impact on the environment through the use of remote sensing and robotic mining systems (RTC 2010; Dunbar 2012b).

To obtain a broader understanding of the impact of producing a particular metal it is useful to consider the total material that has to be handled to produce one tonne of that metal. This is the 'Total Material Required' (TMR), sometimes described as the material 'rucksack'. Values for a range of metals are given in Table 10.2 which illustrates that the TMR factor ranges considerably

Table 10.2. Total material required (TMR) for various metals

Element	TMR	Element	TMR
Iron	8	Scandium	2,000
Manganese	14	Cerium	2,000
Chromium	26	Neodymium	3,000
Silicon	34	Silver	4,800
Zinc	36	Samarium	9,000
Aluminium	48	Gallium	14,000
Magnesium	70	Rhenium	20,000
Tungsten	190	Ruthenium	80,000
Nickel	260	Germanium	120,000
Copper	360	Tellurium	270,000
Cobalt	600	Platinum	520,000
Molybdenum	750	Gold	1,100,000
Lithium	1,500	Rhodium	2,300,000

Source: based on Halada (2011: 18).

from 8 for iron to 70 for magnesium, 360 for copper, 3,000 for neodymium, 20,000 for rhenium, 270,000 for tellurium, and more than a million for gold and rhodium (see Halada 2011).

Initially logistics dictated that mineral exploitation took place in the most accessible regions. Then, as demand increased, exploration and development took place in more remote regions, including desert and artic locations. Approximately seven-tenths of the Earth's surface is under water. The oil industry has demonstrated that with the development of special technologies resource recovery can also be viable from marine areas, initially in shallow waters and then moving into greater depths. At the end of the 19th century nodules of polymetallic material were found to be widely distributed across the ocean floor (Morgan 2011). These nodules contained concentrations of metals such as nickel, copper, and cobalt that would make them viable resources on land. However, to date no cost-effective methods have been discovered to make the recovery of metals from these resources economically viable. With the development of special underwater technologies and treatment systems there are signs that this situation is beginning to change. Many countries are engaged in underwater exploration programmes, even though the legal framework for the development of these resources has not been ratified by all of the major economies and there have already been diplomatic incidents relating to the rights to subsea deposits. A recent article in *China Daily* reported that:

Commercial deep-sea mining by China of polymetallic nodules that contain copper, nickel, and cobalt among other key minerals, can begin as early as 2030, according to the former head of the State Oceanic Administration. 'With the improvement in deep-sea technology, metal resources under the ocean can be explored and mined within 20 years', said Sun Zhihui. (Yannan and Qian 2012).

A Canadian company has plans to develop a sea-floor copper/gold resource located in the Bismarck Sea off the coast of Papua New Guinea (Nautilus Minerals 2013). This 'Seawater Massive Sulphide' deposit, called Solwara 1, is located on the sea floor at a depth of 1,600 m. It has been reported that this resource has average grades of 7 per cent copper and 6 grams per tonne of gold which would make this a very attractive proposition if it was based on land. The plan is to start recovering material from this deposit in 2014, subject to the appropriate financial arrangements being in place.

Significant deposits of REEs have been reported on the Pacific seabed (Kato et al. 2011) indicating that an area of one square kilometre could supply one-fifth of current global demand for these elements (Kato et al. 2011: 535). Yttrium[1] can be recovered from ocean sediment by simple acid leaching and it has been suggested that deep-sea mud is potentially a large resource for REEs.

Before polymetallic nodules and other types of marine deposits are developed, it is important that the potential environmental risks identified by the International Seabed Authority for the International Tribunal for the Law of the Sea (ITLOS 2010) are addressed. The International Seabed Authority is seeking to oversee and regulate the exploitation of marine mineral resources and it has published environmental guidelines (ISA 2011). Taking all of the above considerations into account it is suggested that for most metallic minerals absolute depletion should not be a short-term issue but the production of metals from primary resources has to address a number of challenging trends:

- More expensive exploration (remote and difficult locations, deeper seabed, etc.)
- Declining grades of mineral resource
- Increasingly complex mineralogy (more difficult to treat)
- Higher energy consumption rates (related with lower grades)
- Higher capital and operating costs
- More demanding environmental legislation (need for more sustainable development)
- Difficult/extended permitting process
- Constraints on energy and water availability
- Social opposition to mine developments
- Need to reduce greenhouse gas emissions

Clearly the availability of mineral resources is not the only consideration for the future supply of metals. The following sections will highlight some of the energy and environmental factors.

---

[1] Yttrium is an element often classified as an REE. It is used in a wide range of specialist applications, such as in the manufacture of phosphors used for producing red colours in TV and other applications.

Energy and Environmental Considerations

The growth in the extraction and consumption of fossil fuels since the Industrial Revolution has been fuelled by the demand for the large energy inputs required to convert minerals into the materials (copper, iron, lead, zinc, etc.) used to build modern infrastructures and systems. The developed economies and lifestyles have been based on the exploitation of fossil fuels. However, the development and combustion of fossil fuels has released significant quantities of carbon dioxide, and other greenhouse gases, into the atmosphere. Scientific evidence from the Scripps Institute (Keeling 2007) shows that the carbon dioxide content of the atmosphere, measured in parts per million by volume, has increased significantly from about 285 in 1860 to 315 in 1960 and to 390 in 2010. The significance of this change may appear to be small because it is reported in terms of parts per million in the atmosphere. However, a research group at Oxford University puts this into perspective; it has established a website (<http://www.trillionthtonne.org>) that uses projections, based on the emissions over the past 20 years, to predict the date when the cumulative emissions (from fossil fuel use, cement production, and land use change, since industrialization) will reach one trillion tonnes (1,000,000,000,000 tonnes). At the time of writing this date is projected to be in 2041 but the date will continue to move closer if, despite all the political summit meetings, the global emissions continue to increase. Evidence from work at the Scripps Institute demonstrates the concentration of carbon dioxide in the atmosphere is increasing because it cannot be absorbed by natural sinks at the same rate at which it is being released due to anthropogenic activities.

Oil is often quoted as an example of a resource that is becoming depleted and the concept of 'eak oil' was developed by M. King Hubbert in 1956 (HPOP 2013). However, the example of copper considered above has shown that it is difficult to predict the life expectancy of resources based on current estimates of the reserves available and models of future consumption. The issues relating to the depletion of oil resources have been illustrated in a recent publication (Yergin 2011: 233–41). This shows that, since the start of the industrial exploitation of oil resources in the 19th century, cumulative global production of oil has been about one trillion barrels (about 140 billion tonnes). Today there are at least 5 trillion barrels of petroleum resources of which about 1.4 trillion could be considered to be proven or probable, and based on projections from current and prospective plans it is estimated that production capacity could reach 40 billion barrels per year by 2030 (Yergin 2011: 239). Although consumption rates have increased, developments in the technologies used for exploration and recovery have kept pace and it is still economically viable to produce oil in the volumes required to meet demand. The situation is similar to that for metal ores. New oil reserves are becoming harder to access and/or refine, with more energy and resources having to be deployed to recover them in ways that are environmentally and socially acceptable. However, higher prices mean that more difficult reserves could be developed.

Scarcity may not be a short-term issue, but the major issues associated with the combustion of all fossil fuels are: how to manage 'greenhouse gas' emissions and how the total environmental costs should be distributed or allocated. Legislation was introduced to curb industrial emissions of sulphur dioxide after the environmental impact of acid rain had been recognized (Taylor 2005). Reducing carbon dioxide emissions is proving to be more difficult because most conventional energy systems have been based on fossil fuel consumption.

The production of many of the metals used in modern societies is energy intensive. In many instances fossil fuels are being used, directly or indirectly, to meet the thermal and chemical energy requirements of these processes. Some of the high-volume manufactured materials such as cement and steel have relied on the combustion of fuels for their energy input although, in the case of cement, significant use of secondary fuels (waste oils, solvents, tyres, etc.) has been achieved. In 2011 the global emissions of carbon dioxide reached 33.9 billion tonnes—the highest annual figure ever (Olivier, Janssens-Maenhout, and Peters 2012: 6). The International Energy Agency (IEA) recently reported on trends in emissions, evaluating the performance of different sectors (IEA 2012: 5). In the summary the IEA states that:

> The transition to a low-carbon energy sector is affordable and represents tremendous business opportunities, but investor confidence remains low due to policy frameworks that do not provide certainty and address key barriers to technology deployment. Private sector financing will only reach the levels required if governments create and maintain supportive business environments for low-carbon energy technologies.

The IEA has developed a scenario (2DS) that aims to limit the long-term increase in global temperature to two degrees Celsius (2°C). In this scenario the emission trajectory is consistent with what the latest climate science research indicates would give an 80 per cent chance of limiting long-term global temperature increase to 2°C, provided that non-energy-related carbon dioxide emissions, as well as other greenhouse gases, are also reduced (IEA 2012: 15). Energy-related carbon dioxide emissions would be cut by more than half by 2050, compared with 2009, and continue to fall after that. At present the industrial sector consumes about one-third of the current global energy demand, producing about 40 per cent of global energy-related carbon dioxide emissions (IEA 2012: 32). The IEA has identified five key industries in this sector; iron and steel, cement, chemicals, paper, and aluminium. Between

2000 and 2009 energy consumption increased in all of these sectors, primarily driven by increased production in China and other emerging economies (IEA 2012). In order to meet the 2°C targets, the industrial sector must accelerate the rate of incorporating energy-efficient technologies; recycling, and energy recovery, Carbon Capture and Storage (CCS), alternative materials use, and fuel and feedstock switching. The IEA study suggests that in the medium term (up to 2020) emissions could be reduced significantly (by about one billion tonnes per year) by adopting the most efficient technologies or Best Available Technologies (BATs) when building or retrofitting facilities, and by optimizing production systems and manufacturing practices (IEA 2012: 34). In order to meet the 2°C targets, the introduction of CCS and the deployment of new technologies become crucial. However, in the capital-intensive energy industries it will require strong drivers for businesses to accept the risks associated with the introduction of new technologies.

Global production of steel (primary and secondary) now exceeds 1.3 billion tonnes per year (ISSB 2013)—this is more than the output of all of the other metals added together. Aluminium production is the second highest with a volume of about 60 million tonnes per year (ETSAP 2012), and copper third at about 20 million tonnes per year (ICSG 2013). Thus, in terms of managing energy consumption and greenhouse gas emissions from metal production, steel is a key factor. Steel production accounted for about 7 per cent of global carbon dioxide emissions in 2007.[2] The steel industry has several consortia (EU-ULCOS, US-AISI/DOE, COURSE50-Japan) working on the development of intermediate and radical new technologies that can minimize greenhouse gas emissions, for example through the use of electrolytic or hydrogen reduction systems. However, unless these alternate energy vectors are produced using low carbon technologies the gains will be small. Therefore to support low carbon production of the metals needed by high-technology systems, a more widespread adoption of renewable energy, CCS, and/or nuclear energy systems will be required. An IEA (2012: 61) study suggests that government policies will need to promote the US$24 trillion investments that will be required in the power, transport, buildings, and industry sectors to meet the 2DS targets.

Many of the techniques needed to deliver renewable technologies require the use of advanced materials that utilize special metals and alloys. One strategy for reducing emissions is to promote the use of electrical energy that has been 'decarbonized' through the use of renewable, nuclear, or fossil fuel

---

[2] Author's calculation based on carbon dioxide emissions of 2.3 Gt from iron and steel production (Brown et al. 2012: 4) and total global emissions of 31.4 Gt (Olivier, Janssens-Maenhout, and Peters 2012: 28) in 2007.

energies combined with CCS facilities. Several studies have been conducted to determine what impact this will have on the demand for metals (Kleijn 2012).

It is important for all organizations, large or small, to recognize that the utilization of resources (materials and energy) and environmental impacts are interrelated. Energy is required to recover natural resources and convert them into useful forms. Special materials are often required in the systems that are used to produce and deliver energy more efficiently (for example, elements such as silicon, selenium, and tellurium for photovoltaic systems, chromium for corrosion-resistant alloys in steam turbine systems, and others). At present a high proportion of the global energy supplies are based on fossil fuels, which results in greenhouse gas emissions. Attempts can be made to optimize process efficiencies, but given the trend for increasing global demand, process efficiency improvements alone cannot deliver the reductions in emissions that are required. Research and development on systems for capturing and storing the carbon dioxide generated from industrial processes and on low-carbon energy-generation systems are continuing but would need to be deployed rapidly on a global scale to avoid carbon dioxide levels in the atmosphere rising to levels that are considered to pose a significant risk to the climate. The current growth rate of energy production from sources that are not based on carbon is too low to make an impact on global greenhouse gas emissions. Nuclear energy is one 'low-carbon' source, and some countries, such as France (77.7 per cent), generate significant proportions of their national requirement for electricity from this source (NEI 2013). However, the impact of nuclear accidents such as Chernobyl and more recently Fukushima will constrain the deployment of nuclear technology in many countries. Nuclear and fossil fuel energy systems can generate large quantities of power consistently from relatively small sites, but this is not the case for renewable energy systems, such as photovoltaic, wind, and wave which are more diffuse and intermittent. Although the IEA points out that the transition to low-carbon energy systems offers a real business opportunity, concerted efforts from organizations across the globe will be required to meet the targets set to minimize the risks associated with higher levels of greenhouse gases in the atmosphere (IEA 2012: 61–70). It seems unlikely that this can occur unless government policies create suitable conditions for investment in low-carbon energy systems.

Utilization or Consumption—the Difference Between Metals and Fossil Fuels

The fossil fuels (coal, oil, and natural gas) are residues of ancient biomass originally produced through photosynthesis, altered by long-term processes, and stored in geological systems. When these hydrocarbons are utilized, as fuels or reductants, they are converted into different compounds (mainly gaseous) and standard practice has been to release most of these into the atmosphere. At the end of combustion or reduction processes little or none of the original substance remains, so fossil fuels can be considered to be completely consumed when they are used.

There are some applications where metals may be fully consumed or dissipated in use; for example, in corrosion-protection applications when magnesium alloys are used in the form of sacrificial anodes to protect metallic structures and pipelines from corrosion, or when zinc coatings are used to protect steel. Metals are also consumed in 'metallothermic' processes; when one reactive metal is used to produce another metal from an oxidized state, such as when calcium metal is used to produce neodymium metal. The volumes used in these processes are small, and even in these types of application it may be viable to recover and use the reactive metal, for example when magnesium metal is used in the production of titanium metal using the Kroll process (NST 2002). However, in many applications metals are not fully consumed during the manufacturing and use phase of the life cycle, so significant proportions can be recovered and recycled. This difference between metals and fossil fuels is illustrated in Figure 10.6 (Steinbach and Wellmer, 2010).

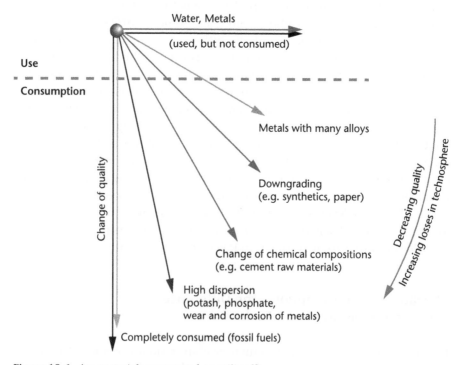

Figure 10.6. Are materials consumed or utilized?
Source: Steinbach and Wellmer (2010: 1412).

For many applications it is possible to recover significant quantities of metallic material from the manufacturing process and end-of-life stage of products and components. This material, often referred to as scrap, can be an important secondary resource. A recent UNEP study has examined the recycling rate of many of the metals now in use (UNEP 2011). The recycling rate for many of the metals that have been utilized in significant volumes (iron, aluminium, copper, chromium, nickel, led, etc.) has reached relatively high values exceeding fifty per cent. However, the widespread use of some other metals is relatively recent, so the infrastructure for the efficient recovery and recycling of these materials has not yet been developed and adopted on a global basis.

Metal production based on the treatment of materials recovered from geological settings is classified as primary production, whilst metal produced from scrap or recycled materials is often referred to as secondary material. The energy required to produce metal from secondary sources is usually lower than that required for primary ores. A figure that is often quoted is that the energy required to produce a quantity of secondary aluminium can be as low as 5 per cent of that required to produce primary aluminium (ALU 2012). The recycling of metals can reduce the demand for primary materials and will often deliver energy savings and thus reduced greenhouse gas emissions in comparison with primary production. However, it is always important to ensure that the basis for comparison between primary and secondary production routes is valid. To obtain a complete picture a full life-cycle analysis is required. 'Life cycle thinking' should always be applied at the product design stage to optimize the selection of materials and the way that they are put together, in order to minimize the overall environmental impact associated with the delivery of a specific social benefit. The UNEP/SETAC Life Cycle Initiative provides a good introduction to the principles and application of life-cycle analysis (UNEP 2009).

Demand for Resources

Before the Industrial Revolution, the supply of metals was constrained by a lack of know-how. The process for obtaining the ores was labour intensive and the technical knowledge and capability was limited, but perhaps the biggest constraint was the availability of a suitable energy source. This energy constraint was removed with the development of fossil fuels—initially coal, and then oil and natural gas. Access to this 'concentrated' form of energy enabled large volumes of materials to be mass-produced and thus to be more affordable for a much larger proportion of the population. The development of mass markets increased demand and delivered economic growth. Combined with developments in the education system this resulted in rapid technological growth, improvements in standards of living, and changes in behaviour. Previously the relatively high cost of materials meant that some products would have a long life and real intrinsic value, sometimes being passed from one generation to the next—as illustrated by the concept of the 'family silver'. The cost of labour was relatively low compared to the cost of materials, so products would be repaired to extend their service life.

Continuous technological development has enabled the development of completely new products and created new demands and opportunities for the rapid growth of entirely different businesses. Today people are used to rapid technological progress and it has become fashionable to acquire new versions every time an updated model becomes available (for example, mobile phones)—but this was not always the case, as illustrated by an early example from the automobile industry. Henry Ford's concept was to build a reliable, durable product, and he standardized the production lines to minimize costs. In 1922 Ford stated that 'We want the man who buys one of our cars never to have to buy another. We never make an improvement that renders any previous model obsolete' (Slade 2006: 32). However, as the market for new automobiles became saturated, manufacturers had to compete for customers in order to keep their large-scale production facilities busy. To retain a share of the market, automobile manufacturers had to offer customers real techno-logical/performance benefits or tempt them with stylistic changes. In his book Slade discusses the concept of 'built-in obsolescence' which he suggests has enabled some organizations to stay in business (Slade 2006: 3–7).

Maximizing the life of products would appear to be advantageous from the point of view of reducing demand for resources; however, rapid advances in technology can moderate this view. For example, older devices may have a high energy consumption rate during use, and/or produce high emissions of pollutants, so a calculation would be needed to determine if it would be beneficial overall to replace the device with a newer, more energy-efficient unit. However, going back to the example of the mobile phone, it is common for people to retain phones when they obtain a new one. These older phones may not be in use but in a sort of hibernation—from which they rarely emerge. This means that all of the materials that were used to make these dormant devices are also taken out of circulation (WIMS 2012). If energy costs are low, the motivation for energy and resource efficiency will be relatively low. This was the case during economic recovery after the Second World War, and growing personal prosperity in the developed economies (measured in terms of GDP per capita) helped to create a 'consumer society'. As the price of manufactured products fell in real terms they were not considered to be worth repairing or recycling when they failed or reached the end of their service life. Energy efficiency was promoted when prices peaked, during crisis periods, but received less attention when prices declined. However, growing concerns in recent decades about the impact of human activity on the environment, in global terms, has prompted re-evaluation of how to manage primary resources, end-of-life materials, and emissions from the combustion of fossil fuels.

What Can Be Done?

Research has shown that improvements in the process efficiency of energy-intensive industries cannot deliver the reduction in greenhouse gas emissions that are required to limit the risks of man-made climate change (IEA 2012; Brown et al. 2012). New ways of designing, using, and re-manufacturing or reusing materials and products must be developed. This will require novel approaches to design and business models. Efficiency across the whole supply chain and product life must be enhanced to deliver an overall improvement in material efficiency (Allwood et al. 2013).

The concept of dematerialization or decoupling the link between economic growth and resource consumption has been recognized for some time (for example, Richardson, Irwin, and Sherwin 2005; UNEP 2009; SERI 2009). Can this be achieved on a global scale by reducing the demand in the developed world? Can new technical developments enable the quality of life to be enhanced in the 'developing world' whilst avoiding waste, low efficiency levels, and the environmental damage caused during the development of 'the industrialized economies'? There is a need to re-examine the basis of modern societies; how can the transition be made from lifestyles based on inefficient consumption of the Earth's resources to ones that take long-term sustainability into account? A worldview is required because a focus on national needs will not deliver global solutions.

The concept of sustainable development for humans is based on a balance between economic, environmental, and social considerations. There are many detailed discussions on how this concept is defined but one succinct way of expressing it has been provided by Tim Jackson: 'Sustainability is the art of living well within the constraints of a finite planet' (quoted in Clift 2011: 4). Clift points out that there is an ethical dimension to the concept of sustainability just as there is with that of justice. 'Living well' must have an ethical base; it is not compatible with enjoying a high quality of life, at the expense of others living now or in the future (Clift 2011:4). Clift has highlighted the need for trans-disciplinary collaborations. Scientists and engineers must not exclude themselves from engagement in social issues. It is important that all 'stakeholder' views are considered and that the impact of human activity on the planet is recognized. There is a danger that breakdowns in social and/or national relations will occur more frequently unless strategies can be developed to address pressures arising from the increasing population and demand for resources (longer human lifespans, pollution of the atmosphere and oceans, loss of biodiversity and habitats).

Interest in the strategic nature of the metal supply chains has been revived recently due to concerns about the availability of some REEs. In fact the name is misleading because some of these elements are relatively abundant in the Earth's crust (BGS 2011). There are 17 elements in this grouping and several have properties that are utilized in advanced technologies including military systems. Most of these applications are relatively new, being developed over the last 50 years, and the annual production of all of these elements is less than 200,000 tonnes. This volume is quite small in comparison with primary production of aluminium, which was 454 million tonnes (World Aluminium 2013), and mine output of copper, which was 17.6 million tonnes in 2011 (ICSG 2013). Two of these REEs, Neodymium and Dysprosium, are used in high-strength magnets that have been developed for a wide range of applications, including electric motors that can be used in wind turbines and hybrid vehicles, and these are markets that are projected to grow (EWI 2011).

Initially, global demand for these elements was met from mines in South Africa and then the United States (Mountain Pass Mine) but these operations were closed when low-cost material became available from mines in China (Humphries 2012). By 2010 China was supplying more than 95 per cent of the world's demand for most REEs. However, China was not content with being a supplier of raw materials; a long-term development strategy shifted the focus from exporting minerals to producing added-value materials and using these to produce advanced technologies for use in China. The Chinese Government began to restrict the export of REE minerals and semi-manufactured products because of the growth of internal markets and concerns over the environmental management of the mining operations. This created shortages in the global supply chain and pushed up the price outside China (Moreland 2012). This has stimulated a lot of political interest with the United States, the EU, and Japan filing a complaint with the World Trade Organization (Baroncini, 2012). It has also stimulated a lot of interest in the exploration for and development of new sources of REEs. The United States Government has supported the redevelopment of the Mountain Pass mine in the United States. The main lesson to learn from this situation is that if one country, or organization, is allowed to develop what is virtually a monopoly supply situation it should be no surprise if they use this to their advantage. Unless a more strategic approach is adopted by end users, similar situations, where the supply chain is dominated by a single organization or small group of operators could arise for other metals, such as magnesium. Although demand for most metals is increasing, it is unlikely that there will be an absolute shortage of mineral or energy resources in the near future. However, meeting the demands based on projections of current trends using existing technologies would place a very heavy burden on global environmental systems and eco-systems. Fossil fuels are still the main resource for meeting human energy demands. Although alternative energy sources and systems are being developed, the current policies will not deliver the changes required quickly enough to reduce the risk of climate chaos. The issues are often approached from national considerations, but a global perspective is required. The development of systems for the more sustainable management of resources can play a significant role in limiting the demand for primary resources and thus reduce some of the impact of man-made climate change.

Japan is a country that has recognized the need for efficient use of resources and sustainable management of the environment. It has a high population density and very few mineral resources. Japan has recognized that the development of their high-technology manufacturing economy has been dependent on imported resources and so they have invested in R&D programmes to promote resource efficiency. They were early adopters of the concept of a circular economy via their '3R programme' (Reduce, Reuse, and Recycle) which has been promoted at all levels of society (MoE Japan 2006). The Japanese Ecotowns programme is supporting the industrial application of systems for recovering resources from end-of-life products and they are actively engaged in promoting the development of programmes that will support the development of 'Circular Economies' in Asia (Nagasawa 2010; Fujita 2009).

In addition to technological development, lifestyle choices will also be important. Businesses engaged in energy-intensive industries such as metal production or energy generation are sometimes depicted in a negative light, but they are responding to market demand and the requirements of society. The conditions in which these companies have a licence to operate should focus on sustainable development and these should be applied across the world because the impacts from their activities are global (ICMM 2012). Engineers and scientists can strive to understand and optimize systems, but they can only work within the ethical boundaries established by society. Since the Industrial Revolution some parts of the world have seen huge improvements in their material wealth, even if there are still questions about how this has impacted on the overall quality of life and well-being. Can citizens in the developing world find ways of achieving an improved quality of life whilst 'consuming' less primary resources (minerals and energy)? Wider discussion across disciplinary and cultural boundaries may help to develop a clearer understanding of the issues associated with meeting the needs of a growing population from a finite resource base. The links between material and energy utilization have recently been highlighted (Kleijn 2012).

A Final Word

It is important that the connections between the development of mineral resources, energy and water consumption, environmental management, population, and lifestyles are recognized. When the global population was smaller the impact of anthropogenic activities may have been insignificant, but that is no longer the case. The future demands on the Earth's mineral resources will be dependent on the size of the global population and the way these resources are valued. The development of cultures based on consumption has resulted in low levels of resource efficiency and degradation of the natural world. New approaches to product design and utilization based on eco-efficiency must become the norm. Unless more sustainable material management systems are adopted, on a global scale, the Earth's ecosystems will be further impaired, to the detriment of future generations. Perhaps drawing inspiration from a well-known phrase from Shakespeare's Hamlet, 'To be or not to be, that is the question', might help. To paraphrase Erich Fromm (2011), the foundation of human well-being should be the quest to develop skills and personality, instead of the accumulation of possessions; 'to have or to be?'

Acknowledgment

This chapter is dedicated to my parents, who lived through incredible times; my brothers and sisters for being there; and my wife and children for their tolerance and understanding. I have been lucky to work in more than 30 countries, and my hope is that with expanding global communication systems we can increase our understanding of the diverse range of human cultures, and recognize our responsibilities to future generations.

References

Allwood, J. M., Ashby, M. F., Gutowski, T. G., and Worrell, E. (2013). 'Material Efficiency: Providing Material Services with Less Material Production', *Philosophical Transactions of the Royal Society A*, 371: <http://dx.doi.org/10.1098/rsta.2012.0496>.

ALU (2012). 'Sustainability', Aluminium for Future Generations (ALU). Last accessed 31 January 2013. <http://recycling.world-aluminium.org/review/sustainability.html>.

Ashby, M. F. and Jones, D. R. H. (2009). *Engineering Materials 1: An Introduction to Properties, Applications and Design* (4th edition). Oxford: Elsevier.

Baroncini, E. (2012). 'The *China-Rare Earths* WTO Dispute: A Precious Chance to Revise the *China-Raw Materials* Conclusion on the Applicability of GATT Article XX to China's WTO Accession Protocol', *Cuadernos de Derecho Transnacional*, 4(2): 49–69.

BGS (2011). *Rare Earth Elements*, Commodity Profile Report, November. Keyworth: British Geological Survey, Centre for Sustainable Mineral Development. Last accessed 27 April 2013. <http://www.bgs.ac.uk/downloads/start.cfm?id=1638>.

Brown, T., Gambhir, A., Florin, N., and Fennell, P. (2012). 'Reducing CO_2 Emissions from Heavy Industry: A Review of Technologies and Considerations for Policy Makers', *Grantham Institute for Climate Change Briefing Paper 7*. London: Imperial College. Last accessed 27 April 2013. <https://workspace.imperial.ac.uk/climatechange/Public/pdfs/Briefing%20Papers/Reducing%20CO2%20emissions%20from%20heavy%20industry_Briefing%20Paper%207.pdf>.

CIM. (2013). 'Standard and Guidelines for Resources and Reserves', Canadian Institute of Mining, Metallurgy and Petroleum. Last accessed 27 January 2013. <http://web.cim.org/standards/MenuPage.cfm?sections=177,181&menu=229>.

Clift, R. (2011). 'An Engineering Approach to the Ethics of Generation and Consumption', Keynote speech, Canadian Academy of Engineering AGM and Symposium, The Sutton Place Hotel, Vancouver, BC, 2–3 July.

COCHILCO (2013). 'Global Copper Mine Production (Yearly)', Chilean Copper Commission (COCHILCO), Ministry of Mining, Government of Chile. Last accessed 31st May 2013. <http://www.cochilco.cl/english/statistics/production.asp>.

Cohen, D. (2007). 'Earth's Natural Wealth: An Audit', *New Scientist* (23 May), 2605: 35–41.

Comendador-Rey, B., Reboreda-Morillo, S., Kockelmann, W., Macdonald, M., Bell, A. M. T., and Pantos, E. (2008). 'Early Bronze Technology at Land's End, North Western Iberia', in S. A. Paipetis (ed.), *Science and Technology in Homeric Epics*. The Netherlands: Springer, pp. 113–22.

CoR (2013). 'The "Limits to Growth"', Club of Rome. Last accessed 31 January 2013. <http://www.clubofrome.org/?p=326>.

Crowson, P. (2011). 'Mineral Reserves and Future Minerals Availability', *Mineral Economics*, 24(1): 1–6.

Diamond, J. (2005). *Guns, Germs, and Steel*. London: Vintage Books.

Dunbar, W. S. (2012a). 'Basics of Mining and Mineral Processing (Part 2)', *American School of Mines 2012 Conference*, Price Waterhouse Coopers, 15 May. Last accessed 27 January 2013. <http://www.pwc.com/gx/en/mining/school-of-mines/2012/pwc-basics-of-mining-2-som-mining-methods.pdf>.

Dunbar, W. S. (2012b). 'Basics of Mining and Mineral Processing (Part 6)', *American School of Mines 2012 Conference*, Price Waterhouse Coopers, 15 May. Last accessed 27 April 2013. <http://www.pwc.com/gx/en/mining/school-of-mines/2012/pwc-basics-of-mining-6-som-a-future-of-mining.pdf>.

ETSAP (2012). 'Aluminium Production', IEA Energy Technology Systems Analysis Programme, *Technology Brief I10*, March. Last accessed 25 June 2013. <http://iea-etsap.org/web/HIGHLIGHTS%20PDF/I10_HL_AlProduction_ER_March2012_Final%20GSOK.pdf>.

EWI (2011). 'Rare Earth Materials: China's Role and Emerging Sources', Rare Earth Roundtable, 24 February. Last accessed 27 April 2013. <http://ewi.org/eto/wp-content/uploads/2013/01/4-Chinas-Role-and-Emerging-Sources-S.pdf>.

Fromm, E. (2011). *To Have or to Be?* New York: Continuum International Publishing Group.

Fujita, T. (2009). 'Eco-Towns for 3R Promotion in Japan', Inaugural meeting of the Regional 3R forum in Asia, Tokyo, 11–12 November. Last accessed 27 April 2013. <http://www.uncrd.or.jp/env/spc/docs/1st_3r_forum_presentation/Session2-2g1_Fujita.pdf>.

GFN (2013). 'Index', Global Footprint Network. Last accessed 27 April 2013. <http://www.footprintnetwork.org/en/index.php/GFN/>.

Giurco, D., Prior, T., Mudd, G., Mason, L., and Behrisch, J. (2010). *Peak Minerals in Australia: A Review of Changing Impacts and Benefits.* Prepared for CSIRO Minerals Down Under Flagship by the Institute for Sustainable Futures (University of Technology, Sydney) and Department of Civil Engineering (Monash University), March 2010. Last accessed 27 April 2013. <http://www.csiro.au/~/media/CSIROau/Flagships/Minerals%20Down%20Under/MinFuturesReport2_MDU_PDF%20Standard.pdf>.

Graedel, T. E. (2008). 'Are Non-Renewable Resources Critical?' Presentation, European Commission's Green Week, Brussels, 3–6 June. Last accessed 25 June 2013. <http://ec.europa.eu/environment/archives/greenweek2008/sources/pres/1_2_graedel.pdf>.

Halada, K. (2011). 'Role of Rare Metals in Material Technology and the Way to Substitute Them', Presentation to the Japan-EU *Substitution of Critical Raw Materials* Workshop, Tokyo, 21–22 November. Last accessed 27 April 2013. <http://www.jst.go.jp/sicp/ws2011_eu/presentation/presentation_08.pdf>.

HPOP (2013). 'M. King Hubbert', Hubbert Peak of Oil Production website. Last accessed 27 April 2013. <http://www.hubbertpeak.com/hubbert/>.

Humphries, M. (2012). 'Rare Earth Elements: The Global Supply Chain', *CRS Report for Congress R4137*, 8 June. Washington, DC: Congressional Research Service. Last accessed 27 April 2013. <http://www.fas.org/sgp/crs/natsec/R41347.pdf>.

ICMM (2012). 'Sustainable Development Framework', International Council on Mining and Metals. Last accessed 31 January 2013. <http://www.icmm.com/our-work/sustainable-development-framework>.

ICSG (2013). 'Copper: Preliminary Data for February 2013', International Copper Study Group (ICSG) Press Release, 22 May. Last accessed 27 May 2013. <http://www.icsg.org/index.php/press-releases/finish/114-monthly-press-release/1538-2013-05-22-monthly-press-release>.

IEA (2013). 'World Energy Outlook', International Energy Association/OECD. Last accessed 31 January 2013. <http://www.worldenergyoutlook.org/opinionleader sonweo/#d.en.34291>.

IEA (2012). *Tracking Clean Energy Progress.* Paris: International Energy Association. Last accessed 27 April 2013. <http://www.iea.org/publications/freepublications/publication/Tracking_Clean_Energy_Progress.pdf>.

ISA (2011). 'Environmental Management Needs for Exploration and Exploitation of Deep Sea Minerals', *ISA Technical Study 10*. Kingston, Jamaica: International Seabed Authority. Last accessed 27 April 2013. <http://www.isa.org.jm/files/documents/EN/Pubs/TS10/TS10-Final.pdf>.

ISSB (2013). 'Global Overview', Iron and Steel Statistics Board. Last accessed 27 April 2013. <http://www.issb.co.uk/global.html>.

ITLOS (2010). 'A Summary of Available Information in the Public Domain on the Likely Impact of Exploration and Mining Activities for Nodules on the Marine Environment', International Tribunal for the Law of the Sea (Case 17, Note from the Legal Council, 25 August) Last accessed 31 January 2013. <http://www.itlos.org/fileadmin/ itlos/documents/cases/case_no_17/ISA_1.pdf>.

Kato, Y., Fujinaga, K., Nakamura, K., Takaya, Y., Kitamura, K., Ohta, J., Toda, R., Nakashima, T., and Iwamori, H. (2011). 'Deep-Sea Mud in the Pacific Ocean as a Potential Resource for Rare-Earth Elements', *Nature Geoscience*, 4: 535–9. Last accessed 7 August 2013. <http://www.nature.com/ngeo/journal/v4/n8/full/ngeo1185.html>.

Keeling, R. F. (2007). 'Understanding Atmospheric Oxygen: The Other Half of the Global Carbon Dioxide Story', presentation dated November. La Jolla, CA: Scripps Institute of Oceanography. Last accessed 28 April 2013. <http://scrippsco2.ucsd.edu/ talks/rfk_birch_aquarium_2007.pdf>.

Kleijn, R. (2012). *Materials and Energy: A Story of Linkages*, Ph.D. Thesis. Leiden, The Netherlands: University of Leiden.

Kooroshy, J., Korteweg, R., and de Ridder, M. (2010). *Rare Earth Elements and Strategic Mineral Policy* (Report No. 2010.02). The Hague: Hague Centre for Strategic Studies and TNO. Last accessed 27 April 2013. <http://static.hcss.nl/files/uploads/33.pdf>.

Meadows, D., Randers, J., and Meadows, D. (2004). *The Limits to Growth: The Thirty Year Update*. White River Junction, VT: Chelsea Green Publishing Company.

MoE Japan (2006). *Sweeping Policy Reforms: Towards A 'Sound Material-Cycle Society' Starting from Japan and Spreading Over the Entire Globe: The '3R' Loop Connecting Japan with Other Countries*. Tokyo: Ministry of the Environment, Government of Japan. Last accessed 28 April 2013. <http://www.env.go.jp/en/wpaper/smc2006/fulltext.pdf>.

Monnet, J. (1978). *Memories*. New York: Doubleday & Company.

Moreland, D. (2012). 'China's Rare Earth Export Restrictions', *International Policy Digest*, 15 August. Last accessed 19 March 2013. <http://www.internationalpolicydigest.org/ 2012/08/15/chinas-rare-earth-export-restrictions/>.

Morgan, C. L. (2011). 'Manganese Nodules, Again?' *Oceans 2011*, 19–21 September. Waikoloa: IEEE Conference Publications.

Nagasawa, T. (2010). '3R Policy and Eco-town Project in Japan', presentation at the *Regional Workshop on Eco-Industrial Clusters: Policies and Challenges*. Tokyo: Asian Development Bank Institute. Last accessed 28 April. 2013. <http://www.adbi.org/ files/2009.12.10.cpp.day3.nagasawa.3r.policy.eco.town.proj.japan.pdf>.

National Geographic (2013). 'The Human Journey: Migration Routes', The Genographic Project, beta. Last accessed 31 January 2013. <https://genographic.nationalgeographic. com/human-journey/>.

Nautilus Minerals (2013). 'Solwara 1 Project—High Grade Copper and Gold', Last accessed 28 April 2013. <http://www.nautilusminerals.com/s/Projects-Solwara.asp>.

NEI (2013). 'World Statistics: Nuclear Energy Around the World', Nuclear Energy Institute. Last accessed 29 March 2013. <http://www.nei.org/resourcesandstats/ nuclear_statistics/worldstatistics>.

NST (2002). 'Technology Trend of Titanium Sponge and Ingot Production', *Nippon Steel Technical Report 85*, January. Tokyo: Nippon Steel and Sumitomo Metal Corportation, pp. 31–5. Last accessed 28 April 2013. <http://www.nssmc.com/en/tech/report/nsc/pdf/8507.pdf>.

NTO (2007). 'Grimes Graves Information Sheet', Fakenham: National Trail Office.

Olivier, J., Janssens-Maenhout, G., and Peters, J. (2012). *Trends in Global CO$_2$ Emissions: 2012 Report*. The Hague, The Netherlands: PBL Netherlands Environment Agency. Last accessed 28 April 2013. <http://edgar.jrc.ec.europa.eu/CO2REPORT2012.pdf>.

Radetzki, M. (2009). 'Seven Thousand Years in the Service of Humanity—the History of Copper, the Red Metal', *Resources Policy*, 34: 176–84.

Ragnarsdóttir, K. (2008). 'Rare Metals Getting Rarer', *Nature Geosciences*, 1: 720–1.

Richardson, J., Irwin, T., and Sherwin, C. (2005). *Design & Sustainability: A Scoping Report for the Sustainable Design Forum*. London: Design Council. Last accessed 27 April 2013. <http://www.designcouncil.info/mt/red/archives/Full%20Document.doc>.

RTC (2010). 'Conceptual Study—Smart Mine of the Future', Rock Tech Centre. Last accessed 27 January 2013. <http://www.rocktechcentre.se/?q=node/62>.

Sass, S. L. (2011). 'The Substance of Civilization', College of Engineering webcast, 2 February. Cornell University. <http://www.cornell.edu/video/?videoID=1085>.

SERI (2009). *Overconsumption? Our Use of the World's Natural Resources*. The Sustainable European Research Institute. Last accessed 6 August 2013. <http://www.foeeurope.org/sites/default/files/publications/FoEE_Overconsumption_0909.pdf>.

Slade, G. (2006). *Made to Break*. Cambridge, MA: Harvard University Press.

Steinbach, V. and Wellmer, F. W. (2010). 'Consumption and Use of Non-Renewable Mineral and Energy Raw Materials from an Economic Geology Point of View', *Sustainability*, 2(5): 1408–30.

Sullivan, K. (2012). 'Copperopolis—World Copper Project Comes to Swansea', Public Relations Office, University of Swansea, 12 April. Last accessed 28 April 2013. <http://www.swansea.ac.uk/media-centre/news-archive/2012/copperopolis-worldcopperprojectcomestoswansea.php>.

Taylor, M. (2005). 'Control of SO2 Emissions from Power Plants: A Case of Induced Technological Innovation in the US', *Technological Forecasting and Social Change*, 72: 697–718.

UNEP (2011). *Recycling Rates of Metal: A Status Report*. A Report of the Working Group on Global Metal Flows to the International Resource Panel. Paris: United Nations Environment Programme. Last accessed 13 August 2013. <http://www.unep.org/resourcepanel/Portals/24102/PDFs/Metals_Recycling_Rates_110412-1.pdf>.

UNEP (2009). *Design for Sustainability: A Step-by-Step Approach*. Paris: United Nations Environmental Programme and Delft University of Technology. Last accessed 28 April 2013. <http://www.d4s-sbs.org/d4s_sbs_manual_site_S.pdf>.

USGS (1980). *Principles of a Resource/Reserve Classification for Minerals*, Geological Survey Circular 831. Arlingron, VA: US Geological Survey. Last accessed 27 January 2013. <http://pubs.usgs.gov/circ/1980/0831/report.pdf>.

WIMS (2012). 'Key Facts', What's in My Stuff? Last accessed 31 January 2013. <http://www.whatsinmystuff.org/key-facts/>.

World Aluminium (2013). 'Primary Aluminium Production', The Website of the International Aluminium Institute. Last Accessed 3 June 2013. <http://www.world-aluminium. org/statistics/primary-aluminium-production/>.

Yannan, T. and Qian, W. (2012). 'China Eyes Developing Deep-Sea Mining Tech by 2030', *China Daily*, 29 May. Last accessed 27 April 2013. <http://www.chinadaily. com.cn/china/2012-05/29/content_15407666.htm>.

Yergin, D. (2011). *The Quest: Energy, Security and the Remaking of the Modern World*. London: Penguin.

11

Governance Matters Most

Ian Goldin

Governance is Key

The question of whether our planet is full cannot be posed simply in terms of numbers, be they of newborns or of carbon emissions and the overall availability of resources. The crucial question is how resources are managed and humans cooperate. The issues discussed in previous chapters are mediated through political and social institutions. The success or failure of the institutions established to manage our collective resources and address our collective challenges significantly raises or lowers the point at which the growth in population or resource use becomes limiting. The current benign neglect of appropriate institutional arrangements which can shape behaviours and influence outcomes undermines the sustainability of our planet and greatly lowers the thresholds for the planet being full.

History Lessons

The importance of political institutions and societal norms in relation to population size is evident historically. Although the Irish famine of the mid-19th century began with a shock to the food supply (with blight withering the source of 60 per cent of the island's calories), the political response was grossly insufficient.[1] Sir George Trevelyan, the British civil servant in charge of government relief efforts, described the famine as 'a direct stroke of an all-wise and all merciful Providence' which exposed the moral failings of the Irish

---

[1] Dependence on a single genetic variety of potato 'cut across all classes' and 'was most absolute among the lower two-thirds of the income distribution' on the eve of the famine (Mokyr 1983: 12).

people (quoted in Bartlett 2010: 287). However, it was technically possible to sustain the population; an early relief program fed 3 million daily. But social norms and political agendas led to the termination of that program after only 6 months and, due to this and subsequent decisions, Ireland's population decreased by half in the coming decades through death and emigration.[2] Geographer and anthropologist Jared Diamond (2005), in his book *Collapse*, describes other societies that failed to maintain population levels through political and social mismanagement. The Rapa Nui on Easter Island lost 80 per cent of its population after overexploiting its natural resources (Diamond 2005: Chapter 2). The Norse who settled on Greenland vanished, in part, due to social inflexibility about their food supply. These coastal peoples and seafarers were unable to adapt to fish eating, even as the climate change of the Little Ice Age reduced their land-based food availability (Diamond 2005: Chapter 7). Amartya Sen (1981) in his groundbreaking book *Poverty and Famines* showed how famine occurs because of the failure of institutions and how inequality in the distribution of food and relief efforts exacerbate existing inequality and poverty.[3]

Resources are managed by societies and, as Tony Atkinson explains in his chapter in this volume, our views on whether we are capable of managing our challenges informs answers to such fundamental questions as to whether 'the current population of some 7 billion, or the 10 billion expected by 2100, [is] the largest sustainable?' Atkinson notes that it may appear that questions of sustainability may require 'experts on water, food, natural resources, and health', but that as economics is fundamentally the science of managing scarcity, economists are also required.

Educational specialists are also required, as there appears to be a strong relationship between education and almost every aspect of human development. In Chapter 4, Sarah Harper considers some of the evidence associated with the demographic transition and shows that education contributes to lower fertility, reduced child mortality, and family planning. These are prominent themes in the literature, although the role of education in development is more wide ranging. In addition to its empowering women and affecting fertility and child mortality, Amartya Sen (2003) has pointed to the significance of a basic education for accessing gainful employment, invoking legal rights, tackling health problems (especially pandemics), reducing deprivation, addressing gender inequalities, and tempering the 'clash of civilisations' (amongst other things). Wolfgang Lutz and Samir KC (2011) explore the empirical relationship and find that better education is associated with lower

---

[2] For information on the debate surrounding blame for the famine, see Daly (2006), Chapter 1.
[3] The question of whether the causation of famine is best viewed in terms of food *availability* or *distribution* has been contested (Nolan 1993; Sen 1993).

fertility and mortality as well as better health and economic outcomes. Their modelling suggests that rapid progress on extending secondary education of girls would lead to a 2050 global population which is over a billion people less than would be the case if constant enrolment rates are assumed.

For economists and other social scientists, many of the challenges regarding the impact of population and income growth, urbanization, and other processes come down to questions of how their management is reflected, enacted, and enforced through political institutions. The structures and decision-making processes of these institutions can have a significant effect on the outcomes, even if the starting points and informational inputs are similar.[4] To add to the difficulty, institutional questions need to be resolved at both the national or sub-national level, and at times regionally and even globally.

Externalities and Institutions

Climate change is one concern which clearly transcends borders. Yet emissions reductions need to take place within the territories of over 200 sovereign states of the world. Even when we are thinking of an issue as global as atmospheric carbon, national institutions necessarily have a central role to play. Similarly, on oceans, it is national governments that will need to restrict their fishing fleets and monitor catches brought ashore.

Although international institutions and regulations have a central role to play, in their application national institutions tend to carry more legitimacy and provide more effective enforcement than global structures. Domestic institutions are often older than their international counterparts and are generally accepted by citizens as a legitimate source of binding law. Nations often possess common values and a common culture, which reduces barriers for communicating policies. Laws that have been produced can be enforced through the existing state apparatuses rather than a bespoke multinational enforcement mechanism. Social norms can also act as a more effective system, shaping individual behaviour via social pressure, and are easier to shift within the denser and more tightly woven networks of national communities, than in the often diffuse and tangled networks of the global communities that transcend borders.

International institutions, such as the UN or the WTO, are more remote and can trigger accusations of infringement on state sovereignty.[5] When nations

---

[4] For more on the relationship between the design of institutions and their effectiveness, see Koremenos et al. (2004).

[5] James Inhofe voted against the UN Convention on the Rights of Persons with Disabilities because 'This unelected bureaucratic body would pass recommendations that would be forced upon the United States if we were a signatory' (quoted in Cox and Pecquet 2012).

sign a treaty, this does not imply enforcement. Many thousands of treaties have been signed but there can be little or no consequence if the signatories fail to implement the agreements. The UN Arms Trade Treaty agreed in June 2013, following ratification by member states, will rely on the weak prospect of negative public opinion to shame arms-dealing nations who admit in their annual reports to have traded with unacceptable regimes, and there is no means to address the prospect of key countries simply not ratifying the treaty, including the United States where approval by Congress is required.[6] In many vital areas, key players refuse to sign up to accords which may limit sovereignty. So, for example, the Kyoto Treaty was ignored by key countries, such as the United States.

One may conclude from global institutions' poor record on addressing pressing issues that it would be best to rely solely on national political institutions. However, the challenges of population growth and economic growth, as well as the growing complexity and externalities associated with globalization, cannot be solved at the domestic level alone. Resource and other challenges increasingly spill over from one country to another. Without global agreements, national management of issues of global commons are necessarily severely compromised. States cannot unilaterally prevent these problems from adversely affecting their citizens.[7] While nations act to address global threats, they are less likely to take unilateral action to address global issues without assurances that other states will follow suit, as few global issues could be resolved by even the most powerful countries acting alone.

Global population and income growth will place extraordinarily heavy burdens on national and transnational governance structures. The World Bank has echoed the IPCC and other authoritative sources in highlighting that climate change will require 'long-term, large-scale integrated management and flexible planning' to prevent temperature rises beyond the limit of 2 degrees Celsius that climate scientists believe is a critical threshold (World Bank 2010: xxi). Achieving this target may require mitigation costs of $140–$175 billion annually in developing countries alone by 2030 (World Bank 2010: 9). Determining how to allocate such costs will be a political decision encompassing contending norms of feasibility and fairness, and of human rights and perceptions of historical legacies. Institutional decisions are likely to be bitterly contested as different countries seek to shape the distribution of future costs and benefits arising from an agreement.

Hartwell's chapter in this book describes the potential riches lying at the bottom of the sea. Resolving territorial disputes in areas like the Spratly Islands

---

[6] There is 'no specific enforcement mechanism' attached to the treaty, according to the *New York Times* (MacFarquhar 2013).

[7] See Goldin (2013), especially Chapter 1.

and South China Sea has already proven difficult, before profitable development of such resources has even begun. As the combination of new technologies which allow deeper drilling and mining, and melting ice resulting from climate change, make the exploitation of the Arctic more attractive to many countries and corporations, the danger of a new rush into this precarious region will severely test and is likely to overwhelm existing agreements. In the Arctic, as elsewhere, the consequences of previous rounds of environmental damage facilitate new forms of environmental degradation.[8]

Without much greater public awareness and political commitment, institutional inertia and reticence to change existing arrangements is likely to stymie institutional reform. In *Divided Nations* (2013) I examine this gridlock but also draw lessons from the instances when institutional reform does happen, sometimes surprisingly quickly. Examples include changing attitudes to same-sex marriage, and the speed at which smoking has been banned in public places in many countries, including in places in which previously smoking may have been considered sacrosanct, as was the case in many jazz clubs and bars. Unfortunately, there are more examples of apparently rational reforms which encounter stiff resistance, not least where there are short-term economic costs or a potential to shirk responsibility.

Governance structures at the local, national, and international level face far greater and more complex decisions than in the past as the number of issues, their interconnectedness, and the blizzard of complexity make it increasingly difficult to discern cause and effect. The extent to which the critical issues may be resolved in a timely manner remains a pressing concern. The capture of political processes by vested interests and lobbying by powerful corporations and groups have compounded the problem of reform. Those that benefit from the existing arrangements are able to capture short-term gains which may be highly profitable. As Joseph Stiglitz (2012) has pointed out, rising inequality means that those in the top percentile of society have a disproportionate ability to influence decision making and support regulations and laws which reinforce these differences, for example through limiting tax increases and cutting back on redistributive policies. The voice of the poor and marginal groups is often weaker in societies, which reinforces their plight. But longer-term and global issues also tend to be marginalized in national politics and have only weak natural constituencies. Short-term and local concerns dominate politics, with the difficult questions regarding institutional reform and global governance pushed down the crowded agendas which focus on the immediate local concerns. Even when they occasionally surface around major global meetings, such as the G8 or UN Assembly, politicians are prone to play

---

[8] I am indebted to David Clark for this point, and many others which have enhanced this chapter.

to the cameras of their national media and only exceptionally are able to transcend the immediacy of short-term national politics. The global institutions are owned and directed by national governments, and it is these governments that have to allow and guide the institutions to deal with the critical global challenges in a manner which at times may well conflict with short-term national objectives of the member states.[9] Similarly, staff seconded to global institutions too often are seen as ambassadors representing national short-term interests, rather than as global civil servants, and this undermines the potential of the international institutions to rise above fractious international politics.

Even on issues of public health, an area about which international political cooperation has been most acceptable, institutional failure is possible. The 'Patient Zero' of HIV/AIDS spread the disease in the late 1970s and early 1980s, but the AIDS pandemic only became a major political and global issue after it spread in the United States, and a growing number of 'famous people became infected' (Arhin-Tenkorang and Conceição, 2003: 493). The WHO did not launch a campaign until 1987, by which time the disease had caused more than 24,000 deaths in the United States alone (amfAR 2013).

At the Crossroads

Global governance is at a crossroads. Key global negotiations, including the Rio + 20 climate talks and the Doha Trade Round have failed. At a time when we urgently need the global community to focus on international institutional arrangements, there is at best benign neglect. In many respects, while globalization and with it economic growth has taken off since the collapse of the Soviet Union, the ending of the Cold War paradoxically has meant that there is less, not more, attention paid to global governance. The Cold War was certainly no golden age for international cooperation, but the bipolar nature of the world system allowed some issues, such as nuclear testing and arms limitations, to be negotiated bilaterally by the United States and the Soviet Union. This facilitated informal negotiating structures with a small number of parties (often just two), as well as manageable enforcement, since only two states needed to be inspected.

Today, up to 200 countries are involved in global negotiations. As the number of official players has increased, so too has the number of civil society, business, and other actors. Growing interconnectedness and the rise in populations, incomes, and connectivity has meant that negotiators and the citizens

---

[9] These questions are the focus of my book, *Divided Nations* (2013).

they represent increasingly face a tightening tangle of connections and knotted alliances. With instant media and rising democratization and transparency adding to the pressure, the demands of special interests and weight of current, rather than looming concerns are major obstacles to the resolution of key global challenges. The perception of citizens and politicians alike is that disentangling cause and effect in global affairs is easier done through simplification and a retreat to localism. Politicians close to home are thought to be more accountable and in touch with local needs. The result is that at a time when the planet is demanding more joined-up governance, we are getting less. The reasons for this are understandable and in terms of democratization and transparency even desirable, but the consequences are an impasse in global governance.

Many, if not most, of the critical factors affecting our personal lives and our country's future will be shaped by forces that come from outside our national borders. The key drivers of change—in terms of opportunities, incomes, jobs, technologies, and other key determinants of economic growth and social health; as well as threats, such as terror, conflict, climate change, pandemics, cyberattacks, or financial crises—are likely to come from across our national borders.[10]

Subsidiarity is a key principal of institutional design. Whatever can best be resolved locally, nationally, or through bilateral or regional relationships, should be. In this respect, global governance should legitimately be seen as a last resort. Unfortunately, a growing number of the challenges facing the planet require a strengthening of both global as well as national governance. The idea that nations would be better off by withdrawing from global or other supranational institutions reflects a failure to understand the nature of connectivity and the extent of our integration, as well as the benefits such integration brings. To secure our future, we need to be more engaged with global political affairs and global or regional institutions, not less.

The importance of institutions in mitigating or exacerbating the effect of the issues discussed in this book exists at all levels of society. The layers of governance and institutions build on each other and global governance cannot be effective without strong local and national institutions. Local authorities, for example, often determine regulations for building construction and maintenance. As buildings consume 40 per cent of the world's energy, mayors and town councils have the power to make a sizeable dent in energy consumption (Long 2012). National authorities set regulations for many products sold within national borders, such as energy efficiency levels for vehicles, light bulbs, or microwaves. In the United States, existing energy efficiency

---

[10] See Goldin and Reinert (2012), Oxford Martin Commission for Future Generations (2013), and Goldin and Mariathasan (2014).

measures, if fully adopted, could produce energy savings equal to 10 per cent of total United States consumption (World Bank 2010: 322). Conversely, national governments often distort the energy market with subsidies directed towards the powerful fossil fuel corporations (World Bank 2010: 211). Local and national institutions therefore create incentive structures that can encourage prudent action, such as tax rebates for insulating old homes, or imprudent action, such as limiting variations on flood insurance, which encourages risky settlement behaviour.

Managing Governance

The current international system tends towards an ineffective decision-making structure. As Pascal Lamy, Director General of the WTO, has argued, 'the main challenge is that the Westphalian order gives a premium to "naysayers" who can block decisions, thereby impeding results. The enduring viscosity of international decision-making puts into question the efficiency of the international system' (Lamy 2012). In a system studded with veto points, states often resist transferring or sharing their jurisdiction with international institutions, while at the same time they are often too busy dealing with domestic concerns to dedicate sufficient attention to issues requiring international agreement.

Further, the current phase of globalization has exacerbated the inability of the global community to take collective action. The United States, Europe, and Japan are greatly diminished in terms of their economic and political standing in the world. As a result of the economic crisis, leaders across the board are fighting for their political survival, and, while cutting expenditures and managing fractured domestic politics, are unable or unwilling to play a global role. The rapidly emerging markets, meeting in the context of the BRICS and other alliances, have as yet been unable to replace the old leadership and take a global lead to address critical challenges. To date, their record has been one of slowing the progress in many global negotiations and they have yet to play a forcefully constructive role in shaping global affairs. In Copenhagen in 2009, we note below that the objections of China and other major emerging nations contributed to the collapse of the negotiations (Rapp, Schwägerl, and Traufetter 2010). Similarly, the leading emerging nations have mirrored the blocking tactics of the most advanced economies to ensure that the Doha Round of trade negotiations, started in 2001, remains stalled.

Global governance is drifting in a period of handover in global power, precisely at a time when issues are bubbling up that need urgent attention. As Kishore Mahbubani (2011) has evocatively noted:

...the world has changed structurally, yet our systems for managing global affairs have not adapted. In the past, when the billions of citizens of planet earth lived in separated countries, it was like having an ocean of separate boats. Hence, the postwar order created rules to ensure that the boats did not collide; it created rules for cooperation. Up until now, this arrangement has worked well. World War III did not follow World Wars I and II. But today the world's seven billion citizens no longer live in separate boats. They live in more than 190 cabins on the same boat. Each cabin has a government to manage its affairs. And the boat as a whole moves along without a captain or a crew. The world is adrift.

Governance and Sustainability

We now examine the implications of the current governance failure for whether the planet is full. For illustrative purposes, and as a chapter such as this cannot be comprehensive, we consider how existing institutional arrangements may impact on four of the dimensions of a fuller planet: cities; climate change; food and water supply; and migration.

The case of cities

Our ability to respond to rising populations and growing complexity over the coming decades is central to our ability to ensure that the planet is not full. This is not simply or even mainly a challenge for central governments. We have argued above that global and regional institutions need to be given greater importance, but so do sub-national institutions and other actors, including business and civil society organizations.

Already, the majority of the world's population lives in cities. By 2050, urban environments may be anticipated to house over 70 per cent of humanity (WHO 2013).[11] Governments at the local and national level are making choices about how to expand their cities, and these choices can have significant effects on the strain that urban dwellers put on their local environment and the global commons.[12] Increasing urban density has been found to decrease carbon emissions; both Sweden and Japan have reduced the carbon intensity of their economies through pro-density incentives (World Bank 2009: 211). In the United States, sprawling cities and the shift of the population towards automobile-reliant suburbs is the outcome of zoning, tax, and other policies.[13] Atlanta, for example, has a similar population to Barcelona

---

[11] See also Satterthwaite (2006).

[12] Los Angeles is an excellent (negative) example of the relationship between government policy, in this case transportation, and development patterns (see Wachs 1996).

[13] In the United States, government policies strongly favour residential investment in peripheral suburbs, as argued in a study by two economists (Persky and Kurban 2001).

but a population density which is lower by a factor of 29.[14] Ninety per cent of the future growth of cities will occur in developing countries, and policies regarding urban management could play a vital role in shaping the response to population and resource pressures. We have already seen how careful management of urban buildings can have a sizable impact on energy consumption. China is among the countries that are most interested in finding alternatives to carbon-intensive growth. It has a particularly large and economically attractive potential for leapfrogging old, inefficient, and environmentally destructive technologies. A large share of China's residential and industrial capital stock of the next decade is yet to be built and with available frontier technologies, and appropriately encouraging open policies on technology transfer, the world's second-largest economy and largest carbon emitter could reduce its industrial energy demand in 2020 by 20 per cent while increasing productivity (World Bank 2010: 291).

Cities can also contribute to the technological innovations that may be needed to address many of the challenges presented by a fuller and more complex planet. In the advanced economies for which there is data, metropolitan areas are home to 96 per cent of innovation (World Bank 2009: 135). As countries advance, cities contribute a growing share of national income and employment (the exceptions are the resource-rich countries where oil or minerals extraction may continue to dominate). One-third of the Mexican population lives in its 10 biggest metropolitan areas, but those cities generate 62 per cent of its value added to the economy (World Bank 2009: 141).

Simply hoping for innovations to emerge from cities is not enough. Regulations, investment in research, and market incentives play a crucial role in driving or stifling innovation and in the transformation of innovation into widely applied products or processes. Investment by governments in their national systems is vital, but so too is investment in collaborative efforts to address key global challenges. The CGIAR is a good example of such collaboration. It lay behind the Green Revolution that led to a doubling of cereal productivity in Asia from 1970 to 1995 and continues to play an important role. This needs to be underpinned with more funding if it is to address the stagnation of yields and the need for developing crops that are able to adapt to depleted and saline water and land, and climate change. The CGIAR agricultural research system reflects a cooperative response to a pressing global challenge. There are many other successful examples of international collaboration to create economies of scale. These include the twenty nations that collectively fund the CERN laboratory which investigates fundamental

---

[14] Author's calculation based on figures from the World Bank (2009: 211).

questions in physics, and the collaboration of a wide range of countries in the International Space Station.

Climate change

There have been a number of attempts to address the global dimensions of climate change. The Kyoto Protocol to the United Nations Framework Convention on Climate Change was adopted in 1997 and places binding obligations on developed countries to reduce greenhouse gas emissions. The Copenhagen Summit in 2009 attempted to advance the climate agenda and bring developing countries into an emissions-reduction regime. These processes have proved inadequate in face of the scale of the global challenge. The United States, the world's largest greenhouse gas emitter at the time, never ratified the Kyoto Protocol and withdrew from it in 2001. By the time of the Copenhagen Summit, China had overtaken the United States to become the largest greenhouse gas emitter. The objections of China and other significant emerging nations to agree to binding obligations for developing countries served to scupper the Copenhagen Summit.[15] These nations argue that it is advanced economies that must make the greatest adjustment, given their historical contributions. Even the advanced economies that acknowledge this point out that as emerging markets already account for over half of new emissions, which are the only ones that can be mitigated, their contribution is vital. As radical action by the largest emitters is required to get off current energy-intensive growth paths, the failure to reach agreements severely undermines the planet's ability to manage the burden of increased populations and growth. When key states lack the willingness to enter into binding agreements that carry the weight of punitive enforcement mechanism, treaties are largely ineffectual.

At the national level political institutions are equally ill-equipped to deal with the looming presence of climate change. What is good on a global scale might conflict with what is best for individual nations acting simply in their own self-interest (see Goldin 2013). Since climate change is a slowly building catastrophe and scientists are uncertain as to the details of its likely timing and impact on any one locality, the uncertainties are exploited by lobbyists, such as the coal industry that strongly opposes reductions in carbon emissions. The effect of this can be seen in the 2012 United States Presidential election campaign. Both candidates avoided discussion of climate change—barring Republican candidate Mitt Romney's dismissal of the issue as of secondary importance in his acceptance speech—and jockeyed during their second

---

[15] See, for example, Bodansky (2010).

debate about who could better increase domestic oil production.[16] Meanwhile, there is the danger that regions with strong 'green preferences' (for example, with restrictive environmental regulation), will outsource either the polluting activity itself or the disposal of accrued waste.

There is debate as to the extent to which pollution is 'exported' as part of globalization, but there is strong observational data that this trend exists.[17] Many examples of pollution havens exist, and it is important to note that the effect not only takes place between countries, but also *within* countries, as a response to regulatory, tax, and other differences. California, for example, has a long history of importing power from coal plants in the American West that produce far greater amounts of harmful gases than would be permitted in the Golden State (Milford et al. 2005: iv–v).

National governments can play a highly significant role in mitigating climate change; pricing carbon (whether through a tax or through a cap-and-trade scheme) is an effective way of both generating carbon finance resources and directing those resources to efficient opportunities. However, without a binding international agreement, adopting such a policy becomes more difficult and less effective, as it may hurt a nation's or state's immediate economic growth or be worked around in a manner similar to pollution havens. It nevertheless may be easier to achieve national agreement or state-level agreements than international agreements, which have proved intractable. The added complication at the international level is that of the rapidly changing power relationship between those countries that account for most of the greenhouse gas emissions (the already industrialized countries) and those that account for most of the new flows (the emerging markets). Nations must therefore balance technical considerations with normative issues of fairness and historical responsibility.

The present stock of greenhouse gases in the atmosphere has been generated almost entirely by the already developed countries. Brazil has insisted that this fact be acknowledged in the Kyoto Protocol with 'historical responsibility' being used as the basis for apportioning future mitigation burdens among those countries with firm targets (World Bank 2010: 238). However, 90 per cent of the increases in carbon dioxide from energy use in the next twenty years will be from developing countries (World Bank 2010: 193). To place the burden on developing countries for a problem caused by the accumulated historical actions of developed countries is unfair and even unethical, especially since it might impede the poorer countries' right to development.[18]

---

[16] Governor Romney said 'President Obama promised to begin to slow the rise of the oceans and heal the planet. My promise . . . is to help you and your family' (NPR 2012).

[17] See, for example, Copeland and Taylor (2004) or McAusland (2008).

[18] This right was codified in the Vienna Declaration and Programme of Action and endorsed by the UN General Assembly.

Yet to allow unfettered carbon usage in those countries that are rapidly increasing their emissions would greatly undermine an effective climate change regime. To navigate this morass of self-interest, competing rights, norms, and social values, rapid technological change as well as massive financial transfers are required within a framework of robust global institutions. As Kyoto and Copenhagen have shown, creating the necessary agreements has proved elusive.

Food and water

Rising populations and incomes mean that growing numbers of people are consuming meat- and resource-intensive diets. Even without climate change and other new pressures, production is stretched to the limit. The failure of institutional responses to rising demand compounds the problem. Food is often a highly regulated product and only a small share is traded globally: subsidies and protectionism result in around 93 per cent of the world's rice and around 82 per cent of the world's wheat being consumed in the same country in which it is grown.[19] Many surplus-producing countries resort to export restrictions in times of high prices to protect their domestic consumers (World Bank 2010: 160). Food production remains heavily distorted, with key producers, notably the United States and the European Union, engaged in highly protectionist policies which exacerbate instability in world food markets.[20] The fact that only a small share of vital food crops is traded on open markets increases the potential for food price spikes. These pose a growing risk for food-importing countries and particularly to poor urban people, who are most vulnerable when food prices rise rapidly.

Extreme weather is anticipated to intensify storms and floods, with more rain predicted in parts of South Asia and less in the interior of sub-Saharan Africa. Increased fluctuations and intensity of weather—rainfall, storms, temperature, humidity, and wind—pose an even bigger threat to agriculture than changes in the annual averages. Agricultural yields in sub-Saharan Africa and Central and South Asia could, as a consequence, fall dramatically. As a result of melting glaciers in South Asia, China, and the Andes, flooding could increase during the wet season and water supplies would diminish during the dry season—potentially affecting more than a billion people. Simultaneously, rising sea levels could lead to the significant loss of coastal wetlands and their food supplies by 2050.[21]

---

[19] These figures are derived from Wailes and Chavez (2012: 8) and USAD (2013) respectively.

[20] For a discussion of the perverse impact of agricultural subsidies see Goldin and Reinert (2012), Chapter 3.

[21] See Brown (2007: 9–10).

Institutions have attempted to respond. The Consultative Group for International Agricultural Research (CGIAR) is a global consortium of food research programmes, which have developed a joint project on adapting to climate change. The UN's Food and Agriculture Organization has sponsored a range of projects, an example being one that has dramatically reduced the overexploitation of aquifers in Andhra Pradesh, India. The Chinese government has had success with a similar project in one of its main wheat-growing regions and has reforested vast areas of its interior highlands to reduce desertification (World Bank 2010: 165).

However, these and many other achievements are small relative to the scale of the problem. Global institutions also have been unable to address the perverse subsidies that undermine sustainability. These are the result of the capture of agricultural policy by powerful interest groups. I have shown elsewhere how agricultural subsidies grossly distort and create instability in global food markets (Goldin and Reinert 2012: 62–3). In the OECD economies these exceed US$360 billion per year.[22] Charles Godfray's chapter discusses how the food trade is mediated through a few multinational corporations and is one of the most protected industries in many countries. The establishment of a level playing field on which farmers in poor countries may compete with those in rich economies is vital to facilitate more inclusive and predictable participation in global food markets. Similarly, access to water and other resources is about power and transparency, not simply about availability. The subsidies to water and energy are even greater than those benefiting farmers in rich countries. In Chapter 5, Ian Johnson estimates that worldwide government subsidies for water total $400 billion annually. A fuller planet demands a more equitable distribution of opportunities to produce food, and that water, energy, and other resources reflect their true value to society.

Migration

Of all the problems that a fuller and more economically advanced planet poses, the most political of them is migration. Historically, the response of people to resource scarcity, as well as to poverty, famine, conflict, and other threats, was to migrate. Over the past hundred years, the invention and increasingly widespread adoption of passports and other border controls has been associated with the rapid rise in the number of nation states. The barriers to movement have gone up, as the opportunities to migrate, through ships, planes, and vehicles have multiplied. As globalization has accelerated in recent years, it is an irony that the movement of people, and particularly

---

[22] The figure quoted is a five-year average (2007–11) that combines the producer support estimate (based on commodity output) with market-based support (OECD 2013).

poor people escaping resource constraints, has become more difficult. Meeting the challenges of a growing population and increasing resource constraints requires that people not be trapped in poverty or environmentally disastrous circumstances. While parts of the planet may be full, other regions are far from their capacity constraints. Migration has historically been the means to address these imbalances and must again be seen as a key means to ensure that we do not exceed our planetary limits.

The movement of people between countries addresses one of the most fundamental questions of political science—who is and ought to be a citizen of one's country—and can trigger passionate controversies about cultural, economic, and human rights. Migration will be of even greater significance in the future. Declining birth rates in much of the developed world threaten the labour supply of those economies and will lead to rapidly rising dependency ratios. In theory, for example, it has been estimated that Europe would need to admit 1.3 billion migrants between 2000 and 2050 if it is to maintain its current ratio of workers to dependants, which is not plausible (Goldin, Cameron, and Balarajan 2011: 248). In practice, however, it is likely that much of the burden imposed by rising dependency ratios will be met by longer working hours, later retirement, smaller pensions, less welfare, higher taxation, and some substitution of machine capabilities for human activities.

The environmental implications of a fuller world could also drive an increase in migration, as climate change and other pressures compel increasing numbers of people to travel across borders. Projections of climate and environmental change in the 21st century from a range of models include scenarios of extreme weather, deforestation, declining fish stocks, pollution of water supplies, and degradation of agricultural land. The 2006 Stern Review on *The Economics of Climate Change*, sponsored by the British Government, noted that without a reduction in carbon emissions the livelihoods of people could be affected by changes in access to water, food production, health, and use of land and the environment (Stern 2006). Climate change would have the most severe consequences for people living in vulnerable areas of the poorest countries because they often live on marginal lands or flood plains and lack the economic and political resources to respond to severe environmental stress. The Intergovernmental Panel on Climate Change (IPCC) has noted that shoreline erosion, coastal flooding, and agricultural disruption can promote human migration as an adaptive response. The debate around the implications of climate change for migration revolves around the magnitude and permanence of displacement by environmental factors.[23]

---

[23] See, for example, McCarthy et al. (2001), Chapter 11.

As with the other factors influencing the supply of migrants in the future, it is impossible to arrive at a reliable estimate of the number of people who will migrate in response to environmental changes. In the words of William B. Wood, official geographer of the United States Department of State, 'there is usually no simple relationship between environmental causes and societal effects' (quoted in Castles 2002: 4). The dramatic forecast of as many as 200 million 'environmental refugees' by 2050 has been widely cited in official reports, but has not held up to wider scrutiny.[24] I believe it is unlikely that, in the coming decades, climate change alone will lead to a tenfold increase in the number of refugees and displaced persons, and a doubling of the total number of migrants, as implied by these guesstimates (see Goldin 2011). The poorest migrants typically do not have the means to migrate internationally. Over the longer term, however, as climate change leads to ocean rises of many metres and makes certain parts of the globe uninhabitable or unproductive, higher levels of migration are an inevitable response. Certain regions of the world, like the far north of the Americas and Europe, may also become more attractive, and migration into previously sparsely populated regions may be anticipated in the longer term. As I show in *Exceptional People*, migration across borders is the exception not the norm for societies, and arises from a multiplicity of economic, demographic, and other factors. For the most part, climate change is likely to compound these underlying drivers of migration, with the effects of climate change and resource depletion on migration likely to become increasingly pronounced in the decades ahead.

In the case of sudden environmental catastrophes, people typically migrate to nearby areas and often return to their homes. Dramatic floods in central and southern Mozambique in March 2000 displaced about a million people from their homes, but within a few months most had been able to return (Black 2001: 7). The 2004 Asian Tsunami caused the death of about 200,000 people and displaced around half a million people. Most of this movement was within the refugees' home region, with only a small number crossing borders to seek refuge (Brown 2007: 16). A year later, in 2005 Hurricane Katrina caused the largest movement of people in the history of the United States. In a period of two weeks, as many as 1.5 million people fled the Gulf coast (three times more than moved in the Dust Bowl migration of the 1930s). With up to a third of the New Orleans residents yet to return, those scattered by the disaster have remained in the United States and the impact on international migration has been negligible (Knight 2009). The size of the United States and the potential for people to find a

---

[24] It should be noted that the United Nations High Commission on Refugees prefers the term 'environmentally displaced person' (Foresight 2011: 34). See also Brown (2007) and Black (2001).

livelihood and live elsewhere in the country has affected the outcomes, as has the failure of even the world's most powerful government to support the displaced persons.

The same remarks apply to man-made disasters such as war, armed conflict, and persecution. The Uppsala Conflict Data Project recorded 29 separate armed conflicts in 2012 (UCDP 2013)—many of which led to displacement and migration. The Syrian crisis alone has forced up to 5 million people to flee their homes since the conflict began and has created more than 2 million refugees in neighbouring countries (BBC 2013a; UNHCR 2013b). The UN estimates that the number of internally displaced people could rise to 8 million by the end of 2014 (BBC 2013b). The impact on the humanitarian system has been overwhelming due to the scale of the crisis (UNHCR 2013a) and the lack of relief organizations in parts of the region (EMN 2013).

Those who cannot return to their homes and must cross borders may find themselves orphans of the international system. While the UNHCR has a clear mandate to support refugees of recognized conflicts or disasters, climate change and environmental loss has not yet been recognized as eligible. There is no UN organization or internationally recognized system for the management of migration (other than for officially recognized refugees, which account for fewer than ten per cent of migrants) (Goldin, Cameron, and Balarajan 2011: 147–9). Migration policies are determined by states, which are not prepared to give away the power to regulate entry into their society. The Schengen free travel area in the European Union is an important exception and is predicated on an agreement among the participating states to control entry into their common border.

Migration offers the most powerful tool for reducing global poverty and inequality and could be a critical mechanism for adjustment to meet the challenges outlined in this book. Its potential to address the critical issues of global resource allocation will become even more important as global populations and incomes rise. Nevertheless, the financial crisis has exacerbated the rising anti-migration sentiment in many countries. Migrants face increasing barriers, with poor migrants who are most in need facing the greatest obstacles to their migration.

The planet may be far from full, and indeed shortages of people, both skilled and semi-skilled, in decades to come will see a reversal of the current preoccupation with keeping people out. However, the mismatch between where, when, and which people wish to migrate and the willingness of countries to accept them is likely to remain a major obstacle to migration realizing its potential as a global adjustment mechanism (Goldin, Cameron, and Balarajan 2011).

Globalization: the Problem with Success

Globalization has led to a decrease in poverty around the globe, as even those with a sceptical view of its successes would agree.[25] The number of people living on less than $1.25 (PPP) per day was as high as 1.9 billion in 1990, but had dropped to 1.3 billion by 2008 and, despite the increase in the planet's population by around 1.5 billion over this period, the poverty headcount ratio decreased from 43.1 to 22.4 per cent over the same period (World Bank 2013).[26] It is predicted that '[b]y 2030, roughly 50 per cent of the world population would fall into the $6,000–$30,000 bracket, up from around 29 per cent currently (and around 24 per cent in the 1980s)' (Wilson and Dragusanu 2008: 10). This growing global middle class owes much to global integration and the dismantling of divisive walls which prevented the flow of ideas, as well as goods, services, and capital, around the world (Goldin and Reinert 2012). The price of this success is a much greater strain on global resources. As incomes rise, individuals eat more meat and fish; consume more packaged and processed foods; use and buy motorized vehicles; travel more; and purchase more energy, water, land, and materials-intensive goods and services, such as heaters and air conditioners, fridges, cookers, TVs and computers, and other consumer appliances.

There is some evidence that the relationship between income and resource consumption is not linear, but that there exists an *Environmental Kuznets Curve* (EKC): an inverted U-shaped relation between income (on the horizontal axis) and pollution intensity (on the vertical axis) (see Goldin and Winters 1995). Supporting the EKC, Daniel C. Esty (2001: 115) reports, that 'environmental conditions tend to deteriorate in the early stages of industrialization and then improve as nations hit middle-income level, at a per capita GDP of about $5000 to $8000'. Different resources have Kuznets curves which peak at different levels and this can also be affected by prices and institutional interventions (Mills and Waite 2009). In general, however, as incomes rise, the demand for planetary resources rises rapidly too, with this peaking as the amount of food, energy, or other resource-intensive goods and services we consume begins to reach our absorptive limits. At around $5,000 to $10,000 per capita, the conversion of every additional dollar earned into the demand for energy, water, and other natural resources is subject to diminishing returns. Thus, although total demand and emissions increase beyond this point, the rate of increase slows down. The coming two decades will see over

---

[25] See, for example, Rodrik (2011), Stiglitz (2006), and Bourguignon (2012). Goldin and Reinert (2012) summarize many of the key arguments.

[26] The poverty headcount ratio is defined as the number of individuals living below the poverty threshold over the total population in the group of developing countries.

two billion people go through this income transition. The result will be a peak in intensity in terms of the rising demand for energy and natural resources, with a wide range of associated environmental and other spillover effects and costs.

More People Means More Systemic Risk, but also More Cooperation

Increased population density combined with increased interconnectedness, both physical and virtual, raises the potential for systemic risk and cascading crises.[27]

Potential crises arising from increasing complexity of the global system are plentiful. Complex system researchers Dirk Brockmann, Lars Hufnagel, and Theo Geisel (2005) simulated the effects of a single SARS-infected individual placed anywhere in the world using data which accounted for 95 per cent of the entire global civil aviation traffic and assuming virulence equivalent to that of SARS. On average, if a carrier took two plane journeys, the vaccination of 75 per cent of the world population would be required to avoid a global pandemic. After one additional flight, global vaccination would be required. The rapidity with which authorities would have to respond stands in stark contrast to past centuries, when epidemics took weeks, months, or years to cover large areas.[28] Parallels can be found in the financial sector, in which complex derivities and overleveraged banks allowed a bubble in the United States housing market to trigger a worldwide financial crisis and recession.

Without greater attention to the management of the global system we are highly likely to see a rise in systemic risks. These include, but are certainly not confined to: growing economic inequality; rising antibiotic resistance and more virulent pandemics; instability of the internet and rising cyberattacks; frequent financial crises; and growing environmental and climate instability.

The response to increased density and complexity may well be that individuals around the world may seek to reduce their exposure to what they perceive as external shocks that come from across their border by seeking to restrict the movement of migrants, withdrawing from international agreements, and exploiting their own resources with little regard for the global commons. If globalization and increased population density is seen to be the source of

---

[27] See Goldin and Mariathasan (2014) for extensive discussions of these issues.

[28] The Black Death reached Western Europe in October 1347, making landfall in Sicily (Ziegler 2003: 27). It did not reach Hamburg, although it was a major trading port, until 1350 (Benedictow 2004: 195–6).

greater risk than opportunity, as the population of the planet increases, we may anticipate growing xenophobia, nationalism, and protectionism.[29]

A fuller planet creates more systemic risks but also provides greater opportunity for problem solving and cooperation. This is urgently required if the escalating challenges associated with economic growth and population growth are to be addressed. The record so far from rising density and connectivity of human activity has been one of remarkable success. The innovative energy which has been released as people connect has led to an acceleration of human learning and what Joseph Schumpeter described as 'creative destruction', from which economic progress comes.

Innovation and integration of markets have brought extraordinary benefits. However, economics and politics, through the increasingly ubiquitous ideas of 'rational economic man' and respect for individual rights, have pushed individuals to act in an atomized manner. With over 7 billion people on the planet and a growing majority able to demand their choice of consumer and other products, the sum of individual rational actions is less and less sustainable.[30] Without urgent action, the apparently rational actions of a growing number of individuals will overwhelm the capacity of the planet to provide sustainable livelihoods.

While we live in a global village, with increasing demands on our common resources, we do not have village elders to guide us. The global governance system is unfit for 21st-century purpose. The drift in global leadership is compounded by the preoccupation of the old G8 powers with domestic crises and the failure of the new powers to take up or even share the burden of leadership.[31] The failure of leadership at the global level may be attributed to a failure at the national level to focus on the critical questions of resource use and the management of the global commons. This failure in turn, at least in the democracies, reflects our failure as citizens to ensure that the politicians we elect focus on these critical questions.

---

[29] Examples of this tendency include the Smoot-Hawley Tariff Act of 1930, which responded to the incipient Great Depression with record levels of trade barriers, and the ultra-nationalist Golden Dawn party, which won 7 per cent of the vote in both rounds of the 2012 Greek elections (Henley and Davies 2012).

[30] Various critiques of 'rational economic man' have emerged. Some have argued that 'thoughtful economic man' (Meeks 1991) is better placed to meet global challenges and promote human well-being (Sen 2009; Phelps 2013).

[31] I describe in *Divided Nations* (2013) how we are entering a perfect storm, with the compounding pressures of income growth and demands on planetary resources reaching a peak of intensity, with no captain at the wheel.

Governance for a Fuller Planet

This chapter has argued that a sustainable and fuller planet will require greater attention to governance. Threats to the global commons, such as carbon emissions leading to catastrophic climate change, or beggar-thy-neighbour fishing policies depleting the food supply of the oceans, require cooperative solutions. So too do threats created by the increasing complexity and connectedness of the globalized world. The blizzard of complexity means it is increasingly difficult to understand and act on a wide variety of interconnected failures of the global commons. Examples include the difficulties associated with tracing the sources of production and the carbon emissions embedded in the goods and services we consume, or pandemics rapidly spreading across travel routes; cyberattacks crippling our technological foundations, or financial crises leading to economic depression and unemployment.

Traditionally, national governments in the advanced economies have responded to issues within their own borders. The United States answered the stock market crash of 1929 with the Glass-Steagall Act and the Federal Deposit Insurance Corporation. It responded to the environmental disaster of Hurricane Katrina with an existing agency to help and house evacuees (FEMA) and assigned a governmental organization to rebuild and repair the levee system (United States Army Corps of Engineers). The global institutions have typically been formed out of major crises—with the UN and Bretton Woods institutions rising out of the devastation of World War Two. The challenge now is how to reform global governance when governments and citizens appear to be content with their benign neglect of the international system.

While nations jealously guard their narrow sovereign interests, they are unwilling to place the necessary pressure on lumbering multilateral institutions such as the UN, World Bank, and IMF to reform. As a result they remain captured by out-of-date mandates and governed by divided nations that are not in a position to proactively address our global needs. The current arrangements were reasonably effective in dealing with the major challenges of the second half of the 20th century. However, they are ill-equipped to tackle the rapidly emerging and dynamic 21st-century challenges.

The question of whether the planet is full or not rests on our ability to address critical governance challenges. However, not all problems require global solutions and we need clear principles as to when and where we need global solutions.[32]

---

[32] The following principles have been developed in collaboration with my Oxford colleague, Ngaire Woods. These principles are discussed in greater detail in *Divided Nations* (2013: 173–6).

First, not all issues require global collective action. A principle of subsidiarity must apply, as many issues are resolvable at the national, regional, or bilateral level, or by non-government actors such as the private sector or civil organizations. Global management must be considered only where public action pursued by governments in cooperation with one another is necessary to address the problem. On many issues of the global commons, such as climate change, fisheries depletion, or preparation for pandemics, only international and regional governmental cooperation can reach the proper scope required. That said, as long as overall national targets are met, the principle of subsidiarity means that nation states and even communities should be able to determine how global rules are adapted to local priorities.

Second, a principle of selective inclusion is required. Not all actors need to be involved in every global negotiation, but those that are most significant must be. In the case of climate change, this means it is essential that the twenty or so countries accounting for over 80 per cent of the emissions are included. Equally, however, countries most affected (such as Bangladesh, in the case of climate change) need to be included in the planning and shaping of global action to ensure that it is legitimate and addresses the concerns of those most affected.

Third, a principle of variable geometry must be applied. Eight leaders sitting around a lunch table at a G8 summit is manageable; 192 members of the UN is not. The process of global management needs to accommodate the minimum number of countries required at each stage of managing a problem, but these states need not be the same for each stage. In negotiations on climate change, Tuvalu and the Alliance of Small Island States will not have a large impact in discussions on how emissions are reduced, but as they will be dramatically affected by climate change; reflecting the concerns of those that are affected as well as those that are affecting is crucial to ensure legitimacy.

Fourth, global management requires legitimacy. This is regularly voiced but seldom defined. Put simply, the rules of engagement in global action have to be understandable and acceptable to most countries. In the case of climate this implies that the biggest polluters—China, Europe, and the United States—need to take action before they can expect smaller players to act.

Finally, for global action to be effective there must be some degree of enforceability at the global level. Governments must do what they promise and defectors must not be allowed to take advantage of their own narrow self-interests by free-riding on the joint efforts of others. Intergovernmental reviews and pressure among governments is one route towards enforcement. Equally vital are wider public pressures which emerge when inactions or failure are brought to light by the media, by the campaigning of NGOs, or by other public institutions.

The world's top policymakers should confine global management to those actions that can meet the basic standards of necessity, legitimacy, and enforceability. However, as the planet becomes fuller and more complex, it is likely that global management will be required on more and more issues. The planet may one day become full, but the level at which that occurs is dependent on our resource consumption, environmental degradation, and economic and technological development; all of which are mediated through institutional arrangements. We can better sustain our planet and its population, whatever that number may be, if we are able to develop the necessary governance arrangements. If not, it may well already be too full. We owe it to ourselves and future generations to redouble our efforts to understand and overcome the current obstacles to managing the collective implications of our individual actions.

Acknowledgements

Chris Oates provided excellent research assistance and support for this chapter. The section on migration draws on Ian Goldin, Geoffrey Cameron, and Meera Belarajan, 2011, *Exceptional People: How Migration Shaped Our World and Will Define Our Future*, Princeton University Press.

References

amfAR (2013). 'Thirty Years of HIV/AIDS: Snapshots of an Epidemic', Foundation for AIDS Research. Last accessed 14 August 2013. <http://www.amfar.org/thirty-years-of-hiv/aids-snapshots-of-an-epidemic/>.

Arhin-Tenkorang, D. and Conceição, P. (2003). 'Beyond Communicable Disease Control: Health in the Age of Globalization' in I. Kaul, P. Conceição, K. Le Goulven, and R. U. Mendoza (eds), *Providing Global Public Goods*. Oxford: Oxford University Press, pp. 484–515.

Bartlett, T. (2010). *Ireland: A History*. Cambridge: Cambridge University Press.

BBC (2013a). 'Syria Crisis', *BBC News*, BBC Breakfast programme (broadcast 8.36 a.m.), 22 October.

BBC (2013b). 'Syrian National Council Rejects Geneva Peace Talks', *BBC News*, 13 October. Last accessed 22 October 2013. <http://www.bbc.co.uk/news/world-middle-east-24513538>.

Benedictow, O. J. (2004). *The Black Death, 1346–1353: The Complete History*. Woodbridge: Boydell Press.

Black, R. (2001). 'Environmental Refugees: Myth or Reality?' *New Issues in Refugee Research Working Paper 34*. Geneva: UNHRC. Last accessed 15 August 2013. <http://www.unhcr.org/3ae6a0d00.html>.

Bodansky, D. (2010). 'The Copenhagen Climate Change Conference: A Post-Mortem', *American Journal of International Law*, 104 (2): 230–40.

Bourguignon, F. (2012). *La Mondialisation de L'inégalité*. Paris: Editions du Seuil et La Republique des Idees.

Brockmann, D., Hufnagel, L., and Geisel, T. (2005). 'Dynamics of Modern Epidemics,' in A. McLean, R. May, J. Pattison, and R. Weiss (eds), *SARS: A Case Study in Emerging Infections*. New York and Oxford: Oxford University Press, pp. 81–91.

Brown, O. (2007). 'Climate Change and Forced Migration: Observations, Projections and Implications,' *Occasional Paper 2007/17*. New York: Human Development Report Office. Last accessed 15 August 2013. <http://hdr.undp.org/sites/default/files/brown_oli.pdf>.

Castles, S. (2002). 'Environmental Change and Forced Migration: Making Sense of the Debate,' *New Issues in Refugee Research Working Paper 70*. Geneva: UNHRC Evaluation and Policy Analysis Unit.

Copeland, B. R. and Taylor, M. S. (2004). 'Trade, Growth, and the Environment', *Journal of Economic Literature*, 42 (1): 7–71.

Cox, R. and Pecquet, J. (2012). 'Senate Rejects United Nations Treaty for Disabled Rights in a 61–38 Vote', *The Hill*, 4 December. Last accessed 15 August 2103. <http://thehill.com/blogs/global-affairs/un-treaties/270831-senate-rejects-un-treaty-for-disabled-rights-in-vote>.

Daly, M. E. (2006). *The Slow Failure: Population Decline and Independent Ireland, 1920–1973*. Madison, Wisconsin: University of Wisconsin Press.

Diamond, J. (2005). *Collapse*. New York: Viking.

EMN (2013). 'Current Humanitarian and Migration Situation in Syria', European Migration Network. Last accessed 21 October 2013. <http://emn.gov.pl/ese/news/9289,dok.html>.

Esty, D. C. 2001. 'Bridging the Trade-Environment Divide', *Journal of Economic Perspectives*, 15 (3): 113–30.

Foresight (2011). *Migration and Global Environmental Change: Future Challenges and Opportunities*, Final Project Report. London: Government Office for Science. Last accessed 21 August 2013. <http://www.bis.gov.uk/foresight/our-work/projects/published-projects/global-migration/reports-publications>.

Goldin, I. (2013). *Divided Nations: Why Global Governance is Failing, and What We Can Do About It*. Oxford: Oxford University Press.

Goldin, I. (2011). 'DR3: The Future of Global Migration and the Impact of Environmental Change', *Foresight Report*. London: Government Office for Science. Last accessed 15 August 2013. <http://www.bis.gov.uk/assets/foresight/docs/migration/drivers/11-1172-dr3-future-global-migration-impact-environmental-change.pdf>.

Goldin, I. Cameron, G., and Balarajan, M. (2011). *Exceptional People: How Migration Shaped Our World and Will Define Our Future*. Princeton, NJ: Princeton University Press.

Goldin, I. and Mariathasan, M. (2014). *The Butterfly Defect: How Globalization Creates Systemic Risks, and What to Do About It*. Princeton, NJ: Princeton University Press.

Goldin, I. and Reinert, K. (2012). *Globalization for Development: Meeting New Challenges*, New Ed. Oxford: Oxford University Press.

Goldin, I. and Winters, L. A. (eds) (1995). *The Economics of Sustainable Development.* Cambridge: Cambridge University Press.

Henley, J. and Davies, L. (2012). 'Greece's Far-right Golden Dawn Party Maintains Share of Vote', *The Guardian*, 18 June. Last accessed 16 August 2013. <http://www. theguardian.com/world/2012/jun/18/greece-far-right-golden-dawn>.

Knight, S. (2009). 'The Human Tsunami', *Financial Times*, 19 June. Last accessed 15 August 2013. <http://www.ft.com/cms/s/0/bb6b0efc-5ad9-11de-8c14-00144feabdc0. html#axzz2c3RKlq6E>.

Koremenos, B., Lipson, C., and Snidal, D. (2004). *The Rational Design of International Institutions.* New York: Cambridge University Press.

Lamy, P. (2012). 'Local Governments, Global Governance', Oxford: Oxford Martin School. 8 March. Last accessed 15 August 2013. <http://www.oxfordmartin.ox.ac. uk/event/1256>.

Long, M. (2012). 'C40, World Green Building Council and the U.S. Green Building Council form New Global Partnership to Advance City-Led Green Building Efforts', US Green Building Council, Press Release, 16 November. Last accessed 21 August 2013. <http://www.usgbc.org/articles/c40-world-green-building-council-and-us-green-building-council-form-new-global-partnership->.

Lutz, W. and KC, S (2011). 'Global Human Capital: Integrating Education and Population', *Science*, 333: 587–92.

MacFarquhar, N. (2013). 'U.N. Treaty is First Aimed at Regulating Global Arms Sales', *New York Times*, 2 April. Last accessed 15 August 2013. <http://www.nytimes.com/ 2013/04/03/world/arms-trade-treaty-approved-at-un.html?pagewanted=all&_r=0>.

Mahbubani, K. (2011). 'A Rudderless World', *New York Times*, 18 August. Last accessed 15 August 2013. <http://www.nytimes.com/2011/08/19/opinion/19iht-edmahbubani19.html?_r=0>.

McCarthy, J. J. Canziani, O. F., Leary, N. A., Dokken, D. J., and White, K. S. (eds) (2001). *Climate Change 2001: Impacts, Adaptation, and Vulnerability* (Contribution of Working Group II to the Third Assessment Report of the Intergovernmental Panel on Climate Change). Cambridge: Cambridge University Press.

Meeks, J. G. T. (1991). *Thoughtful Economic Man: Essays on Rationality, Moral Rules and Benevolence.* Cambridge: Cambridge University Press.

McAusland, C. (2008). 'Globalisation's Direct and Indirect Effects on the Environment', paper presented at the OECD's *Global Forum on Transport and Environment in a Globalising World*, 10–12 November, Guadalajara, Mexico. Last accessed 21 January 2013. <http://www.oecd.org/env/transportandenvironment/41380703.pdf>.

Milford, J., Nielsen, J., Patton, V., Ryan, N., White, V. J., and Copeland, C. (2005). *Clearing California's Coal Shadow from the American West.* Environmental Defence. Last accessed 18 July 2013. <http://www.westernresourceadvocates.org/energy/pdf/ CA%20Coal%20Shadow.pdf>.

Mills J. H. and Waite, T. A. (2009). 'Economic Prosperity, Biodiversity Conservation, and the Environmental Kuznets Curve', *Ecological Economics*, 68 (7): 2087–95.

Mokyr, J. (1983). *Why Ireland Starved: A Quantitative and Analytical History of the Irish Economy, 1800–1850.* Abingdon, Oxon: Routledge.

Nolan, P. (1993). 'The Causation and Prevention of Famines: A Critique of A. K. Sen', *Journal of Peasant Studies*, 21 (1): 1–28.

NPR (2012). 'Transcript: Mitt Romney's Acceptance Speech', NPR [formerly National Public Radio; now known solely as NPR], 30 August. Last accessed 15 August 2013. <http://www.npr.org/2012/08/30/160357612/transcript-mitt-romneys-acceptance-speech>.

OECD. 2013. 'OECD.Stat Extracts'. Last accessed 30 August 2013. <http://stats.oecd.org/>.

Oxford Martin Commission for Future Generations (2013). *Now for the Long Term: The Report of the Oxford Martin Commission for Future Generations*. Oxford: Oxford Martin School. Last accessed 21 October 2013. <http://www.oxfordmartin.ox.ac.uk/commission>.

Persky, J. and Kurban, H. (2001). 'Do Federal Funds Better Support Cities or Suburbs? A Spatial Analysis of Federal Spending in the Chicago Metropolis', *Discussion Paper*, November 2001. Washington, DC: The Brookings Institution Center on Urban and Metropolitan Policy. Last accessed 15 August 2013. <http://www.brookings.edu/~/media/research/files/reports/2001/11/metropolitanpolicy%20persky/ persky.pdf>.

Phelps, E. S. (2013). *Mass Flourishing: How Grassroots Innovation Created Jobs, Challenge, and Change*. Princeton, NJ: Princeton University Press.

Rapp, T., Schwägerl, C., and Traufetter, G. (2010). 'The Copenhagen Protocol: How China and India Sabotaged the UN Climate Summit', *Der Spiegel*, 5 May. Last accessed 15 August 2013. <http://www.spiegel.de/international/world/the-copenhagen-protocol-how-china-and-india-sabotaged-the-un-climate-summit-a-692861.html>.

Rodrik, D. (2011). *The Globalization Paradox: Democracy and the Future of the World Economy*. New York and London: W. W. Norton & Company, and Oxford: Oxford University Press.

Satterthwaite, D. (2006). 'Urbanisation and Third World Cities' in D. A. Clark (ed), *The Elgar Companion to Development Studies*. Cheltenham: Edward Elgar, pp. 664–70.

Sen, A. K. (2009). *The Idea of Justice*. London: Allen Lane.

Sen, A. K. (2003). 'The Importance of Basic Education' (Full text of Amartya Sen's speech to the Commonwealth education conference, Edinburgh), *The Guardian*, 28 October. Last accessed 16 August 2013. <http://www.theguardian.com/education/2003/oct/28/schools.uk4>.

Sen, A. K. (1993). 'The Causation and Prevention of Famines: A Reply', *Journal of Peasant Studies*, 21 (1): 29–40.

Sen, A. K. (1981). *Poverty and Famines: An Essay on Entitlement and Deprivation*. Oxford: Clarendon Press.

Stern, N. (2006). *The Economics of Climate Change: The Stern Review*. Cambridge: Cambridge University Press.

Stiglitz, J. (2012). *The Price of Inequality*. New York: Norton.

Stiglitz, J. (2006). *Making Globalization Work*. London: W. W. Norton & Company.

UCDP (2013). 'UCDP/PRIO Armed Conflict Dataset', Uppsala University, Department of Peace and Conflict Research. Last accessed 21 October 2013. <http://www.pcr.uu.se/research/ucdp/datasets/ucdp_prio_armed_conflict_dataset/>.

UNHCR (2013a), 'UNHCR says it is "Stretched to the Limit" by the Rising Number of Refugees', UN Refugee Agency, News Stories, 1 October. Last accessed 22 October 2012. <http://www.unhcr.org/524ae6179.html>.

UNHCR (2013b). 'Syria Regional Refugee Response', Inter-agency Information Sharing Portal, United Nations Refugee Agency. Last accessed 21 October 2013. <http://data.unhcr.org/syrianrefugees/regional.php>.

USAD (2013). 'Table 4: World and U.S. Wheat Production, Exports and Ending Stocks', Foreign Agricultural Service, United States Agricultural Department. Last accessed 21 August 2013. <http://www.ers.usda.gov/datafiles/Wheat_Wheat_Data/Yearbook_Tables/World_Production_Supply_and_Disappearance/wheatyearbooktable04.xls>.

Wachs, M. (1996). 'The Evolution of Transportation Policy in Los Angeles: Images of Past Policy and Future Prospects' in A. J. Scott and E. Soja (eds), *The City: Los Angeles and Urban Theory at the End of the Twentieth Century*. Berkeley and Los Angeles: University of California Press, pp. 106–59.

Wailes, E. J. and Chavez, E. C. (2012). 'World Rice Outlook: International Rice Baseline with Deterministic and Stochastic Projections, 2012–2021', *Staff Papers SP 01*, Research in Agricultural and Applied Economics, University of Minnesota. Last accessed 21 August 2013. <http://ageconsearch.umn.edu/bitstream/123203/2/March%202012%20World%20Rice%20Outlook_AgEconSearch_05-01-12%20final.pdf>.

WHO (2013). 'Urban Population Growth', Global Health Observatory (online). Last accessed 15 August 2013. <http://www.who.int/gho/urban_health/situation_trends/urban_population_growth_text/en/>.

Wilson, D. and Dragusanu, R. (2008). 'The Expanding Middle: The Exploding World Middle Class and Falling Global Inequality', *Global Economic Papers 170*. New York: Goldman Sachs. Last accessed 15 August 2013. <http://www.ryanallis.com/wp-content/uploads/2008/07/expandingmiddle.pdf>.

World Bank (2013). 'Poverty & Equity Data [Global Poverty Indicators]', Data Portal. Last accessed 16 August 2013. <http://povertydata.worldbank.org/poverty/home>.

World Bank (2010). *World Development Report 2010: Development and Climate Change*. Washington, DC: World Bank.

World Bank (2009). *World Development Report 2009: Reshaping Economic Geography*. Washington, DC: World Bank.

Ziegler, P. (2003). *The Black Death*. Stroud, Glos.: Sutton Publishing Ltd.

Index